THINKING FROM WITHIN

THINKING
from WITHIN

A Hands-on Strategy Practice
Johan Roos

With contributions from
Madeleine Roos

Peter Bürgi

Mark Marotto

and Roger Said

palgrave
macmillan

First published 2006 by
PALGRAVE MACMILLAN
Houndmills, Basingstoke, Hampshire RG21 6XS and
175 Fifth Avenue, New York, N.Y. 10010
Companies and representatives throughout the world

PALGRAVE MACMILLAN is the global academic imprint of the Palgrave
Macmillan division of St. Martin's Press, LLC and of Palgrave Macmillan Ltd.
Macmillan® is a registered trademark in the United States, United Kingdom
and other countries. Palgrave is a registered trademark in the European
Union and other countries.

ISBN-13: 978–1–4039–8670–2
ISBN-10: 1–4039–8670–3

This book is printed on paper suitable for recycling and made from fully
managed and sustained forest sources.

A catalogue record for this book is available from the British Library.

Library of Congress Cataloging-in-Publication Data

Roos, Johan.
    Thinking from within : a hands-on strategy practice / by Johan Roos ;
with contribution from Madeleine Roos ... [et al.].
    p. cm.
    Includes bibliographical references and index.
    ISBN 1–4039–8670–3 (cloth)
    1. Strategic planning. 2. Creative thinking. 3. Intellectual capital—
Management. 4. Knowledge management. 5. Organizational effectiveness.
I. Roos, Madeleine. II. Title.

HD30.28.R6623 2006
658.4'012—dc22

2005054968

10 9 8 7 6 5 4 3 2 1
15 14 13 12 11 10 09 08 07 06

Printed and bound in Great Britain by
Antony Rowe Ltd, Chippenham and Eastbourne

This book is dedicated to
Kjeld Kirk Kristiansen
for his constant support and encouragement
in both good and bad times

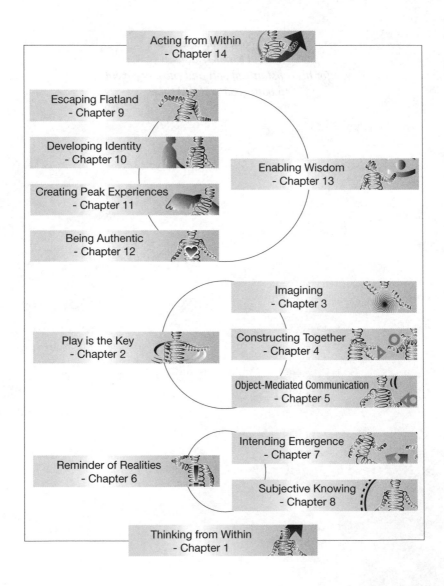

Acting from Within
- Chapter 14

Escaping Flatland
- Chapter 9

Developing Identity
- Chapter 10

Creating Peak Experiences
- Chapter 11

Being Authentic
- Chapter 12

Enabling Wisdom
- Chapter 13

Imagining
- Chapter 3

Play is the Key
- Chapter 2

Constructing Together
- Chapter 4

Object-Mediated Communication
- Chapter 5

Intending Emergence
- Chapter 7

Reminder of Realities
- Chapter 6

Subjective Knowing
- Chapter 8

Thinking from Within
- Chapter 1

Contents

List of Exhibits

Preface

It is easy to criticize the status quo, but much more demanding to find thoughtful and useful alternatives. In this book we have tried to do both. *Thinking from Within* critiques how strategy is conventionally practised in organizations, but this is just the starting point. In 13 of the 14 chapters we describe, illustrate and reflect on alternative ways of thinking and doing strategy – *Thinking from Within*.

The early traces of the ideas behind this book stem from research I was doing in the early 1990s, especially in dialogues with Georg von Krogh and Ken Slocum. At that time I was Associate Professor of Strategy at the Norwegian School of Management. Later, when I was Professor of Strategy and General Management at IMD in Lausanne, these ideas matured significantly especially in dialogues with Bart Victor. Six years ago I seized the opportunity to launch, develop and lead an independent research foundation devoted to some of these ideas – Imagination Lab Foundation. This was made possible by generous donations and encouragement from Kjeld Kirk Kristiansen. That is why I wholeheartedly dedicate this book to him.

The dozens of people who have worked with Imagination Lab Foundation have presented theoretical and empirical research findings at some 60 academic conferences, primarily in Europe and the US; staged two international academic conferences; generated some 70 research papers of which quite a few are gradually being converted into peer-reviewed academic articles and book chapters; and experimented with more than a 1000 practitioners in research-based engagements. In addition, over these years I have continued to consult with curious and reflective managers as well as contribute to executive education programmes. These activities have not only grounded the initial concepts in organizational realities, but also propelled my own ideas about how to improve managerial practices in general and strategy practice in particular.

Thinking from Within brings together the cross-disciplinary theoretical foundation and 'hands-on' illustrations of how the ideas can be put into (strategy) practice.

Just as I have learnt from, as well as challenged, theory and practice over the past decade, I hope this book will contribute to the advancement of both.

JOHAN ROOS
Lausanne

Acknowledgements

Ideas emerge from the interaction among people. In addition to the four co-authors in this book, I would like to thank the following people who have contributed in various ways. For collaborative research work: Francois Grey, Claus Jacobs, Hugo Letiche, Marc-Olivier Linder, Joachim Maier, David Oliver, Kari Oppegaard, Richard Randell, Matt Statler and Bart Victor. I especially recognize the contributions of Matt, David and Claus, who preferred to remain with our earlier collaborative work. For managerial insights: Nassim Aldahoud, Cliff Dennet, Kai Denzel, Ingrid Engström, Scott Frondorf, Jennie Gertun-Olsson, Susan Mackie, Jens Mogaard, Kendra Overall, Stephany Parry, Lewis Pinault, James Prouty, Göran Roos and James Rowe. For great design ideas and work. Craig Austin, Marshall Clemens and Jesse Moran For editorial assistance: Carla Svehlik and Antoinette Price. Finally, I thank Stephen Rutt, Jacky Kippenberger and Rebecca Pash of Palgrave Macmillan – for their rapid responses and supportive ways of working – and Linda Norris and the superb team at Aardvark Editorial.

Although the roots of the ideas presented in this book go back a decade, I want to acknowledge that the very notion 'from within' emerged from sparkling conversations with my wife, Madeleine Roos, during the early summer of 2005. Then, it all suddenly made so much more sense.

JOHAN ROOS

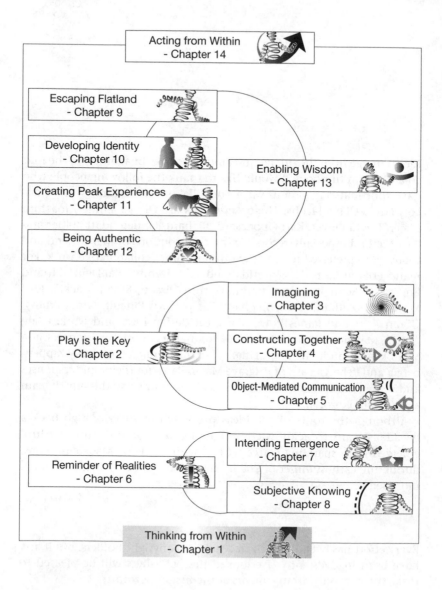

1
Thinking from Within

Johan Roos

Introduction

In the mid 1990s I worked as an action researcher with several companies to find out more about what leaders were thinking and doing when they practised strategy. After a few leadership meetings in one of these firms, a newspaper, it was obvious that there was no passion for strategic issues and the editor consistently arrived late. In a world of 24-hour cycles, the whole group was noticeably uninterested in the long-term and abstract tasks of strategy, the editor being the most detached and impatient. During these meetings the group exercised and discussed a range of analytical tools similar and sometimes identical to the ones used in the previous year.

At one meeting midway through the strategy process, the editor arrived even later than usual, bursting in with the freshly printed edition of the newspaper squeezed into his hand. Red-faced he interrupted our conversation and called out 'Look, the margin on the front page is 1 mm to the left', followed by a series of unprintable expressions describing his sentiments about the people in production. Rather than dismissing this episode as 'daily and operational' and not relevant to the few precious hours set aside for strategy conversations, the rest of the group immediately latched onto the perceived problem.

At first, I was astonished to see the sudden passion, enthusiasm and activity (including strong swearwords) that followed and totally changed the dynamic of the meeting. Nobody remained seated, they moved around waving their hands, argued face-to-face, and took turns to grab hold of the newspaper issue. Suddenly they were subjective and close to the issues discussed, not distant and objective; they were emotionally engaged, not just intellectualizing; they were touching things and using their hands to express their views and feelings, not just engaged in abstract talk.

1

Taken aback by their enthusiasm and passion for an issue that was apparently close to their hearts, I wondered what was needed to make the strategic discussions equally interesting for them. It is only partly true that the 'missed margin' gave them an excuse to escape from a difficult and uncomfortable, and perhaps boring, conversation about 'strategy'. Perhaps newspaper managers have a particularly short time-horizon as they produce a new paper every day and, consequently, are prone to jump on an emerging discussion about an operational problem. Regardless whether this is myth or reality, on a deeper level the story says something about the way we think and do things when we practise strategy.

On a surface level this episode reminded me of what poet-consultant David Whyte said in his book *The Heart Aroused*: organizations today 'must also honor the souls of the individuals who work for them' (1994: 9). He defined soul in terms of belonging, 'the way human beings belong in their world, their work or their human community' (ibid. p. 13). His message is that unless there is a sense of belonging there is little sense of soul. When we do not feel this belonging, we not only feel that we are 'running on the spot', he argued, we also feel as if we are 'dying'. During the strategy meetings the managers in the example above did not show much sense of belonging and contributed accordingly. Some of them probably felt they were running on the spot, wasting their time. Perhaps some of them even felt they were dying of boredom. This contrasts with how they engaged after the interruption, now with their 'hearts aroused'. Yet, in strategy practice this is not heart of the matter.

The problem

Despite good intentions and decades of conceptual progress, strategy is often practised as if circumstances remain reasonably stable. The typical outcome of such practices is well-defined action plans suitable for dealing with the expected, rather than increasing the readiness of individuals, groups and the entire organization to seize fleeting opportunities and avoid emerging problems. When I confront senior executives with these observations and views, few disagree and most say they wish things were different in the way they practise strategy. They also seem to be at loss about how to remedy the situation.

The problem is not new. Leading scholars have discussed the problem of organizational strategy practices for decades. In their textbook on the topic Chakravarthy and Lorange (1991) noted that that a more formal, integrative approach to strategy practices is appropriate only when the business faces predictable situations and when it has several distinct competencies. Few company leaders appear to heed their advice. Starbuck (1992) argued that to help firms operate more effectively, strategy practice must preserve uncertainty and allow for contingencies, which is typically not the case. Mintzberg (1994) argued that strategy practice even risks destroying commitment, discouraging change, and breeding a damaging political atmosphere. Strategy practice (in the guise of 'planning'), he argued, should be about synthesis rather than analysis. Despite such observations and good advice, 'dominant logic' (Prahalad and Bettis 1986) or rather the way strategy is practised in organizations seems to evolve very slowly.

Insanity?

It has been said that the definition of insanity is doing the same thing over, and over, and over again, and, for some reason, expecting a different outcome. According to this definition we are perfectly sane when we keep repeating what we do and how we think, while expecting the same old outcome, regardless if we claim otherwise. Over the years I have met, taught, researched and consulted with quite a few managers who belong in this category. According to the same definition, however, we are 'insane' if we expect a *different* outcome from repeating the same old concepts, models, tools and techniques year after year. Frustrated by this situation some managers are eager to break this routine.

Over the past decade a growing community of researchers have argued that it is high time we knew more about what managers are actually *doing* when they engage in strategy practice (see for example Johanson et al 2001; Whittington 2003 ; Wilson and Jarzabkowski 2004). The phenomenon of practice is a tricky one that has been conceptualized by grand sociologists in a variety of ways.[1] For our purposes in this book it suffices to conceptualize practice in terms of 'thinking' and 'doing'.

The problem with strategy practice Is in both its 'thinking' *and* its 'doing' aspects: *strategy practice remains biased in favour of deductive, unimaginative analytical thinking and routinized ways of doing*, what I call 'prescribed thinking'. In this book we shall describe, illustrate and reflect on another way more suitable to enhance preparedness for the unexpected.

The framework

The overall message of this book is: *To be prepared to deal effectively and responsibly with the unexpected our thinking should be more imaginative and our doing should be spontaneous.* This is easier said than done, especially within organizations.

Using more senses to fuel our imagination

Imagination is about what we think, what we do and what we use, and is intertwined with our senses. Research has demonstrated how our sensory-motor system stimulates our abstract thinking in general. What we think or understand is shaped by, made possible by, and limited by our bodies and our embodied interactions in the world:

> There is no such fully autonomous faculty of reason separate from and independent of bodily capacities such as perception and movement. The evidence supports, instead, an evolutionary view, in which reason uses and grows out of bodily capacities. (Lakoff and Johnson 1980: 17)

Just like black-and-white, colour and infrared are three different ways of presenting an image, our thinking can be stimulated by many rather than few senses. To imaginatively develop 'new outcomes', seeing and hearing may not be enough. Other senses can be used to both deliver existing knowledge to the table and generate entirely new insights.

Making way for the spontaneity of our wisdom

Routines are repetitive pattern of activities (Nelson and Winter 1982), which emerge when there are available cognitive schema, categorizable clues, action rules, minimal effort required and few sub-routines, interruptions and surprises (March and Simon 1958). The benefits of repeating the currently known best practices lie primarily in creating stability (Cyert and March 1993; Nelson and Winter 1982). *Routines are not supposed to result in new outcomes.*

Different from routines is the notion of spontaneity, a concept that has been treated by philosophers (for example Immanuel Kant), political observers (for example Rosa Luxenburg) and psychologists (for example Jacob Levy Moreno), who all refer to the *possibility of freedom*. Unlike routines, spontaneous actions are generated from natural inclinations and unconstrained feelings.[2] Spontaneity is unplanned and by definition of short duration.[3]

Thinking from Within

Exhibit 1.1 depicts the conceptual framework of this book. For analytical purposes, I have separated the thinking and doing aspects of 'practice'. The bottom left-hand corner of the model represents the routinized, deductive, unimaginative *analytical* thinking that I call 'prescribed thinking'. The upper right-hand corner represents the imaginative thinking

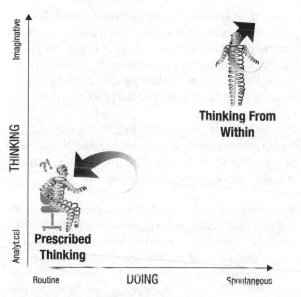

Exhibit 1 1 Conceptual framework

and *spontaneous* doing that come 'from within', which I simplify into the term *Thinking from Within*.

In subsequent chapters we will describe and illustrate how thinking from within helps managers escape the conventional flat papers and screens, develop organizational identity, up the ante for peak experiences and enhance authenticity in what they do. By thinking more from within they also nurture their (internally generated) wisdom, which makes them more prepared to deal with the unexpected. Rather than being threatened by new circumstances, they thrive on them. Rather than talking about new outcomes, they generate them.

Commencing this journey frequently seems difficult. Why? Perhaps due to the lack of vocabulary we use to describe what managers actually do when they practise strategy. Perhaps due to the dominant logic and tools of mainstream management practice. Perhaps because of invisible assumptions of people involved, shaped by education and ritualized through 'best' practices. Yes, yes, and yes. But there is more to it.

The human side

All people 'think from within', but management practices in general and strategy practices in particular (see Johnson et al. 2003) do not for various reasons encourage this sufficiently. Strategy practice is, or at least should be, a *human* activity rather than like short-cycle assembly work following standard operating procedures. When it isn't, we have a deeper problem.

Rooted in the rationality of natural sciences, strategy theory and practice has for long admired objectivity and avoidance of personal views, which works contrary to *Thinking from Within*. By disregarding human qualities in strategy practice, both the theory and the practice risk becoming amoral.

The late Sumantra Goshal (2005) recently delivered a sweeping and harsh critique of the academic management discipline, which illustrates the consequences. The amoral theories professed by business schools profoundly shape managers' worldview. In his own words:

> In courses on corporate governance grounded in agency theory ... we have taught our students that managers cannot be trusted to do their jobs – which, of course, is to maximize shareholder value ... In courses on organization design, grounded in transaction costs economics, we have preached the need for tight monitoring and control of people to prevent 'opportunistic behavior' ... In strategy courses, we have presented the 'five forces' framework ... to suggest that companies must compete not only with their competitors but also with their suppliers, customers, employees, and regulators. (ibid. p. 75)

Based on this Goshal argues that we have created a generation of managers who, left to themselves, will exhibit what society will deem to be unacceptable behaviours, for example excessive greed.

Grounded in many years of research under the auspice of Imagination Lab Foundation, the conceptual foundation of *Thinking from Within* rests firmly on the idea that strategy is inherently normative (Statler and Roos 2005). Our stance in this book is that it is *good* to encourage the inner human potential and qualities by using more of our senses and welcome the freedom of spontaneous action. Moreover, we suggest that *Thinking from Within* is appropriate to deal with and prepare for the unexpected.

To illustrate how the practice we call *Thinking from Within* may appear in a strategy setting I will use two contrasting tales. The first is the tale of OilCo and the second is the tale of RedCo.

Case: Generating commitment in OilCo[4]

OilCo distributes petrol and associated products in a large country in the world. Over the past few years OilCo acquired and integrated into its growing organization several competitors distributing petroleum-based products in adjacent geographical areas. In addition to its traditional focus on large customers, such as truck fleets and large farms, the CEO had recently taken the initiative to acquire several retail outlets for consumers, that is, gas stations. In mid 2005 the CEO summarized the situation:

> Over the last two years we got our act together after the acquisitions, and today we are a reasonably unified organization. We have no more territory to develop so our strategic challenge is to create more value from our existing business.

To this end, six months earlier the CEO had initiated and launched a new initiative to make his organization more customer oriented. Labelled a 'customer service programme' his idea was to gradually transform the culture of the organization from its traditional product-orientation, to become more aware of the needs of consumers and what must be done to be successful in the retail business. Within this programme, the key concept was 'Customer Service Champion,' which was to define a new, customer-oriented *role* for each senior leader, and eventually for others throughout the organization. The underlying idea was to respect local customers much more than was the case today, thereby creating better relationships, as well as customer satisfaction in general. The CEO said: 'We know the production process by heart, but we really do not know so much about our customers.' Despite the talk, not much happened in practice. He continued: 'We just talked about the concept a few times, and I haven't really pushed it since everybody has been too busy.' He also said he had not pushed for a specific definition beyond vague notions of customer focus.

When I met him, the CEO was somewhat ambivalent vis à vis the entire Champion idea: Was this really what they should be doing, he asked me, and if yes, how could they gain momentum in this transformation process? He elaborated:

> Phase 1 was about integrating and extracting value from our acquisitions. Phase 2 is about getting more out of who we are now and this ought to require customer focus: we need to know what they want, what we can do and then close the gap.

Through our initial conversations I learnt that the leadership team was a relatively homogenous group of people, who also knew each other well socially. The group consisted of three geographical business managers, the CFO, the officer responsible for health, safety and environmental issues, the business development manager and the CEO. As a group they met once a month. Three times a year they met at overnight strategy retreats, dedicated to specific business issues.

The ways of working in the company were relatively informal. The CEO summarized: 'We are not big on written things. I ask my managers what they need in order to do what they need to do. Then, we simply agree on resources, recognition and authority.' Despite this aversion to written plans and strategies, the CEO had nevertheless formulated a written set of corporate 'objectives'.

The CEO and I agreed to stage a one-day strategy retreat to encourage his leadership team of seven people to share more of their inner thoughts and feelings about the concept and take a stance about what it implied. Our joint expectation was that anything could happen during this retreat, including total chaos. The CEO was prepared to go ahead with this uncertainty.

The retreat

During the first few hours I spent time ensuring that the leaders were comfortable constructing things out of hard and soft physical construction materials as well as capable of using such objects to mediate communication (both practices are explained in subsequent chapters). Encouraging them to articulate and share their unique individual views of the concept, I first asked them to create their own personal models of Customer Service Champion. These individual models were rather rudimentary and consisted of only a few hard and soft pieces combined. As Chapter 12 will expand on, I subsequently asked them to take on the role of their creations and present their understandings in the first person which would answer the question 'who am I?' (that is, 'I am a Customer Service Champion):

> Geographical business manager 1: 'I am different from other managers, but they think they are as good as I am in customer service. I am part of creating a complete cultural change in the company, but I do not understand where the company wants to go, and my role in it. I think I am a one to two year story.'

> Geographical business manager 2: 'I am a hard job. Customers are not happy and I have to deal with it. Others are dropping obstacles in my way, and I must smooth the path out. I need to kill attitudes and even people who have the wrong attitude, like the bottom line is most important.'

Geographical business manager 3: 'I am on a constant journey filled with barriers and rewards. I am A Better Offer of goods and services. [Then he slipped out of the first person mode when he continued:] We do not offer anything different from competition so we simply need to do things better.'

CFO: 'It is about barriers ... I think the concept is about attitudes of mind' [despite several attempts, the CFO was unable to express his construction in the first person].

Safety officer: 'I am a culture; the missing edge on a five-edged star. I am about adopting standards. I must be precise. I must be communicated. I must be measurable. I must be transparent. I must not let the staff be in any doubt about what I am.'

CEO: 'I am a frightening journey on a tightrope into the future, and I am struggling to keep the right balance. I am engaging my customers and ask them about today and tomorrow to try to get more balance and security into my journey. Both office and field people support me and I want to engage more with them. I am halfway through the journey ... no, in fact I am just starting out. I get energy from feeling what I do is risky. Although I want to mitigate the risk I do not want to lose sight about where I am going.'

Business development manager: 'I am a set of processes to deliver to customers. I might be talking with them, gathering information. I communicate to meet customers' needs.'

Following this initial exercise I asked them to try to construct together a new model that captured what each one of them considered an important aspect of the Customer Service Champion concept, manifested but not constrained by their previous narratives and models. This process took considerable time but resulted in a new construction to which all of them had contributed. As they revisited each of the hard and soft objects included in their model they added, removed and connected things as they saw fit. Throughout this sharing exercise all of them, the business manager included, seemed to enjoy themselves, evidenced by their relaxed body language, use of humour, and frequent laughter. One of them said: 'I could have kept going constructing, only time prevented me.' (Compare this with the story about the newspaper managers above.) When I asked for a volunteer to describe in words what they had captured in objects, one of the business managers eagerly jumped in (I asked him to continue to use first person):

> I am a journey about delighting our customers in the future. I am knocking down barriers and involving lots of people. I am a universal approach and I demand that every manager join me. I begin by engaging customers in an open, knowledgeable and passionate way. I am ready to change and to knock down barriers [illustrates this by pushing aside and removing things in the model].

His story provoked much approval among the others, indicated by nods, 'yes' statements, and scattered applause. From here I engaged them in a process to extract the key or foundational ideas that the Customer Service Champion concepts rested on according to them, and manifested in the model. At this stage they were all stirred up. They moved around the room and pointed at the constructions and at the list of words. They did not so much reflect over which words to use, but rather seemed to offer their top-of-mind reactions: *journey, openness, engagement, knowledge, passion, universal, many people, diversity, customer delight, flexibility and knock down barriers.*

Following this exercise, we agreed that each one of them, individually, should try to write their own personal story about what the Customer Service Champion meant to them, still *by playing the role of the model*. The CEO encouraged them to be personal, to make it 'their own thing'. While he said this, the rest of the group searched for whatever pieces of paper were available (not much), borrowed pens from one another, and started writing. During this process most of them stood up, walked to the table and studied the model from different angles.

This exercise resulted in seven individual statements that all wove most of the words on the board together, but in different ways. Then they each took turns to read how they had given meaning to the concept of Customer Service Champion. Immediately following this sharing, one of the business managers exclaimed: 'These stories are different, and yet similar!' Although it was late in the afternoon, the ambience was cheerful and relaxed, manifested by smiles, handshakes to congratulate one another for what they had achieved, and laughter. The CEO concluded the workshop with these words:

> I am happy we have captured what WE mean. I know now that any one of you can stand up in front of anyone in this organization and, using your OWN words, explain what Customer Service Champion means.

After the formal workshop we gathered in a local restaurant to relax over a drink. After a while the CEO came over to me, raised his glass, and said: 'I really struggled with this concept of ours. I didn't want to push it onto them and yet, I didn't take the time to invite them to co-own this idea with me – until today. This has really helped.'

The CEO of OilCo chose to involve others in making sense of the new customer-focus concept in their own personal way and share this among themselves. He did not push his own meaning onto the others and as a result their sense of belonging increased dramatically. Moreover, even as his group homed in on a handful of words they felt captured the essence of the concept, he did not push for a standardized statement to be inculcated into the rest of the organization. Instead, he explicitly invited his leaders to describe the concept to the people in their respective units *in their own words*, framed by their shared sense-making. Having gone through a process in which his leaders appeared to *authentically* bring forth their own ideas and interpretations of the concepts, he was confident they 'co-owned' the essential meaning of it. Every one of them was ready and committed to transform the organization from within.

In this book we will *step-by-step* describe and illustrate how the OilCo leaders came to this state of readiness. To make the point I will start with an anecdote that illustrates contra-practices, which are perhaps the 'prescribed' thinking and doing more common in organizations. Midway through the journey of the book we make a halt – to again remind you of such realities and the assumptions they rest on.

The anti-case

Driven by increased competition the CEO of the financial service company RedCo launched a new customer-focus concept (at about the same time as OilCo launched the concept of Customer Service Champion). To ensure immediate implementation of the new concept, the CEO recruited a well-known marketing professor to develop a standardized, two-hour, online 'worldwide implementation' workshop. Then he instructed his leadership team, ordering them to tell their staff to do the workshop within a month. To help his leadership team he authored a standardized e-mail, which he recommended they used in their own name. As was common practice in this firm, the initiative was linked to the bonus system, and doing the workshop was a must. Yet, to the CEO's frustration, despite these mechanisms people did not sign up for the workshop at the expected rate and in mid-2005 it looked inevitable that the whole project would be delayed.

One of the executives who was asked to help implement this initiative in his region explained the problem: 'The concept is owned by the CEO but he hasn't found a way to spread it even to us on the next level.' He continued, 'some of my peers went as far as to warn me not to touch it.' Reflecting over the history of such a corporate initiative he continued, 'these initiatives often lack coherence; they do not go well.' As far as I could tell a few months later this strategic (and expensive) initiative had met the same fate as previous ones: an important topic in meetings without deeper impact.

Quick reflection

There are striking similarities and differences between the two tales. The two organizations have a similar strategic need, that is, to become more customer oriented, which naturally means different things in their respective businesses. New circumstances called for a new outcome. In both cases the CEO initiated and launched a new concept to capture the essence of this need and, *in principle*, both of them decided to push this initiative further down the organization. Here is where the similarities end.

In RedCo the CEO chose to package his understanding and definition of the problem and enforce this meaning onto the next level managers, and, in turn, asked them to 'cascade' this approach further down the hierarchy. To efficiently and effectively steer the organization in the new direction, the leadership standardized both the meaning of the new concept (set definition), and the process for how to interpret it correctly (the 'implementation' workshop). The CEO's prescription was experienced as prescribed by the people on the next level, who in turn pushed the prescription further down the ranks. Having followed RedCo over time and seen the failure of a major strategic initiative a few years ago, I was not surprised to hear about their continued habits of prescribing new practices just as if they were reprogramming computers. Yet, I could not help wondering why they expected it to work this time, but as the people I talked with appeared quite sane, perhaps few had expected a different outcome this time. This way of working is truly inefficient, seems to be a waste of resources and managerial time, and rarely provides the desired results. It is also an opportunity loss for the organization. Just imagine how much the initiative might be improved if the vast resources that lie *within* people could be aroused.

In the world of prescribed thinking, we need to conform to what others think and suppress our own thoughts and feelings. When we are engaged in a necessary routine work to create value in stable circumstances this make sense. But, this is not the best way to prepare our minds for the new outcomes needed to meet new circumstances. The upcoming delay described in the RedCo anecdote exemplifies this failure. Until the CEO invited his leaders to think from within he faced this same risk, and we saw that nothing happened for quite some time after he first tried (but not very hard) to prescribe the new concept.

The OilCo tale illustrates the idea and practice of *Thinking from Within*, which I seek to convey throughout this book, and the RedCo tale illustrates what it is not. The OilCo tale illustrates how in a safe and secure environment it is possible to create the conditions to engage people's senses in ways that stir conventional thinking. It shows us what can happen when we let strategy emerge from within our thinking, how we can migrate from relying solely on routine and deductive analytical thinking towards nurturing our incredible imagination and making way for the spontaneity of our wisdom.

Objective facts and figures about the world are of course also important, for both strategy and other managerial practices. But only when we let the external information in to meet and merge with the inner world can we make any new meaning of it. This is what differentiates humans from expert systems. When we seek different outcomes to *also* meet new circumstances, strategy practices should become an opportunity to reflect on the world as we subjectively see it, just like the people in OilCo did. When we embrace spontaneity and imagination in our doing and thinking, strategy becomes a practice that helps organizations not only to efficiently adapt to given circumstances, but also to imaginatively shape their worlds. The distinction is clearly visible in the difference between the two tales above. When we grow our strategy practices from prescribed to 'from within', we delve into the world as we subjectively see it here and now. Conversations can focus on how to shape the world of which we are already an integral part, like they did in OilCo. Achievements of the strategy practice are manifested in wiser people, prepared to spontaneously seize fleeting opportunities and cope with emerging problems called for by changing circumstances.

Before we describe and further illustrate in more detail what the OilCo managers went through let's dig a bit deeper into the roots of the prescribed practices manifested in the RedCo anecdote and strategy practices in many other companies around the globe. After all, in order to change something we must first understand and acknowledge what it is we want to change.

Intellectual heritage

Prescribed strategy practices are rooted in an intellectual tradition that views leaders as cold-minded intellectuals, 'heads', separated from the 'body' of the organization. Knowledge is best acquired through deductive, analytical reasoning free from the fallibilities of our senses, and the specificity of the situation. When defending his 1641 treatise *Meditations on First Philosophy*, René Descartes famously coined *cogito ergo sum* ('I am thinking therefore I exist') to capture his thesis about the dualism of mind and body. Anyone who has meditated knows that it is indeed possible to pretend not to have a body, but not for too long. Eventually we need a bio-break. For the past centuries, Descartes has come to symbolize the paradigmatic separation between mind and body that underlies much of western organizational practices (as I will discuss below, this portrayal is unfair), such as strategy. For many leaders strategy practice is nothing but an austere exercise of passionless and pure reasoning, often conceptually and physically detached from the body of the organizations.

The Cartesian ideas developed further during the 18th century in the European philosophy we call the Age of Enlightenment. In principle, this philosophical movement advocated rationality as a means of establishing an authoritative system of ethics, aesthetics and knowledge. By objective study of nature and the physical universe, the intellectual leaders of this movement, Blaise Pascal, Gottfried Wilhelm von Leibniz, Galileo Galilei, Carl von Linnaeus, Denis Diderot and Isaac Newton among others, regarded themselves as courageously leading the world out of a long period of irrationality, superstition, and tyranny (from the church and sovereigns). In the Age of Enlightenment scientists were convinced strict laws could grasp Nature in full. It was the dream that man finally could be in control, to master the world rather than be left to the whims of a potentially dangerous Nature.

The coherent system of verifiable predictions, based on axiomatic proof and physical observation, in Newton's *Philosophiae Naturalis Principia Mathematica* (1687) and Linnaeus's *Systema Natura* (1735) are perhaps the most visible and famous example of the ideal of the Enlightenment. The idea of uncovering uniform laws for natural phenomena mirrored the greater systematization in a variety of studies by these scholars. Diderot's *Encyclopédie* (1751–1772) evidenced that in his fight against the unpredictable Nature, man had finally put his fist around all available knowledge centred on 'reason'.

This intellectual heritage is visible in much academic research in the field of organization. It is also the root of the term 'physics envy', which is used derogatively to describe social science's dream of emulating the paradigms of the natural sciences. It is particularly visible also in the field of strategy and this is a problem.[5] When strategy practice is seen as pure intellectual reasoning based on the ideals of rationality and prediction, we risk engaging only parts of the human potential and what people can contribute. When we eliminate from strategy practice what makes us human, it risks becoming as lacklustre, trivial and empty as many texts describing it. In David Whyte's terms, there is no sense of belonging. This practice may be good enough for those increasingly rare stable, predictable circumstances that do not call for new outcomes, but not for the rest of life.

The embodied mind

In the face of changing circumstances calling for new outcomes, how can we activate more of the human potential in an important organizational practice such as strategy? The mature Descartes lets us see a way. Towards the end of his life Descartes abandoned his early views and wrote in *Les Passions de l'Ame* (1649) how emotions are intricately intertwined with thinking. Descartes' refined ideas fundamentally challenged the 'tripartite soul' doctrine of Plato (impulses and reason mediated by emotions – Gr. *thumos*).

He came to this conclusion by pondering how feelings like passion, pleasure, hunger and pain were not disembodied, but rather appeared to have a lot to do with our body. There is indeed something intrinsically opaque about the sensory data we receive when the body is stimulated by, for instance, touching something or when we recklessly fall in love. Feelings are vivid and intense, often dramatically influencing our bodies in unpredictable ways and do not lend themselves to be analysed with the transparent rationality of the Enlightenment, but carry their own much deeper logic that is based on a wider and richer well of inputs. This suggests that knowledge, or rather 'knowing', involves not only 'pure' reasoning but also intuitive and embodied practice.

Like Descartes, who eventually questioned his famous distinction between mind and body, we should consider strategy practice to be more than pure and emotionless reasoning. As we gradually include more of our senses into the picture, we must also question the assumptions of rationality and prediction that underlie much of contemporary strategy practice (and research). When we *do* strategy, not just *think* strategy, we engage internal resources that otherwise would never be triggered. This 'doing' is not about mindless execution of, for instance, an 'implementation workshop' for the sake of just doing something; it is about the kinds of doing that describe, create and challenge what we know in ways pure intellectual reasoning cannot. *Through inclusion of our senses and personal thoughts, we engage more of the uniqueness and potential of our minds –*

we think 'from within'. This way we can avoid the apparent insanity by both expecting and getting a different outcome.

As a picture is said to convey more than a thousands words I will illustrate the difference between prescribed thinking and 'from within' with two pictures (Exhibits 1.2 and 1.3 in plate section), which depict the same group of people practising strategy in two very different ways. As an observer I took these pictures during a strategy session with the divisional leadership team of a multinational service company.

When I show such illustrations to managers and ask what they see their first reaction is typically 'what a mess'. They see the scattered documents, the projector, the laptop, the flipchart and the whiteboard, as well as the coffee, water and fruits. Focusing on the people they see a group of managers sitting around a table. One of them is using his hands to make a point, others watch him, a facilitator is standing in front and one guy is, yes, peacefully asleep. Following the laughs about the extremeness of the fleeting moment captured in this photo, I have enjoyed many serious conversations with managers about what they actually do when they practise strategy.

Of course, Exhibit 1.2 captures a brief moment of thinking and doing. Although we cannot see what they think, we can see what these managers do, at least then and there: talk, read papers, watch slide presentations, write text on the whiteboard and so on. As an observer I can report that they also used the occasion to regularly check their e-mails. As captured in this photo they spent most of the time listening, talking and reading – while sitting. From my recollection they were quite bored and detached.

What is not visible is their thinking, which for all except one seems to occur consciously. As an observer I noted how most of the time was spent reacting in a politically correct way to facts and figures. In my experience this photo reflects what managers do when they practise strategy, regardless whether they gather in an off-site retreat setting, as in this case, or work at the office. It may also represent the practice during just another meeting, on just about anything.

Managers often like to view themselves as hands-on, execution oriented and sometimes even passionate about what they do. Yet, when they practise important things like strategy they tend to become 'hands-off', emotionless intellectuals who thrive on abstract models. Perhaps they are too inspired by the notion of the thoughtful, superior, but passionless philosopher of ancient Greece, who also was an inspiration for the early Descartes? During this cerebral activity personal, subjective views are not welcome because they risk polluting the pure reasoning centred on objective facts about how things 'really are'. Noting a gender difference, former US secretary of state Madeleine Albright said the inclusion of feelings into serious conversations may sometimes make a man look 'strong', but typically makes women be described with the less positive term 'emotional'.[6]

Now look at Exhibit 1.3 (in plate section), and remember that it is the same group of people practising the same thing: strategy. The paradigmatic differences are that they have now allowed their senses to be engaged in service of creative expression from within, which in turn engaged their minds in new ways. Their knowing about the issues discussed did not just come from pure intellectual reasoning, but was also influenced by signals from their bodies in general and their hands in particular. These managers were freely engaging their ability to describe, create and challenge what they saw, and they took a stance about what they worked on. What comes from within becomes a part of us that we naturally commit to and take responsibility for. Just like the leaders of OilCo did, that day these managers were *Thinking from Within*.

By engaging more of our senses and emotions, as exemplified in Exhibit 1.3 and the OilCo story, we fuel our minds in ways that have tremendous benefits. We learn new things, we interact in new ways and we can more easily reach the deeper emotional levels of ourselves, which we believe are an important source for new ideas. When we think from within, as individuals and in groups, we can reduce the inefficiency, ineffectiveness and opportunity loss of contemporary organizational practices, such as strategy, and we can more easily belong to the thinking and doing involved. Instead of imposing the thinking on the next level of the organizational hierarchy in terms of a standardized and readymade training package attached to a bonus system, the CEO of OilCo invited his leaders to think from within. They left the meeting room ready and eager to execute: engaging others in something they both understood and agreed with. None of them used the occasion for a micro-nap and potential bonuses were not discussed.

Roadmap

Thinking from Within is grounded in the human practice called 'play'. By transforming important work such as strategy to become more play-like and play-ful, as illustrated in Exhibits 1.2 and 1.3 (in the plate section), we have to go beyond the deeply rooted folk conception that 'leisure play' has nothing to do with 'serious work'. Chapter 2 describes the possibilities of play for expressing deep and important thoughts, through the quality of ambiguity, from a range of perspectives, including philosophy, anthropology, sociology and, in particular, psychology. Seen as an important and inherent human practice, particularly important when dealing with changing circumstances where a new outcome is required, play serves as the overall conceptual foundation for *Thinking from Within*.

Practices

Grounded in this ambiguity of play *Thinking from Within* consists of three separate but interrelated practices, to be expanded in Chapters 3, 4 and 5: imagining, constructing together and object-mediated communication. Exhibit 1.4 depicts how these practices, grounded in the notion of play, make up *Thinking from Within*.

When we play we engage our imagination to describe, create and challenge the dynamic world as we see it. As described in Chapter 3 imagination has a conceptual, behavioural and an often neglected material dimension. To nurture and practice our full imagination we need to take on different symbolic roles, like being handymen, storytellers and architects. The story of ChemCo and other cases in this book illustrate how managers can do this in practice. Chapter 3 is devoted to how we can engage more of our imagination.

Delving further into the concept of *Thinking from Within* the material dimension of imagination deserves more attention. The very act of constructing things with our hands, and doing this together, is particularly beneficial for our imagination. Chapter 4 describes the concept behind and the practice of *constructing together* as an important element of *Thinking from Within*. The case of PrintCo illustrates the discussion.

But *Thinking from Within* is yet more imaginative than constructing together; it is about using what we co-construct to mediate communication about matters that concern us. Working with objects makes us think,

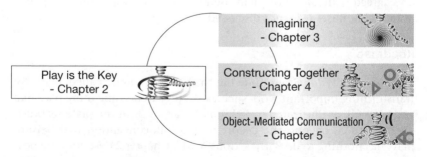

Exhibit 1.4 Thinking from Within practices

agree and cope differently, which will be evident in the cases provided throughout this book and already indicated in the tale of OilCo. Chapter 5 describes the third practice of *Thinking from Within*, *object-mediated communication*, and the case of TelCo illustrates what we mean.

Assumptions

On a deeper level *Thinking from Within* rests on two philosophical assumptions, which we need to grasp: how we view the world (ontology) and how we can know about it (epistemology). As esoteric as this may seem at first glance, such deeply formed assumptions influence our thinking and actions every day and are manifested also in how we practise strategy. To make this discussion more tangible Chapter 6 provides two longer case stories of conventional strategy practices, which did not include any of the thinking and doing described in this book. These two cases, framed in Chapter 6 as *a reminder of realities*, also serve as a comparison against all of the ideas presented in the book.

As depicted in Exhibit 1.5, Chapters 7 and 8 focus on the stance we must take when we think from within. Specifically, Chapter 7 claims we should view the world as inherently dynamic and always expect things to suddenly happen: the required ontology for *Thinking from Within* must be *intending emergence*. The BrassCo and TechCo cases presented in Chapter 6 and ChemCo of Chapter 3 serve to illustrate the necessary shift of ontology. In addition the tale of PackCo illuminates the key points made in this chapter.

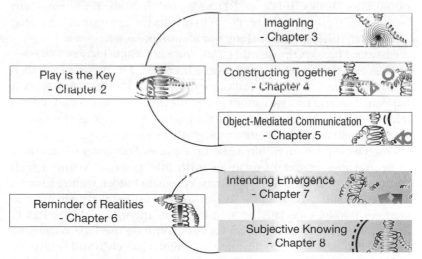

Exhibit 1.5 Assumptions of *Thinking from Within*

Chapter 8 describes and illustrates that what we perceive depends on who we are. *Thinking from Within* requires an epistemology of the *subjective way of knowing*. The BrassCo and TechCo cases presented in Chapter 6 and ChemCo of Chapter 3 serve to illustrate the necessary shift in ways of knowing (epistemology) for *Thinking from Within*.

The emergent benefits from *Thinking from Within* are manifold. Recall that this not an idea about better philosophizing, or abstract reasoning for the sake of thinking, nor is it about mindless execution for the sake of just getting things done. The next few chapters are devoted to describe and illustrate the emergent, potential benefits of *Thinking from Within*, which is described in Exhibit 1.6.

Chapter 9 suggests that the content of our thinking becomes influential and enduring when we escape from the 'flatland' of text and pictures so often used in strategy practices. *Thinking from Within* encourages us to develop three-dimensional imagery that, when co-constructed with our hands, remain with us. The focus of this chapter is on the three-dimensional imagery our imagination and hands produce and the narratives these images both capture and give rise to. Yet another case of strategy practice, that of HandyCo, illustrates the benefits of escaping the flatland in strategy practice.

Another emergent benefit of this practice stems from the very foundation of play: developing organizational identity. In Chapter 10 we focus on organizational identity, describe what it is and how it is socially constructed and, in our case, also physically constructed. We use two additional case stories, InfCo and DiscCo, to illustrate these emergent benefits. Using these cases, we go on to discuss the intrinsic benefits that all play activities have in shaping our identities.

Chapter 11 makes the case that *Thinking from Within* increases chances of peak experiences among the people involved. The literature on such phenomena in other fields indicates the tremendous benefits when it happens, but also that we cannot just make them happen. An additional tale of a management group, ConglomerateCo, as well as the case of TalkCo, illustrate peak experiences and what they are good for.

When we think from within we become aware of our inner self and how to bring those important qualities forth into practice. Without such authenticity, imagination and spontaneity remain hidden within. Chapter 12 describes and illustrates how we can enhance authenticity when *Thinking from Within*, especially by learning from theories and practices of drama. In this chapter we revisit PackCo, continue the TalkCo case and provide two new stories to illustrate out point, GadgetCo and UtilityCo.

Thinking from Within paves the way for the spontaneity of our practical

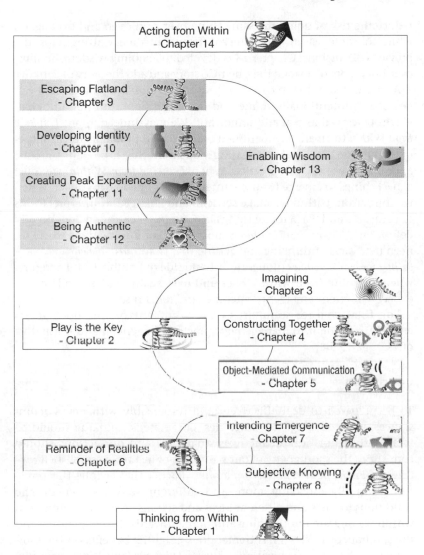

Exhibit 1.6 Emergent benefits of *Thinking from Within*

wisdom. When we are wise we use our inner potential of imagination and spontaneity to size up novel situations, make decisions and take action that promotes not only ourselves but also the community that sustains us. *Thinking from Within* cultivates our split-second swiftness to do the right thing when real-life situations call for it. With increased wisdom we reduce the risk of doing the same thing over, and over, and over again, while, for some reason, expecting a different outcome. Cutting across the previous discussions, Chapter 13 is devoted to enabling wisdom. To illustrate our points we extend the ChemCo story and add the story of BankCo.

As illustrated in Exhibit 1.6 *Thinking from Within* is a practice that can be used to intentionally frame and deal with opportunities and challenges perceived as real and important. We may indeed apply *Thinking from Within* to an already identified and specified problem. Yet, as subsequent chapters will make increasingly apparent that is perhaps the least appropriate use for this practice. When *Thinking from Within*, we must expect things to emerge from the interactions of people involved. When we think from within we make sense of and change our interpretations of the world and we perceive things in ways pure reasoning does not. By definition, *Thinking from Within* is most pertinent for situations where we need new ways of thinking and acting, that is, for *unstable circumstances calling for new outcomes* (upper right-hand side of Exhibit 1.1). Therefore, when we think from within, over and over again, we can and should expect a different emergent, outcome (and remain sane).

The final chapter summarizes the argument of this book in its entirety, relating it to management practices in general and normative ones in particular.

Conclusion

To be prepared to deal effectively and responsibly with new circumstances, while seeking new outcomes, our strategic thinking should be imaginative, not only deductively analytical and our actions should come from the spontaneity of our wisdom, not just from established routines. *Thinking from Within* is a play-like practice that enables this transformation. By engaging more and different senses we create the conditions for new and different ideas and actions. When we think from within we migrate our thinking and doing towards the imaginative and the spontaneous, which has tremendous potential benefits on the individual, social and organizational levels. *Thinking from Within* complements existing strategy practices in organizations with ways of working more astute for meeting new circumstances in new ways.

Because of my own background this book focuses on strategy practices, but that should not be seen as a constraint, just a starting point. *Thinking from Within* is a way of thinking *and* doing that can and should be applied in whatever fields that make sense to you. The only limitation is your own imagination, spontaneity and perhaps how well you play.

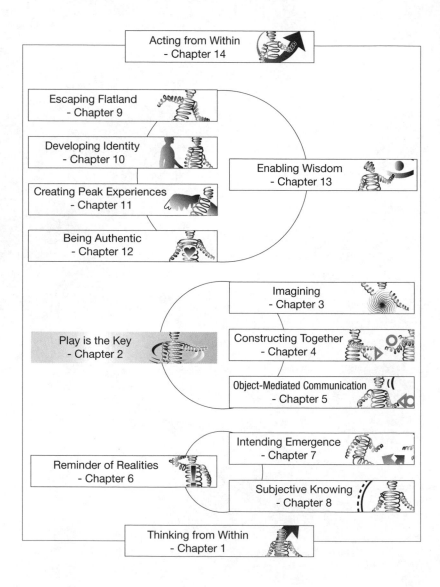

2
Play is the Key

Johan Roos and Madeleine Roos

Introduction

Play forms an important conceptual foundation for the practice of *Think ing from Within*, which subsequent chapters will describe and illustrate. Play is a natural human activity that has been widely acknowledged to have significant emotional, social and cognitive benefits for children and adults. Based on a traditional view on play as a tool for building up the minds of children, adult play is usually regarded as frivolous and of questionable value at work. It is hence chiefly the 'childish' aspects of play that are officially recognized while the ambiguity, imagination and other qualities of play that benefit humans of all ages are rarely regarded as play. For instance, play as described by Whitilcott (1971) is far from an aimless activity or simply having fun, although that may be part of it. Play involves the capacity to relax our control needs and become more open minded about what might emerge. Thus, to think from within we need to be able to play.[1]

The purpose of this chapter is to describe play from several theoretical perspectives. To this end we review in brief the philosophical, anthropological and sociological literature, and in depth the psychological literature. This review reveals the deep, intrinsic characteristics of play, which in turn characterize *Thinking from Within*. The emergent benefits of play include the fundamental principles (studied in philosophy) that guide decisions concerning the purpose of work itself via the overall identity of an organizational culture (studied in anthropology), the social bonds and relations between individuals (studied in sociology) and the core of the emotional and cognitive dimensions within the individual (studied in psychology). This multifaceted view of play serves as a solid building block in the foundation of *Thinking from Within* and also indicates the emergent benefits of this practice.

The ambiguity of play

There is an incredible diversity of activities referred to as 'play', which has given rise to an equally wide range of theories that seek to explain the purposes and processes of the activities themselves. Brian Sutton-Smith (1997) describes these theoretical perspectives as 'rhetorics' that function both descriptively and normatively to explain and perpetuate play as certain forms of social and cultural activities. Although we regard play as an important dimension for pushing the achievements at work to new, hitherto unknown heights, we realize that, at first glance, work and play might appear mutually exclusive (as some researchers claim). Over the years, derived from the modern cultural and economic heritage of Protestant capitalism (Weber 1958), work has attained the status of something serious = good, and play has attained the status of irresponsible = bad. This worldview is developed in our childhood.

Children benefit naturally from play while growing up, and enjoy playful methods for their early education. As we approach adulthood something happens, as we can see from the differences between kindergarten and schools. In kindergarten we are encouraged to play and the adults guiding us do not separate play from other activities. Most of what we do is playful, even when we learn. When we enter school most of us are hit by the sudden separation between play and classroom activities, like 'teaching', 'instruction' and 'learning'. Play is relegated to the space in between classes, but considered legitimate in sports, music and arts classes. As adults we tend to lose our earlier ability to play well, especially at work where play is often seen as a frivolous activity with no purpose other than enjoyment. With increasing responsibilities and formal positions, most of us become even less playful and more serious, except when we are allowed to 'play' at company parties, dress down on casual Fridays, or during the token 'outdoor' exercise at business school and perhaps during 'brain storming'. Unless we are a recognized 'creative type', during the rest of our work-life we should stay away from any play-like behaviour.

The positivist and rationalist traditions of management theories that advocate this view have been broadly critiqued during recent decades, although not with any significant impact on the mainstream literature in the field. The relationship between work and play remains under-defined and tenuous. This lack of a clear definition pertains especially to the shallow claims about the benefit of 'having fun' often included in company statements of 'core values'. This practice denies the deep dimensions of the intrinsically human activity called play. A solid definition of play in organizations requires clear definitions of the play–work relationship.

Before entering the review of play we would like to pay attention to play in relation to art. We acknowledge the difficulty of defining the exact differences and precise similarities between play and art. The two words are intertwined linguistically as well as semantically. It is not as simple as play being an activity and art the result of an activity. Expressions like 'The Art of …' and 'The State of the Art of …' exemplify the wider meaning of art; and 'a theatre play' shows that play can be used to describe a static phenomenon (that actually is a piece of art). We are contented to state that play is an important factor in art-making, and that the experience of art can trigger the imaginative and ambiguous qualities of play that we discuss above and below. Furthermore, there is art which comes about without play (for example photo realistic painting) and play that does not fit into the description of art (for example playing games). To avoid confusion, we will in the following text use *play as a verb and art as a noun*, and also try to be as clear as possible in general with what we mean.

Perspectives on play

Philosophy

In philosophy the concept of play relates to metaphysical questions concerning the world and to questions about knowledge and knowing, epistemology (see Chapter 7) as well as to ethical questions concerning humanity. First, philosophers view play as a fundamental characteristic of our world. This view dates from the beginning of the western philosophical tradition and continues today with complexity and chaos theory (to be discussed in Chapter 8). An influential formulation of this notion characterizes the universe metaphorically as an instance of child's play in which all order emerges, is destroyed over time and then, in turn, is replaced by new, fundamentally different laws and regularities (Nietzsche 1964). This claim is tempered by arguments that maintain that the apparent processes of chaotic transformation visible in the natural and physical world are in fact based on the ancient Greek principles of form and order, which do not themselves undergo change. This distinction between an 'apparent' world of 'becoming' based on 'play', in contrast to a 'real' world of 'being', has itself undergone significant critique. Recent philosophical endeavours have characterized the contingent, dynamic and 'playful' character of reality in terms of difference (Derrida 1978), identity (Heidegger 1968), and alterity (Levinas 1969).

Play has a corresponding epistemological and ethical significance: a truly ethical society can only arise if all parties acknowledge the inherently playful character of meaning and communication (Rorty 1991). Philosophers argue that the freedom of the will differentiates us from the 'causal determinism' that governs the world around us (Kant 1781/1950), because our free will is precisely what allows us to cope with choices. Whenever we judge our actions as good or bad, we must refer to ethical principles about what is considered right or wrong, which require both imagination and understanding. Following this argument even the notion of 'common sense' refers not to a common understanding based on compulsory agreement, but to the possibility of reaching such agreement, when all people enjoy the free play of imagination in harmony with the understanding (Kant 1790/1987). Thinkers in the Enlightenment tradition (Kant 1781/1950; Schiller 1983), already alluded to in Chapter 1, have argued that an essential component of human rationality is the capacity to imagine the world 'as if' it was different from empirically manifest reality. The human imagination has been shown to involve the 'playful' construction of abstract, even fantastic ideas that differ from empirical sense data. But in a corollary line of argument, philosophers have demonstrated that the imagination serves a greater function than the generation of mere fantasy (Chapter 3 expands on the topic of imagination and how we practise it).

In sum, from a philosophical perspective play sets conditions for ethical judgement and imagination. The philosophical literature suggests that our playful imagination help us to recognize ethical principles and act accordingly.

Anthropology

With the fundamental principles of play described in philosophical terms we now zoom in one level closer to the private worlds of human beings when we move into the anthropological literature. From this viewpoint play is a cultural activity through which a society frames itself. Play is an expressive and/or narrative activity to construct collective and cultural identity. Play allows people to create and recreate cultural identity in light of their reality (see Sutton-Smith 1997).

Researchers debate to what extent play is similar across cultural differences and if the cultural identity can be challenged from the play activity as such. For example, through play, cultures encounter aesthetic, moral and metaphysical dimensions of their identity (Geertz 1973). This theory suggests that through play people within a culture collectively imagine themselves as others, which helps them to reflect on their own identity and the values that sustain it. Whenever a culture – national or organizational – constructs itself by imagining an alternate image of itself, this alternate image draws direct attention to the 'liminal' aspects of the culture under construction. Hence, not only can the individual imagine the self as another in play (see role-play in Chapter 12), but the entire culture within which an individual comes to understand the meaning of self–other relationships is imagined through collective play. Carnivals, festivals, parades, national anniversaries and other forms of collective play exemplify this (for additional examples see Sutton-Smith 1997).

In light of these ideas, how can work be identified and pursued? Some scholars claim that the excesses of play serve as a necessary counterpoint to work, sustaining and reinforcing the overall order of society (Bakhtin 1984). Other anthropologists have shown that while play may be completely 'unproductive' in the sense that it results in no direct value artifact, in the way that work and art should, it can produce certain higher-order benefits for cultures as well as for individuals.

In sum, in the anthropological literature play is a narrative process through which cultural identity is created and transformed. Imagination in play is an important dimension for understanding the meaning of relationships with others, on both individual and social levels (within the culture). Anthropologists also take an interest in the relation between play and work for the understanding of cultural identity, and different views are put forward on this matter (Chapter 10 expands on the notion of organizational identity seen as a benefit).

Sociology

In our journey of studying play at different levels of human dimensions we have seen diverse yet similar patterns emerge. On the overall level of fundamental principles, (imaginative) play is important for ethical judgement, and on the more specific cultural level it is important for our understanding of who we are and how we can understand others. The play literature also addresses the meaning of play within a society because individuals within a culture use play as a means for interactions. Sociologists have dealt with the concept of play from several distinct, but interrelated standpoints. Play is a process by which individuals become familiar with societal symbols, identify themselves in relation to others and acquire skills required to function effectively in the social community (Mead 1934/2001). The sociological literature discusses how the concept of self (identity) involves seeing oneself as another. Thus, individuals playing are always playing-at-something, or imagining themselves 'as if' they were someone else. Working from these insights, an important stream of research in sociology explores the relationship between particular forms of play and the overall structure and significance of society at large. From this vantage point play has contributed greatly to the formation of civilization as such, influencing and giving rise to institutions such as war, law, art and philosophy (Huizenga 1950). Play activities also allow society to adapt and survive (Smith 1982) and some even claim that plays is 'the primary place for the expression of anything that is humanly imaginable' (Sutton-Smith 1997: 226). This definition of play moves us towards 'potentiation of adaptive variability' (ibid. p. 231) for people and society, that is, preparedness. Subsequent chapters will pick up this thread in terms of increased spontaneity (Chapter 12) and wisdom (Chapter 13). In other words, through play, humans imagine new possibilities and become more prepared to realize them, should circumstances call for it.

Sociologists have also examined play as a metaphor for human communication, demonstrating that the rule-based frames imagined through play also organize the individual's experience of society (Goffman 1974). Play develops our capacity to understand meaning in contexts and social rules and how to act and communicate in accordance with them.

In sum, the sociological literature addresses play primarily as an activity through which social relationships are developed and adapted. Spontaneity is increased through play, which helps us become both more poised for imagining new possibilities and able to put them into practice.

Quick reflection

Let's make a short stop on our journey from the outer framework to the inner mind and get an overview of what we have seen so far. Already from the three grand perspectives of humanism we can better understand and frame the ambiguity of play, summarized in Exhibit 2.1. The philosophical literature suggests that our playful imagination helps us make ethical judgement, which can in turn effectively guide work activity.

Philosophy	Anthropology	Sociology
Play helps us recognize and act according to ethical principles	Play is a narrative process to create and transform cultural identity	Play develops and adapts social relationships

Exhibit 2.1 Framing play
Source: Statler et al. (2002).

The anthropological literature demonstrates that play allows people to develop and adapt cultural identities, within which the purpose and value of work may be determined. The sociological literature casts play as an activity through which people frame and adapt the social contexts and relationships necessary for work and living together.

With a good idea of the philosophical, anthropological and sociological perspectives for what play means, we will now enter the inner world of humans and explore what qualities play is attributed from the psychological perspective. We believe that by this action we will further comprehend human practice in organizations in general and set the stage for the notion of *Thinking from Within* in particular.

Psychology and play

Since the surfacing of psychology as a scientific discipline, and the subsequent emergence of psychotherapy in the late 19th century, during the 20th century psychotherapy branched into three related yet distinct traditions: *behaviourism, psychoanalysis* and *humanistic psychology*, which treat play in different ways.

The late 19th century was a time of intensive and rapid scientific and technological advancement. The pursuit of objective knowledge focused also on the human mind and behaviourism was born. A milestone in this process was when Wilhelm Wundt created a laboratory for studies in psychology and observed human behaviour in various experimental situations (1874). This stream of research systematically excludes all the subjective data of human consciousness and denies that it is possible to know, much less intervene therapeutically in the 'inner complexity' of the human personality and its development. It is only indirectly connected to the subsequent appearance of two dominant paradigms in psychotherapy: first psychoanalysis and later humanistic psychology, which is the home for most of the playful ideas in psychology.

Psychoanalysis

Parallel to behaviourist researchers (for example Skinner 1974), others interested in individual differences sought to go beyond the surface of human behaviour and develop a more profound understanding of the depths of the human mind. Breuer used cathartic methods to release symptomatic emotional tensions that he thought were the result of forgotten past events (Breuer and Freud 1895). Furthermore, Sigmund Freud studied hypnosis with Charcot in the 1880s (Owen 1971), who practised this method as a means of accessing the unconscious part of the mind, which was believed to contain repressed emotions and basic human instincts.

Freud subsequently became the father of the concept of the 'unconscious'. He went on to develop the psychoanalytical technique of free associations, as well as interpretation of dreams as ways to disclose the hidden depths of the unconscious, which he regarded as a very personal entity.

One of Freud's closest followers was Carl Gustav Jung. Like Freud he believed not only that unconscious signals revealed themselves in symbolic forms, but also that by exploring revelations through analysis, a patient could identify his or her 'true self'. But whereas Freud believed that the unconscious mind only communicated with the conscious mind passively, in dreams and through free associations, Jung's method additionally involved 'active imagination' which he defined as a sequence of fantasies produced by deliberate concentration, or dreaming the dream onward (Hopcke 1989). In this regard, Jung theorized the unconscious not just as a receptacle for repressed material à la Freud, but also *as a positive resource* (1965). He furthermore believed that the unconscious psychic life went beyond the personal, to include a 'collective unconscious' of humanity itself, something he described as the unlearned tendency to experience things in a certain way (Hopcke 1989). Jung illustrated symbolically the different functions of the collective unconscious in Archetypes, that is symbols structurally similar to Freud's notion of biological instincts.[2]

Another of Freud's colleagues, Otto Rank (1989), researched therapeutic practices on the active, or constructive, forces within the individual psyche, including what he considered to be 'a will to health' (Lieberman 1985; Freedheim 1992).

In contrast with Freud himself, Freudian-trained analysts who later went their own ways saw the unconscious less as a passive entity that could be explored objectively, but more as a positive resource for active personal development. Instead of regarding the hidden insights brought to the surface in therapy with defeatism, patients were helped to actively use their new understanding to create a healthier future.

Play and art in psychoanalysis

There is a close relationship between play and art in psychoanalysis. We will see below how play is an important aspect for art-making, and art an important source for symbolic communication that in its turn triggers the imaginative and other qualities of play in a continuous feedback loop (of psychotherapy).

In the early days psychoanalysts used play to better understand the unconscious mind of children and they soon noticed that children differed from adults. They were unable to describe their anxieties verbally as adults did, and they seemed not the least bit interested in free-associating, exploring their past or discussing their earliest memories (Landreth 2002). In the early 20th century Freud published the first case in which play was used in psychotherapy, 'Little Hans', involving a five-year-old boy with a phobia (Freud 1955). Based on Hans's father's notes about Hans at play, Freud conducted the treatment by advising the father how to respond to the child at play.[3] Working with adults, Freud asked some of his patients to express themselves by creating drawings (Malchiodi 1998).

Jung is the father of both play therapy and 'creative arts therapies', and the latter is the recognized term for this activity. But in view of how it is carried out it could also be called 'playful arts therapies' because the word creative refers to the imaginative and spontaneous qualities of play that imply creating new material. Creative arts therapies are usually carried out in groups, and characteristic are the three phases of warm-up, action, and the subsequent sharing of insights and experiences. The one or several media that are chosen for the process can be of conceptual and/or physical nature (see Chapter 4).

After his emotional break with Freud in 1912, Jung opened himself up to inner impulses and remembered a boyhood experience playing in the dirt and constructing a miniature town. He was drawn to the idea and, overcoming his embarrassment at appearing childish, he started to build in the dirt again. Jung found this activity allowed him not only to express his emotional turmoil better, but also to process and reintegrate the emotional material in a less threatening way (Jung 1965; Schaefer 2003). Jung went on to explore both play and art as methods for unleashing the symbolic and communicative powers of practising imagination (more about this in Chapter 3).

Melanie Klein (1955), Anna Freud (1946) and other psychoanalysts used play therapy in their work with children, whereas educator Margaret Naumburg (1947, 1950, 1953; Cane et al. 1983) and psychoanalyst Beatrice Hinkle (1923) in the USA, and Adrian Hill in the UK (Malchiodi 1998) brought forth Jung's theories in the name of art therapy for both adults and children.

Among the psychoanalytical play therapies, we focus specifically on *sand play*, which is a technique derived from two sources: the 'World Technique' where children were asked to use small toys in wet and dry sand on trays to 'make their world', hence the name (Lowenfeld 1979),[4] and the analysis of Dora Kalff (1980), a Jungian analyst who came in contact with the 'World Technique' in the 1950s. Assuming that play could establish a dialogue between the unconscious and the conscious mind, Kalff used sand play to encourage her patients to symbolize and express pre-verbal experiences and blocked energies. She believed that the medium of sand, in combination with projective figures, allowed the child to naturally express both the archetypal and intra-personal worlds, while providing a direct, physical connection between the inner world of the mind and outer, everyday reality. She hypothesized that the effect of using this medium for expression would be to activate the child's regenerative and healing energies. More specifically, she thought that when all these dimensions blended within the safe and protected space created by the therapist, a vital connection between the ego and the self could be re-established. And once the ego-self axis was reactivated, Kalff theorized, the child would act in a more balanced and congruent manner.[5]

The acceptance of creative arts in psychotherapy, especially with adult patients, was more difficult, even though the pioneers found it highly effective to replace the verbal approach with art therapy, with its use of symbolic language and imagery, in their analytical work with both children and adults. One can speculate as to why creative arts, despite its shared roots with analytical play therapy, came to stand outside the established traditions of psychotherapy for several decades, while play therapy with children thrived within the respected institutions. Play was probably seen as a secondary alternative when the analytical 'talking cure' was not possible, and thus not needed with mature and verbal adults. The communicative power of making and interpreting art was not yet fully recognized. Therapists considered toys as symbolic words in the child's play language (Landreth 2002). Psychoanalyst D.W. Winnicott summarized: 'It is in playing and only in playing that the individual child or adult is able to be creative and to use the whole personality, and it is only in being creative that the individual discovers the self' (1971: 63).

The past decades have seen adult versions of play therapies, like for example sand play (see Mitchell and Friedman 1994), to be practised within the realm of established adult psychotherapy. The non-directive technical aspects of sand play are the same for adults as for children. It remains important for the therapist to establish a safe and protected space, within which whatever emerges in the tray should be regarded as appropriate and acceptable. Adults, like Jung, often experience uncomfortable feelings of embarrassment when thinking about playing in the sand, and if they are reflective about the technique, then the playfulness can be constrained by a fear of what might be unexpectedly revealed in the tray.

Humanistic psychology

Towards the mid-20th century, the active and future-oriented versions of psychoanalysis attracted much attention and inspiration for psychotherapy was also found in other humanistic fields, for example existentialism (Heidegger and Farrell 1993; Kierkegaard et al. 1996). Psychologist Carl Rogers' ideas resonated not only with ideas from Jung, Rank and other early followers of Freud, but also strongly with Kurt Goldstein's idea of self-actualization. This is a holistic view that extends the scientific finding of how other parts of the human brain compensate for brain damage and to consider this function to be valid and possible for the entire organism (Goldstein 1939, 1963). The time was ripe for Carl Rogers, Abraham Maslow and Rollo May to found the concept of humanistic psychology, which sought to bring about healing through reconciling the true self and ideal self to a 'fully functioning' person (Rogers 1961). Rogers talked about the 'actualizing tendency', which can be defined as the built-in motivation present in every life-form to develop its potential to the fullest extent possible. He believed that all creatures strive to make the very best of their existence. This new category of thoughts was both an evolution of, as well as a reaction to, psychoanalysis. Rogers' non-directive technique was later referred to as client-centred therapy and today is known widely as 'person-centred therapy' (Rogers 1951, 1961).

Play and art in humanistic psychology

One of Roger's students, Virginia Axline (1947), developed a version of Roger's client-centred therapy called 'child-centred play therapy'. The idea was to avoid controlling or changing the child, but instead trust the child's drive for complete self-realization. As the child plays freely in a well-stocked playroom, the therapist actively reflects on the child's thoughts and feelings, seeking to help the child accept and deal with these thoughts and feelings once they had been expressed, identified and accepted.

Adler, who originally was a disciple of Freud but later became closely associated with the humanistic psychology movement, also came up with a play-based psychotherapeutic method based on the holistic assumption that people are socially embedded, goal directed and view reality subjectively (Ansbacher and Ansbacher 1956). The Adlerian play process uses toys, art materials, and books to go through four stages.[6] Over time the safe space of the playroom provides a forum within which the child can practise healthy skills and attitudes. Adlerian play therapy has been shown to work well with children who suffer from acting-out behaviour, as well as for anxious or perfectionist, and gifted children, who seem especially responsive (Schaefer 2003).

On the parallel track of creative arts therapies, we can see how its basic concepts developed and also, with great success, came to embrace the qualities of humanistic psychology. Otto Rank, one of the strong sources of inspiration for Carl Rogers, was deep into creativity and the arts and its relations to personality development. Rollo May, himself also an artist, argues that psychological well-being comes from the act of making (1985). Carl Rogers' daughter Natalie has integrated her father's ideas with creative arts therapies (or expressive arts therapies as it is called when several media are combined within the frame of a creative arts process), to a concept she calls 'person-centered expressive arts therapy' (1993). Thus, creative arts within the realm of humanistic psychology does not reduce the importance of the symbolic communication that was so strongly accentuated by the psychoanalysts, especially Jung, but the emphasis here is even more on the experience of the creative process as healing in itself, something that Jung also vividly described. Since the foundation of humanistic psychology, the traditional institutions have gradually accepted creative arts therapies as valid also for adult psychotherapy (Malchiodi, 1998). During the 1950s and 1960s several national associations for different kinds of creative arts therapies were founded.[7]

In sum, from both the psychoanalytical perspective as well as that of humanistic psychology, playful processes such as creative arts therapies promote *symbolic communication from within* and are also *healing in themselves*. Similar processes, but with the dimension of psychotherapy replaced by non-clinical issues, like for example personal development or counselling, are called creative arts processes. As will be evident in this book, *Thinking from Within* is a representative of this category.

Emerging benefits of play

By now it is clear that we reject the view that play is frivolous and only marginally important in organizations. In a simple phrase suggested by Statler et al. (2002) play in organizations 'ain't misbehavin'. On the contrary, it is imaginative, ethical and by its potentiation of adaptive variability nurtures spontaneity, which is something we relate to as 'intentional emergence' (see Chapter 7). The OilCo example (Chapter 1) and several other cases in this book exemplify such emergent benefits.

The consequences are straightforward. On the one hand, the apparently frivolous has to be taken more seriously. From an anthropological perspective, play is integral to the orderly function of organizations (as social systems or cultures). It is precisely through play, seen as liminal experiences, that people come to associate themselves with a particular cultural (organizational) identity in the first place. Moreover, the ritual process of playful activities is what allows cultures (organizations) to adapt to change. In other words, not only might play activities allow organizational identity as such to emerge, or be strengthened, but they may also help that organization to prepare for changing circumstances. As depicted in Exhibit 2.2, play is imaginative, ethical and intentionally emergent.

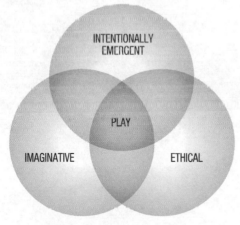

Exhibit 2.2 What play is
Source: Adapted from Statler et al. (2002).

In terms of the language of Chapter 1, play can transform the 'prescribed thinking' of conventional practices to *Thinking from Within* (see Exhibit 1.1).

Conclusion

The ambiguous concept and practice of play is fundamental to humankind and by implication to human interaction in organizations. From the literature review in this chapter we can now summarize that when we practise *Thinking from Within* in organizations we need to nourish the relationship between play and work. Play has a value in itself because it creates the context for emergence. Thus, by making work more play-like we can create the context for the emergent benefits of play to be brought into work.

In the beginning of this chapter we said that play and work should not be each other's opposites, but integrated with the aim of increasing the quality of work as well as the well-being of those working. To achieve such a symbiosis of play and work, play has to be imaginative, ethical and by nurturing spontaneity, also intentionally emergent.

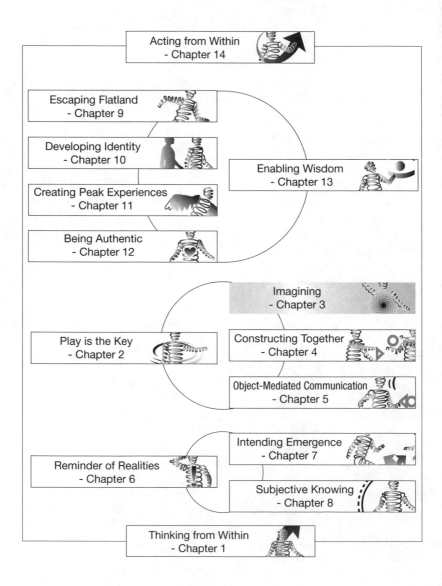

3
Imagining

Peter Bürgi and Johan Roos

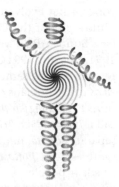

Introduction

In Chapter 2 we learnt that one of the distinguishing characteristics of play is that it is imaginative. The starting point for *Thinking from Within* is to see imagination as a practice that thrives in the ambiguous context of play (discussed in Chapter 2). This chapter serves two purposes: to provide a conceptual framework for the ancient and tricky notion of imagination and to describe and illustrate what it means to practise it. First, we describe three fundamental dimensions of imagination: conceptual, behavioural and material. Grounded in these dimensions we then present three roles that we should take on when practising imagination: handymen, architects and tellers of stories that drive action. Finally, we illustrate with the case story of ChemCo how two groups of leaders had an opportunity to practise imagining in these ways, helping them think from within rather then rely on their existing, prescribed thinking.

More than an act to develop new ways of pursuing business, imagination is a deep and multidimensional construct at the heart of what it means to be human. As evidenced in the OilCo story and depicted in Exhibits 1.2 and 1.3 (in the plate section), imagination is not just a cerebral and meditation-like exercise. Imagination is a whole-body experience, so to imagine means to also use the body, including the hands. To better understand the practice of imagination, we need to dig deeper into the meanings of imagination as it has evolved over the past two millennia. Imagination has several profound dimensions.

The concept of imagination

The historical record of how notions of imagination developed begins with the Greek philosophers Aristotle and Plato, but the meaning of the

41

concept has evolved continuously, taking on new energy through the philosophy of the Enlightenment and Modern periods to the present (see Bundy 1927; Warnock 1976; Kearney 1988; White 1990; Brann 1991; Cocking 1991). Various terms have been used, all of them basically referring to the same concept: the Greeks used the terms *phantasia* and *eikasia*, the Romans called it *imaginato*; Germans use the two denominations *Einbildungskraft* and *Phantasie* and both the English and the French call it *imagination*. Rooted in the Germanic tradition, Swedes (like Johan) separate *föreställningsförmåga* (the ability to visualize things) and the more esoteric *fantasi*, which means fantasy. In daily practice, though, Swedish people use the latter to mean the former, so it follows that most tend to imply *fantasy* when they use the English term imagination. This practice means many Swedes view issues of 'imagination' with a certain scepticism. While all these terms share the basic idea that humans have a unique ability to 'image' or 'imagine' something, the variety of uses of the term imagination implies not one but several meanings, which are deeper than to describe, create and challenge.

In the philosophical literature imagination is persistently seen as some property that mediates between experience and understanding. Thus, experience does not present itself as meaningful to the mind in and of itself but becomes meaningful because of the imagination. The Greeks' treatment of the concept is characterized by serious attempts to come to grips with the conceptualization processes of the mind, beyond their devotion to pure reason and rationality. Although they do not name it as such, Aristotle and Plato illuminated the concept of imagination as a 'faculty of inner representation' (Brann 1991).

Plato used the word *eikasia*, translated as building and representing images in the mind, to refer to an ability to recognize images as images. Aristotle used the word *phantasia*, meaning a process for presenting inner appearance of sensation in the mind. Given Plato's predisposition against the possibility of apprehending reality through the senses except as a derivative and debased body of experiences, he equates *eikasia* with a form of trickery and misrepresentation. Thus, *eikasia* is the suspect derivation of the reality accessible to the senses. For Aristotle, there is no world of forms behind or beyond what we perceive. Like Plato, he tries to come to grips with how the physical world is represented to the intellect. *Phantasia* is the concept he uses to describe the process whereby the physical properties of things appear in the mind, that is, how we describe things, even if they are not physically present. For these philosophers, 'imagination' is about the integrity of experience in our thinking, which in turn help our pure reasoning.

While the philosophical writings of the next one and a half millennia offer occasional glimpses of attempts to wrestle with the concept of the imagination, it is only in the Enlightenment that the topic really gathers strength again. At that point, Immanuel Kant famously develops the notion that mind furnishes our experience of reality with the properties of being 'in space' and 'in time', rather than 'space' and 'time' being independent of subjectivity. Our capacity to understand is our capacity for mental experiences characterized by the 'synthetic unity' of antecedent, simpler and less mediated 'representations' of the world in the mind. At the same time there are also straightforward 'sensations', made possible through the faculty of the mind he calls the 'sensibility'. Imagination, in his schema, is what integrates understanding and sensibility: it allows for judgements to form integrated representations *as concepts* (Brann 1991).

At the heart of these three classic approaches lies an idea that cuts to the very root of the supposedly pure 'objectivist worldview' of rationalists: namely, the recognition that we do not experience the world in an unmediated way, but instead experience it *mediated* through interpretation. Plato's 'image-agency' presenting 'images' to the mind, the *phantasia* of Aristotle, and Kant's (1781 and 1790) 'representations' all suggest that to understand the world is to interpret it, and, more importantly, that imagination is the 'interpretative aspect of perception' (Thomas 1997: 106).

During the Romantic movement of the 18th and 19th centuries, however, the vitality of the concept of the imagination changed, and the meaning of imagination came to be seen not as a property of all minds, but as one more limited to 'creative minds' – it came to be thought of as the pre-eminent source of artistic creativity (Abrams 1953). This change of meaning segregated imagination from 'normal' human mental faculties, and made it a special characteristic of gifted individuals. This hobbled the imagination concept for the next two centuries, so that, moving into the 20th century, the meaning of imagination had come to mean the capacity for fantasy, whimsy, or delusional, non-actual ideation (Thomas 1999). In a word, imagination was something that 'artists' had, but it was not something relevant to the condition of the great mass of striving, productively working citizens. Thus, picking up strands of objectivist thought from the Enlightenment, imagination was seen as opposed to the supposedly more robust, practical and socially valuable processes of reasoning and rationality that underpin logic, science and technological development. Just consider the public's reaction if Isaac Newton or Carl von Linneaus had said they *imagined* their treatises.

During the second half of the 20th century, however, the concept of the imagination has been rethought as part of the wider human experience (Kearney 1988; White 1990; Thomas 2001). The descriptive, creative and destructive forms of imagination discussed by Kearney (1988) and extended by Roos and Victor (1999) exemplify this attempt. A parallel and influential strand of the discourse on imagination focuses on imagination's role not apart from, but as an integral component of, the development of science, the shaping of scientific paradigms and the formulation of scientific concepts (Tweney et al. 1981; Miller 1984; Brown 1991; Holton 1996). Albert Einstein's famous utterance that imagination is more important than knowledge illustrates this idea. And while the relationships among the concepts of imagination, image, imagery and mental processes are still being debated, a whole current of cognitive science is mapping out how tightly interwoven they are.

There are exciting convergences between philosophy and cognitive science that further illuminate the contemporary understanding of what 'the imagination' is. Thomas, for instance, points out that the folk and Romantic understanding of 'imagination' sees it as a 'capacity to comprehend the meaningless welter of incoming sensation, synthesizing it into a coherent, meaningful whole: the secret ingredient that turns mere mechanical receptivity into mental apprehension' (1999: 236). For him imagination is the capacity to 'see as', that is, a fundamental cognitive faculty though which complex reality is made understandable. For Deacon (1997), the distinguishing aspect of the human mind is its propensity and capability to collect from experiences the potential patterns and correlation that can compose a robust representation of the world.

Humans have a unique ability not only to label and sort events in the world as experienced, but also to analyse these relationships into a general conceptual fabric of reality. This capacity to imagine the world, interacting with the cycle of experience and analysis, is the essential character of our thinking. As discussed above and as illustrated by the examples throughout the book, this idea certainly applies to strategy practice.

Dimensions of imagination

Imagination is practised in three primary dimensions: in what we do (behaviour), in what we use (materials) and in how we think (concepts). While each of these three dimensions is exclusive of the other two *in the abstract*, human imagination *in practice* almost always embodies at least two of them. Anything that is imaginative in human experience – our descriptions, creations and even our challenges – is typically a blend of these dimensions. As subsequent chapters will describe and illustrate in the context of strategy practice, *Thinking from Within* involves all three dimensions simultaneously.[1]

The conceptual dimension

The conceptual dimension of imagination consists of using abstract ideas to interpret reality. Although ideas are experienced in many ways, we often share them as stories or as highly emblematic images, as the Chapter 1 tale of OilCo illustrates. The conceptual dimension of imagination can shape the very way we look at the world – and even how we behave. Imagine the compelling, arresting image of what the OilCo leaders' customer service concept meant and implies, and how this image can reshape how work gets done, or is initiated in the first place. From an abstract idea uttered by the boss six months earlier, Customer Service Champion became a difficult but potentially rewarding and passionate 'journey'. This did not seem to be the case in the RedCo company (Chapter 1), where people perhaps imagined something similar to the meeting depicted in Exhibit 1.2 in the plate section (Chapter 1) when they were instructed to sign up for the compulsory 'implementation workshop'.

The images, stories and concepts we create and deploy to frame and reframe reality and make sense of our actions is this conceptual dimension of imagination. To become aware of new patterns and ways of interpreting what goes on in organizational life is imaginative in and of itself, but it is a new story, metaphor or image that integrates the new information in a way that makes it socially accessible, or even compelling. In sum, the conceptual dimension is what we *think* (and what we think about) when we imagine.

The behavioural dimension

The behavioural dimension consists of behaviours that help us interpret reality. Although certain arts (for example dance, acting) immediately come to mind, imagination is more than acting imaginatively. We are all imaginative, to some degree, almost all the time and this capacity to be imaginative inheres in everyone's behaviour as well.

Recall again the image of the managers in the messy conference room in Chapter 1 (Exhibit 1.2 in plate section). A fairly predictable scene, perhaps, until one takes into account that these managers are conducting their discussion not solely with words and the usual array of flipcharts, whiteboards, slides and spreadsheets, but also with their hands and their bodies. One of them uses his hands to gesticulate as he makes a point. At other times some of them sketch out a quickly conceived graph showing the interrelationship of two important factors. Another participant leans back in his chair, maybe making faces to convey frustration. Others may doodle in the margins of a piece of paper, or grab a marker pen and energetically underline in several thick lines what they believe to be the most important element in the factors being considered. One of them seizes the opportunity for a well-deserved nap.

Now, recall how they behaved on the second day, as depicted in Exhibit 1.3 in the plate section, or your own image of the OilCo group of leaders. People are all standing, walking around and leaning over the conference table. Some of them are busily moving variously sized models into a cluster near the centre of the table, while others are manually building up new models with bricks, soft materials, magnets and metal spheres, and so on. In essence, they are using their hands and their bodies to think about and examine aspects of their business they consider important by doing the dexterous and fine work of building a detailed model of what it means to them.

While this managerial behaviour may be unusual, is it imaginative? In the first place, the use of alternative communication media is a direct example of the interpretative, 'seeing-as' nature of imagination. In this case, the managers see their strategic situation as the direct result of how they physically construct the detailed model. Such physical construction work, as much as it may be – inaccurately – hobbled by assumptions that manual activities are inferior to non-manual ones, is replete with imaginative potential. This is a potential both to stimulate new and innovative ways of looking at reality to be conceived and to represent these conceptions through the astoundingly fine and focused motor skills at work when constructing together a three-dimensional model.

The ending of the OilCo workshop crystallizes the imaginative impact of this activity. They used the model to extract words that captured the essential meaning to them as individuals. During this process they leaned back and forth, removed, replaced and moved elements. Some of them reshaped some of the soft material to make a point. They moved around and looked at their model from different vantage points, urging others to do this too. While talking, one of them was squeezing some soft materials in his hands to make a point, another was just fiddling with a brick. In other cases, people tossed materials at the model, whilst others sought to repair and defend it. The point is that their very actions embodied the meaning they wanted to convey. Behaviour is an integral part of our imagination. In sum, the behavioural dimension is what we *do* when we imagine.

The material dimension

The material dimension concerns the deployment of objects and physical effects, which produce an interpretation of reality. The way in which materials shape our interpretation of the world is perhaps best seen in architecture and, of all things, in doors and rooms.

Architecture of private homes illustrates with startling clarity how important the built environment and architectural products are for our understanding of reality. The so-called in *enfilade* layout promoted not privacy, but sociability and the constant traffic of people. Only in the 17th century did the habit catch on of creating corridors or spaces specially designated for traffic, with rooms accessible off of the corridors via single doors. Instead of gregariousness and constant availability, such 'terminal rooms' specifically segregated spaces where people could isolate themselves *in privacy* (the terminal rooms) from spaces where people moved in public around the building from room to room (the corridors). Architecture reminds us that material, especially in constructed spaces, is intimately intertwined with our understanding of reality.

Recall again the tales of OilCo and the team depicted in Exhibits 1.2 and 1.3 in the plate section. Taking the contributions of philosophers at face value, the imagination is the faculty that brings patterned meaning to the many perceptions we gain in daily experience. And so it was with these groups, whose use of soft and hard media in three dimensions broke them free of the holding pattern they'd been in about what a Customer Service Champion meant. In the case of the service group, using different materials (day 1, papers and visual text, and day 2, an assortment of soft and hard materials), they modelled very differently the architecture of their situation. The gradual accumulation of co-constructed objects during day 2, like in the OilCo experience, helped them to interpret and change their views about important matters. The impact and effect of material on thinking has a century of precedents. Thus, the material is an important dimension of our imagination. In sum, the material imagination is about what we *use* when we imagine. Exhibit 3.1 depicts the three dimensions of imagination in practice.

Quick reflections

Imagination, by definition, comes from within us. The conceptual, behavioural and material dimensions help us break down and better understand the intrinsically human practice of imagining. To ' imagine'

	Behavioural	Material	Conceptual
Description	Behaviours to interpret and create our reality	Use of objects and physical effects to interpret and create our reality	Shaping how we perceive and create our worlds
Arts analogue	Performance art, dance, theatre	Sculpture and painting	Literature, playwriting, poetry
In context of strategy	What we do when we practise strategy	What we use when we practise strategy	How we think and what we think of when practising strategy
Organizational literature	Mintzberg's (1987) 'crafting'	Doyle and Sim's (2002) 'modelling'	Morgan's (1997) images of organizations

Exhibit 3.1 Three dimensions of imagination

implies all three dimensions. Through our exposé on imagination we can already now see the role of play discussed in Chapter 2. In both work and play we have the opportunity to imagine, but if we do not imagine we do not really play.

In the language of Chapter 1, we have now further explained why *Thinking from Within* is not about 'pure reasoning' or 'deductive analysis' but about what we do and what we use when we engage our human capacity to describe, create and challenge the world as we and others perceive it. When we think from within, we do things and we use things. Unlike what we learn from young Descartes, *Thinking from Within* is about practising, that is, doing something that engages our senses and fuels our thinking in ways pure reasoning or meditation does not. Precisely because imagination in practice causes us to act, we will now consider what roles the behavioural, material and conceptual dimensions of imagination suggest we take on.

Roles

The behavioural dimension calls us to be the resourceful *bricoleur*, or handyman. Organizational theory and practice cultivate the illusion that the more senior the individual in an organization, the more abstract the issues are that they confront, and the more cerebral is the way they should deal with them. The labels used to portray leaders as 'heads' and workers as 'hands' are very revealing. Deeply woven into our cultural preferences, but rarely examined consciously, is the notion that what one does with one's head is much more consequential and important than what one does with one's hands. Only when we recognize how powerful the behavioural imagination is can we appreciate how wrong this image is. Using one's hands to craft, create, or construct some representation of a complex reality, as illustrated in Chapter 1, can be a tremendously powerful stimulant to create new ideas. To cultivate the behavioural imagination we need to trust our hands to lead their heads, metaphorically taking on the role of *handyman*.

With handiwork comes close engagement and contact with materials, which in turn allows us to make discoveries about the world we work in. These discoveries may often lie dormant until we actually mobilize materials and discover – in action – what we did not know beforehand: the act of building itself creates designs and not only implements them. As in the example of the development of 'terminal rooms', architecture is material deployed in a way that has a great power to shape how we live. Just as the handyman uses materials at hand to solve a problem, so the architect uses materials to create a space in which work is done – not only house, temple, arena, but also factory, office, headquarters. As the OilCo story illustrates, by designing and building three-dimensional models of their abstract customer concept, they move from being 'heads' only, to also become the 'hands' that fuel the thinking of their heads. In addition to being handymen, to use the imaginative possibilities of material we need to sometimes also be *architects*.

Architecture depends for its effects, in part, on the stories associated with buildings. The cathedral of Notre-Dame de Paris comes with its story about the hunchback Quasimodo, the Taj Mahal with the story of the raja's wife. Other stories immortalize their architects, like Gustav Eiffel's tower in Paris, or the aspirations or despair of people, like the Berlin Wall. The fact that buildings themselves come alive in stories reminds us again of the importance of narratives, which embody the conceptual imagination, the employment of abstract ideas to produce an interpretation of reality. Often, explanations of the importance of stories return to the centrality of language in human life, but stories are perhaps even more important because they require the imagination. Consider how often leaders use stories to spark action, convey values, articulate aspirations and share knowledge.

While one can behave unimaginatively, or use materials unimaginatively, one cannot make any of these types of stories without imagination. This is perhaps why stories are so tremendously motivating and why a good story often provides us with a good reason to act, as illustrated by the satisfaction of the OilCo leaders after creating their own personalized stories (Chapter 13 expands on this topic in terms of authenticity). Like these managers nurtured and used their behavioural and material imag-

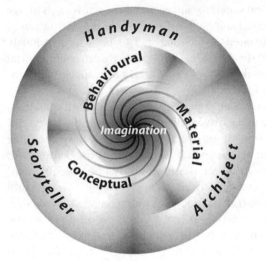

Exhibit 3.2 Dimensions of imagination and associated metaphorical roles

inations, we should also become *story-makers* and *story-tellers*. Exhibit 3.2 illustrates how these roles attach to the three dimensions of imagination, when we practise it.

From Chapter 2 we learnt that imagination is a fundamental aspect of play, but not necessarily of work. In this chapter we have described and reflected on how imagination is more than an intellectual exercise but is implied in both thinking and hands-on activities. Consequently, *Thinking from Within* is fundamentally a practice of imagining, in a context of the ambiguous activity of play. To think from within means taking on the roles of handyman, architect and storyteller.

To further illustrate how these ideas may play out in organized life we illustrate our claims with a story of how two leadership teams get an opportunity to imagine in new and different ways in the important work of strategy.

Case: Practising imagination in ChemCo[2]

The corporate top management was not happy. 'The new divisional strategies are too similar to the ones from the previous planning cycle', the concerned top corporate strategy officer told us. More importantly, he noted, the plans didn't address the quickening pace of change in their industry, or even the obvious changes in the business environment in the intervening years. How, he wondered, could he help divisional management recognize that its individual plans were out of sync with a rapidly changing business environment and in need of vigorous new directions? And how could he encourage these managers to see their strategies not as a trajectory they were locked into, but rather as a resource permitting adaptive action when the unforeseeable occurred?

ChemCo – a Europe-based, mid-sized specialty chemicals firm with a worldwide workforce of approximately 4000 – was experiencing a problem typical of the growing number of organizations facing disruptive change in the business environment. It was striving to balance the disciplining effects of a structured plan against the need for innovative, adaptive action. For ChemCo, like most organizations, the dilemma was deeply problematic, but finding a way of reconciling these seemingly opposed demands was seen by the leadership to be crucial for its long-term success. How could corporate management help the divisions work towards finding such a way?

Controlling the details of implementation

Formal strategic planning was a relatively new phenomenon at ChemCo. In the words of one of the senior managers:

> there was not any formal strategy at ChemCo until about five years earlier. Up to that point we simply made money by producing high-quality, desirable products for an industry that was organized like a sort of big club in which everyone had a place and a role.

This cosy situation changed when corporate management decided that a more formal planning process was needed, and instituted a tri-yearly process of developing strategic plans for the different divisions of the corporation. The first of these tri-yearly strategy-making cycles, undertaken in 1999, was internally referred to as the 'X3' strategies. Because each of the three divisions had a different market focus, they were allowed some autonomy in developing these X3 strategies. However, all had used commonly accepted strategy-making tools in their efforts during the X3 cycle of strategy development.

The Fragrances division had reviewed a variety of financial performance indicators (prior revenue, costs, projected sales) from its many clients, segmenting its client base into various grades and especially identifying 'preferred clients, who represented >70% of the potential' revenue stream. This analysis led it to conclude that clients who fell into this segment would provide the best 'forward cumulative EVA' for its stakeholders. Intensified R&D (more staff, increased budget), and a new HR initiative for hiring and retraining staff to align its workforce with organizational performance targets supported the strategic focus on these 'preferred clients'.

ChemCo's Fine Chemicals division had also completed a comprehensive financial review of its performance. Specific targets for contribution to the corporate bottom line had been set, but its strategic situation was especially complex. For historical reasons, this division had evolved to serve internal clients, providing basic components to the Fragrances division, as well as providing these same components to other organizations, often the direct competitors of the Fragrances division. The ability to judge the financial trade-offs, both year-on-year as well as in terms of the more extended time horizons involved in straddling internal and external markets, had become compromised by the growing size of the organization, as well as accelerating changes in alliances among competitors. A decision had therefore been taken to manage this complex situation with the 'Balanced Scorecard' approach. The leadership hoped that this could help neutralize any tendency to develop a bias towards either the internal or the external clients that might not serve ChemCo's overall long-term interests.

By early 2002, the second of the tri-yearly cycles of strategy development was nearing completion. The resulting strategic plans, called the 'X6' strategies, had not departed in any radical way from the previous ones (see Exhibit 3.3).

In fact, many in the firm felt that, if the X3 strategies had suffered any deficiency, it had not been in the analysis but in the way the strategy had been used. Thus, interviews with executives and management in early 2002 were very consistent across all divisions in emphasizing that

Division	Market	Standing in 'ChemCo'	X3 Strategy	X6 Strategy	Means of dissemination
Fragrances	Perfumes	Oldest division of corporation, very high profile	'Preferred client' determined via financial measurements	Review and update X3	PowerPoint slides of financial graphs, mission and objectives statements, specific actions to be taken
Fine Chemicals	Chemicals	Basic engineering, corporate wide logistics and budgeting	Market analysis, begin Balanced Scorecard approach	Extend Balanced Scorecard	PowerPoint slides of Balanced Scorecard components

Exhibit 3.3 ChemCo's X6 plans

Source: Bürgi and Roos (2004).

the strategic planning groups were concerned with controlling the details of how the new X6 strategy would be implemented. One senior manager said:

The strategic vision of X3 was not lived through people. People were reassured that we had such a plan, but it wasn't critical to what they did on a daily basis. We now want to bring it closer, bring it home to people, and make it tangible in their behaviour.

A senior member of another strategy development team put it this way: 'The X3 didn't address implementation. In fact, we had success with the strategy despite the lack of implementation focus.' And, in the words of the number two executive in the largest division, 'The Balanced Scorecard is the primary input to our strategy. It drives the level of detail about what has to be done down very far – it's a very detailed process.'

But there were clearly dissenting voices who argued that strategy development had quickly become routinized and bureaucratic and that the obsession with controlling the details of implementation carried with it diminishing returns. A senior vice-president at the division using the Balanced Scorecard approach observed, 'It's a heavy process. There's so much formalism that it is quite difficult to use.' Although they were in the minority, there were some divisional managers who shared the corporate impression that the X6 strategies were 'too similar to the X3 ones'. After talking about the review of the competition they had conducted to develop their X6 plan, the senior strategist in the one division had declared, 'Porter would be proud of us.'[3] A senior colleague from another division had promptly rejoined, 'and the way we've gone about it is ridiculous.'

Complementing the conventional strategy practice

From his vantage point overseeing all corporate-wide strategy development, the corporate strategy officer at ChemCo recognized that the divisional processes had stagnated and he began to challenge the content of the divisions' strategic plans. One way to remedy the situation, he believed, called for a complementary *practice* that might yield additional, complementary content. To this end he approached us for ideas. As a result we designed and staged workshops for the strategists and senior managers of both divisions. The idea was to take another look at both the organization and the business landscape (see Exhibit 3.5 in the plate section). In both cases we provided a range of playful construction materials to be used to construct and deconstruct in various ways.

What happened?

Each of the workshops stimulated interesting and unexpected ideas, which, in turn yielded new inputs to the planning process.

Fragrances division

The 'looking inside' phase evolved to focus the organization's workflow. The model the group built was very linear, and laid out along a single long axis, which began with an 'innovation engine' and culminated in a set of stairs rising up to a 'client project', represented by a large animal. A small, mobile, piloted vehicle, bristling with emblems of the specialty products that this division provided to clients, was moving along the axis. It represented the continuous efforts to bring value to clients and when it was produced, the participants united in seeing their organization in these common terms.

In the next phase of the workshop, the key element that attracted most attention was the building of a large 'windmill' or 'propeller' representing the 'winds of change', which were sweeping across the industry and were likely to change things in the near future. This was by far the largest and most imposing structure on the table, constructed together by several people in a variety of materials. This construction occasioned considerable discussion about how much the current X6 strategy reflected these forces of change in the organization's environment.

During the final debrief the group became acutely aware of further omissions in the X6 plan. Sitting at the head of the table, their corporate vice-president, who had participated in drafting the plan and in the early phase of the workshop had shown signs of resistance to changing anything in it, stated bluntly: 'The X6 strategy should be anticipating and reacting to the winds of change, but all we've really put into that plan is how to take care of today's business.' Another person said: 'If you look at the X6 plan, where is the emotional part that is such a big part of our products? It's not there.' And a third person, reflecting on the vivid representation of the organization in its complex competitive landscape, said:

> One of the things that's clear to me is why all the two-dimensional ways of communicating strategy, like charts and laptop slide shows, just don't work. To really understand what our strategy should be, you have to experience it like this, in 3-D.

Postscript

When the divisional strategy finally rolled out, the basis structure of a 'preferred client' strategy remained in place, but it was supplemented in two important ways. First, the strategists had concluded that they would have to adopt a new perspective towards their strategic plan: no longer seeing it as a predetermined set of activities, they would regard it as a key point of reference, which left them with enough tactical room to take advantage of opportunities where they presented themselves, or where they needed to adjust to the 'winds of change'.

Fine Chemicals Division

After an initial attempt to create a very orderly depiction of the organization merged with elements of its context, participants in this group focused on several problematic *internal* relationships. Returning to the model they had constructed together, they converged on the image of a 'flat information surface' in which an interwoven network of relationships knitted together production, marketing and planning, with an emphasis on the quality of the links. The manager who oversaw the entire engineering function was especially emphatic about indicating blockages in the links between people, insisting 'We have to show how it really is.' The final version showed that the Number 2 man in the division was connected, it seemed, to everything and everyone everywhere. The division president, by contrast, noted that while he himself was an active and mobile supervisory component on the 'information surface', he 'wasn't really connected to anything' except the computerized data system of the organization.

The landscape in which this 'flat information surface' was located became populated by a very wide variety of external elements, representing not only competitors and joint ventures, production sites and out-sourced production sites, but also several regulatory agencies and university research alliances. The participants were especially interested in how the vice-president of purchasing showed distinctions between the several competitors, represented by 'pussy-cats, grumpy bears, and devious snakes'. 'I really like how the competitors are shown as different species of animals,' one of his colleagues said; 'it clearly shows how and why they're different.' This group too was struck by the fact that populating the Balanced Scorecard model had led them to neglect several crucial strategic implications of their organizational setting.

During the debrief the division president commented to the group: 'I'm really glad I didn't send out the memo I've been working on about the 'state of the division. I've got to redo it completely in light of what we've now learnt about the way we all work together.' Another participant added, 'It's surprising that when you work on seeing how you see

Division	Key insight of workshop	Outcome and impact on strategic plan
Fragrances	We have great processes, but we're not prepared to respond to the inevitable 'winds of change'	Use the strategic plan as a point of reference, and leave the room to adjust where needed. Cascade strategy with simple ideas rather than numbers
Fine Chemicals	Our role in the centre of the corporation means that we are intensely interdependent with all parts of it	Focus more on inter-divisional relationships as a counterbalance to the Balanced Scorecard approach

Exhibit 3.4 Summary of insights from two workshops

yourself, you don't have to put so much effort into wondering what the future will be.' The person sitting next to him nodded, and commented, 'When you heed all the things surrounding you, the ideas just seem to come.' Hoping to frame subsequent conversations with colleagues and subordinates around the model they had just built, they carefully packed it away in large boxes in order to be able to reconstruct it later on. During subsequent meetings between this top management team and their several dozen direct reports, this reconstructed model served as the basis for how the entire strategic situation of the division was discussed.

Exhibit 3.4 summarizes what we identified as the key insights and conclusions from the two workshops.

Quick reflections

The ChemCo story illustrates many of the points made in this chapter. Additionally, it illustrates what happens when people involved in such serious practice as strategy begin to work in more playful ways, which in turn nurture their imaginations. We saw evidence of how they described the world as they uniquely saw it at that point in time and space (for example 'we are an information flow'), how they created new knowledge (for example using animal images to capture the important characteristics of clients), and how they challenged existing thinking (for example realizing the division president must be more connected).

The story also illustrates the conceptual dimension of imagination, that is, what and how they thought about strategy. From our pre-workshop interviews we realize that the way these managers thought about strategy practices was in conventional ways of thinking and doing, very much like the (boring) 'analytical' practices of pure reasoning depicted in Exhibit 1.2. They thought about strategy practices as 'prescribed thinking,' as portrayed in Exhibit 1.1 (Chapter 1), fed by routines and deductive reasoning. During these workshops the way these people thought about strategy practices changed, to also include their imagination and welcome the spontaneity of their wisdom; they moved towards *Thinking from Within* (see Exhibit 1.1).

Perhaps more visible in the case story is how ChemCo managers behaved differently. Rather than sitting motionless around a table (which was their expectation), they moved around and used their hands in ways previously unheard of in strategy practice (see Exhibit 3.5 in plate section).

Perhaps most apparent is the material dimension, manifested by their use of construction materials rather than the usual flipcharts, documents and PowerPoint slides used while practising strategy.

As they thought and acted, described, created and challenged they took on the three roles we have characterized in metaphorical terms above. As *handymen* they rolled up their sleeves and dug into a pile of materials to find construction solutions to the problematic aspects of the things, events and processes they considered important. As *architects* they designed and changed the evolving constructions into meaningful buildings maquettes – of their intentions and aspirations. As *story-makers* and *storytellers* they mobilized their constructions in conveying to one another emotionally powerful stories describing what was going on in their business. Unlike their previous practice in developing the X6 (and X3) plans, in a playful context they brought more of their existing, personal knowledge to the table and together developing entirely new insights which they enjoyed doing. This, we argue, made them readier to meet the new circumstances they realized they, de facto, faced the nex day.

Conclusion

This chapter has moved in two tightly related directions: providing a conceptual framework for the ancient and tricky notion of imagination; and describing and illustrating what it means to *practise* imagination, especially in light of changing circumstances. Often cloaked in mystery, the imagination can be seen as a black box process, described with terms such as thunder bolts, 'god given' talent and genius. However, as we have seen, imagination is far more than the 'creative genius'. With its ancient roots and historical evolution, imagination relates to both embodied and mental processes, especially through images and language but also through action. When we do things and when we use things, we imagine too.

How we think, act and use materials is an all important part of how we imagine, and as such makes up the core meaning of *Thinking from Within*. When we practise our behavioural, material and conceptual dimensions of imagination, we are not just motionless and feelingless intellectuals, but active and sometimes passionate handymen, architects and story-tellers who can impel very meaningful organizational action.

The ChemCo case illustrates these points. In the language of Chapter 1 the corporate director of strategy had a hunch that changing circumstances called for more than the usual outcome. We are not sure about how content the leaders in the two ChemCo groups were with the previous outcome, nor how much they expected a different one. However, as the tale illustrates, the new outcomes generated by *Thinking from Within* made them more prepared to deal positively (and sanely) with those circumstances.

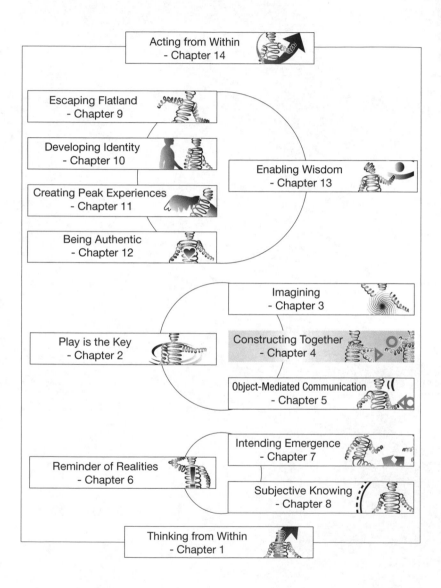

Acting from Within
- Chapter 14

Escaping Flatland
- Chapter 9

Developing Identity
- Chapter 10

Creating Peak Experiences
- Chapter 11

Being Authentic
- Chapter 12

Enabling Wisdom
- Chapter 13

Imagining
- Chapter 3

Play is the Key
- Chapter 2

Constructing Together
- Chapter 4

Object-Mediated Communication
- Chapter 5

Intending Emergence
- Chapter 7

Reminder of Realities
- Chapter 6

Subjective Knowing
- Chapter 8

Thinking from Within
- Chapter 1

4

Constructing Together

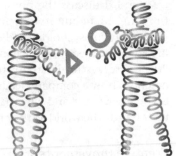

Johan Roos

Introduction

Recall how the OilCo leaders of Chapter 1 shaped the meaning of the new and rather abstract customer-focus concept with their hands. Recall also how the ChemCo leaders of Chapter 3 visually displayed their X6 strategy and reflected and engaged with the messages embedded into their construction. Unlike what occurred during the many meetings preceding the workshop, their construction work challenged sight and touch as well as stimulated emotional arousal and consciousness. Like artists they expressed the basis for their evolving customer-focused strategy, not just metaphorically but by manipulating a range of devices with their hands. They could have used brushes to paint their views on a canvass, but in this case they crafted meaning in three dimensions with their hands. They used the material dimension of their imagination to an extent previously not done. They were *Thinking from Within*.

The approach taken by the OilCo and ChemCo managers challenged conventional strategy practice. Rather than taking the role of cold-minded intellectuals reasoning their way to a shared meaning or at least agreement, these leaders engaged in a manual activity not usually associated with high value 'white collar work'. By breaking the tradition of dealing with strategic issues as high, value-added white-collar work, like the RedCo leadership, it was the more manual work of the OilCo and ChemCo leaders that generated value (Chapter 6 provides in-depth stories about traditional strategy practices without such manual work). In OilCo the verbal communication was also inspired by drama, which, as we will explain in Chapter 12, was key to the positive outcome.

The purpose of this chapter is to discuss the importance of hands-on, construction work for the practice of *Thinking from Within*. The starting point is the importance of movement for creative expressions illustrated by a well-known metaphor about a potter shaping clay.[1]

Second, I discuss the physiological significance of the hand for our thinking, including its role in human evolution. Third, I move from physiology to psychology to discuss how human development and learning are associated with the concrete activity of construction. The case of PrintCo serves to illustrate the main points in the chapter. This tale describes how a company leadership team spends a day to 'discuss strategy in a new way' and what happens when they begin to construct with their hands the world as they now perceive it, together.

Creative movements

Grounded in the combined theories of Cartesian philosophy and ideas from the Age of Enlightenment, the intellectual heritage we have grown accustomed to views creation, in art or in management, as brainpower acting alone. Yet, how we move our bodies and how our brain works are so interconnected, no scientific discipline has been able to explain what is going on. Art therapist Shaun McNiff argues that this is a myth because artists engaged in creation 'collaborate' with their personal repertoire of expressive movements and gestures within a particular milieu. Creation, he argues, always happens in a 'field of action' where thinking and motion interact. In his words: 'In order to paint effectively I need to commit myself to exercise with brushes, pencils, oil sticks, and other implements of expression. Each device, like a new dance partner, calls for a different sensitivity' (1998: 17). When we dance some of us prefer bold swirls and sweeping motions whereas others enjoy modest spins and more restricted movements. Our favourite motions and forms of dance manifest our personal basis for creative expressions, just like our preferred material and devices in painting.

McNiff's point is that we rarely realize how our expressiveness is influenced by how we move our bodies. When he studied films of Picasso painting and drawing he was: 'struck by his fluid lines and graceful body movement ... The gestures on paper and canvas extended from his stance and lower body motions as much as his hands and arm' (ibid. p. 17). McNiff realized that accomplished artists like Picasso used every part of their body to achieve 'total expression' (see Chapter 11 for more on aesthetics-based peak experiences). So, just sitting still around a table for a day seems to be an ineffective way to stimulate creative expressions. Personally, when stuck or asked tricky questions I tend to stand up and walk around, often gesticulating, to get my thinking moving again.

Strategy scholar Henry Mintzberg likened the work of strategists with how the potter works the clay:

The potter sits before a lump of clay on the wheel. ... She has an intimate knowledge of her work, her capabilities, and her markets. As a craftsman, she senses rather than analyzes ... All these things are working in her mind as her hands are working the clay. (Mintzberg 1987: 66)

His conclusion was clear: strategists are not only intellectuals but like craftsmen they 'shape' strategy. In addition, in this metaphor about hand-work we also see the active involvement of the person's entire body; leaning back and forth and sideways, lifting shoulders and the movement of the feet to control the speed of rotation. I envision the whole person in anticipation of and engaged in a creative and emotional experience, which initially includes moving materials around until they suddenly find their place, which is an important and integral part of the imaginative process. Artists call this transition *motus*, which happens when the artist leaves the warm-up phase of 'manual scouting' and opening up the mind for new ideas, in order to enter the action phase of dedicated creation of art (see Belensky 2001). Later on in this chapter I will discuss in more detail the three phases that make up a creative arts process, with particular emphasize on the initial, warming-up phase.

By using the image of how an artist works and interacts with materials, Mintzberg bridges the traditional, conventional and early Cartesian-inspired idea that strategy formulation (thinking) is separate from implementation (doing). The potter working the material with her hands (and the movements of her entire body) is bound to discover in her mind new possibilities as she shapes the clay. In the language of Chapter 3, the potter and other artists practise their material and behavioural imaginations, and it really helps them to simultaneously conceptualize. Yet, Mintzberg did not follow through on the practical implications of this metaphor. As Peter Burgi, Claus Jacobs and I have argued in one of the articles behind this chapter (Bürgi et al. 2004), and as illustrated throughout this book, crafting, or rather *constructing* strategy together it is not just a metaphor. It can be a practice.

Pottery and other creative expressions are all part of a very basic form of activity in human experience. Archeologists have found traces of not just cave paintings but also pottery throughout the world, and going back tens of thousands of years. Pottery remains with us today in both commodity and artisan forms. Yet, in the increasingly industrialized and knowledge-driven society manual work such as pottery has gradually been devalued. In organizations 'blue collar' manual work is seen as less value-added than the white-collar 'knowledge' work. This simplified dichotomy has led many people to assume that manual activities add less value to organizations than ostensibly 'thinking' activities. As illustrated with the tales of OilCo and RedCo in Chapter 1 and ChemCo in Chapter 3, this may not always be the case.

The hand is the key

Artists know that images in our mind grow from the interaction between hands, the entire body and senses; and the hands are at the core of both our thinking and our expressions of thoughts. There is a clear and strong connection between cognitive and manual activity, and correspondingly, between the hand and the brain. The intimate link between the hand and the brain is a primordial component in human physiology and a very significant milestone in the development of human beings. As early as 1840 Sir Charles Bell, a Scottish surgeon and respected anatomist of his day, published a treatise that highlighted the relationship between movement of various body parts, perception and learning. His message was that all serious accounts of human life simply must acknowledge the central importance of the hand (Bell 1840).

The hand is not only an instrument for manipulating the physical world, but is also a large source of feedback for the brain. The hand or rather its functions are widely represented in the brain. The Canadian neurosurgeon Wilder Penfield developed a 'map' of the brain, known as the 'motor homunculus', which shows the proportions of it dedicated to controlling different parts of the body (Penfield and Rasmussen 1957). The often-reproduced image of his theoretical findings, illustrates how much of the brain is devoted to processing input from and providing instruction to the hand. The Musée de la Main in Lausanne displays a three-dimensional version of this map, reproduced in Exhibit 4.1 in the plate section. It is a grotesque looking statuette that quickly conveys the message about the profound interconnection between the hand and the brain. Beyond this map of input–output proportions, it is also increasingly evident that neurological and biomechanical elements of the hand and its movement are very prone to spontaneous interactions and change. Just, for example, consider how we use our hands to express emotions.

Scientific research into human origins verifies the profound interdependence of the hand and mind in the evolution of human beings. For example, from an evolutionary perspective the five-fingered precision grip with the opposable thumb, the enlargement of the brain and the elaboration of the brain's speech centres co-evolved with the development of the brain (Gibson and Ingold 1993; Tattersall 1998). From an anthropological perspective, the appearance of the five-finger grip is reflected in the label *homo habilis*, or 'handy'. From a biomechanical perspective, the hand is a remarkable device where each part has a specialized structure and particular purpose. From a neurobehavioural perspective it sheds light on how our hand movements relate to our thinking patterns. In other words, when we move our hands and fingers neurons fire in ways they do not while sitting still on the very same hands.

The hand in many ways remains the centre of human evolution and contemporary practice of everyday life, even organized life. These various roles of the hand illustrate its importance for individual skill and performance in all walks of life. The hand is an important part of the developing powers of human thinking, and also in managerial work.

Frank Wilson, a leading researcher of the hand and an admirer of Charles Bell's early insights, summarized the role of the hand for human intelligence:

any theory ... which ignores the interdependence of hand and brain function, the historical origin of that relationship, or the impact of that history on developmental dynamics in modern humans, is grossly misleading. (Wilson 1998: 7)

The hand is also intimately connected to language and the most obvious example is perhaps sign language. In addition to a standardized set of hand configurations, in practice sign language involves the entire body. Sign language experts testify how people intentionally and unconsciously shift their bodies, change their facial expressions and move their limbs while making the appropriate sign, which is visible for the rest of us watching. Some people call this to 'talk with their hands'. Yet, experts point out, sign language is not just an extension of gestures. What makes sign language such an effective and efficient form of communication is the code-like, opaque relationship between signs and meanings that evolves with practice. One of the leading researchers on the topic of communication via gestures, Robert Krauss (1998) suggests we make movements with our hands to help us think. The term 'gesture' also suggests coordinated vocal *and* limb movements. In some western languages, interestingly, the evolutionary strong link between hand and language is obvious. Verbs for understanding in German *'begreifen'*, Swedish *'begripa'* (in slang *'fatta'*) and French *'comprendre'* all point to the function of the hand – to grasp.

This account of the role and importance of the hand for being human sheds light on Mintzberg's crafting metaphor. We naturally use our hands in all aspects of our daily life and the hand has tremendous importance for how and what we think. We may type in a few more words on the PC, draw a figure on a piece of paper, manipulate some materials, gesticulate to make a point or squeeze the hand in anger under the table when our demands are not met. The message is clear: when we engage our hands we change our thinking, and we do this all the time and everywhere, no matter who or where we are.

Constructivism

Moving from the physiological to a more conceptual consideration, we turn from anatomy to educational psychology and in particular to the theories of the Swiss child psychologist Jean Piaget, who devoted his research to the relationship between action and cognition. The basic idea of constructivism is that we make ideas about the world *from within* as opposed to getting ideas from the outside. As a philosophy of learning, constructivism suggests that when we reflect on our experiences we generate our own ways of making sense of them. Learning, therefore, is the process of adjusting our mental models to accommodate new experiences (Piaget 1958, 1971). In Piaget's terms we accommodate new inputs rather than assimilate what they mean on deeper levels. To really change how we think and act we need practical experience, 'actions-in-the-world'. Until we have developed knowledge from within, we do not change other than on the surface.

In a much-cited example, he observed that young children often associated tall glasses with larger amounts of water and wider glasses with smaller amounts. If the same amount of water is poured from one shape to another, these children will often assert that the amount of water has changed. Their theory of the relationships of shape and amount would not change until the children 'constructed' it for themselves out of their own activities. Based on this research, Piaget claimed that concrete acts of constructing things in the world, like manipulating objects, constructed knowledge in the mind. He proposed that knowledge was psychologically constructed in the mind alongside the action of physically engaging with the world. In his own words: 'every act of knowing includes a mixture of elements furnished by the object and by the action. These elements are intrinsically united and linked to each other' (Piaget 1958: 49). Put another way, knowing is an active engagement with the world, hence, 'constructivism'.

Others like Jerome Bruner (1960, 1986) have applied Piaget's ideas to learning theories. Constructivism suggests that learning is an active process, ideally including hands-on problem solving. Learning is a search for meaning. The purpose of learning is for individuals to construct their own meaning, not just memorize the 'right' answers and regurgitate someone else's meaning. Therefore, instructors rely heavily on open-ended questions and promote extensive dialogue among students so that they can make connections and discover principles for themselves. It follows that standardized curricula should be replaced with customized curricula adapted to the learners' prior knowledge. To experience meaning requires understanding the whole as well as parts, and parts must be understood in the context of the whole. Thus, the learning process should focus on primary concepts, not isolated facts. In order to teach well, we must understand the mental models that learners use to perceive the world and the assumptions they make to support those models.

Let us exchange the term learner in this framework for education with a manager practising strategy. The implications are straightforward. Rather than imposing our own meaning upon others, we need to create the context in which people can make sense of and create their own meaning about the issues at hand. Thus, we should not expect people to learn from the 'outside'. Instead, people interpret what they hear in light of their own knowledge and experience. We do not easily learn or change our basic views from external perturbations, like someone sending us instructions by e-mail telling us to attend a two-hour implementation workshop (see the RedCo anecdote in Chapter 1).

To really learn and change we need to interact with the world, people and things included, ideally using our hands to fuel our minds in new ways. In other words, we need to think from within. This is what the ChemCo (see Chapter 3) and the OilCo leaders did, and what the RedCo leaders did not (see Chapter 1). Effective learning is not only an intellectual exercise in deductive reasoning based on 'instructionism'.

Constructionism: stressing the material dimension

Like Bruner and others, Seymour Papert, a student of Piaget, strongly advocated a 'constructionist' approach to learning (Harel and Papert 1991). Papert dislikes traditional classroom-based instructions where information is imparted by teachers and retained by students, who subsequently reciprocate by handing in the filled-in test-sheet. Papert stresses Piaget's ideas about the importance of simultaneously constructing things in the world and knowledge in the mind. And to Piaget's ideas he adds the notion that learning happens most effectively when the learner is consciously engaged in constructing a public entity, whether it's a sand castle on the beach or a theory of the universe. Papert's ideas help us understand and appreciate the importance of different *media*, for example digital media, for shaping and expressing ideas in various contexts. To him, projecting our *inner ideas and feelings* is a key to learning. By expressing our ideas in tangible forms, not only can we communicate them, but the very act of physically shaping our ideas changes them.

Simply put, a constructionist approach ensures that learners are given access to appropriate materials, in relevant contexts, and are given tasks directly related to the learning outcomes sought. This sets in motion a virtuous circle of growth and development since, as new knowledge is built, the supply of means by which to interact with the world is increased and new approaches can then be undertaken for building still more things (Kolb and Fry 1975; Jarvis 1995). This line of reasoning questions the privileged position that knowledge is abstract, impersonal and detached from the knower, analogous to the early Cartesian notion of a disembodied mind. These ideas are closely connected to the Russian psychologist Lev Vygotsky's (1934) work on the role of cultural artifacts as resources for tapping into and increasing people's cognitive potential. Whereas Papert focuses on digital media, scholars in the so-called 'socio-constructivist' tradition, like Vygotsky, experiment with artifacts and language.

Piaget's knowledge theories, Bruner's learning theories and Papert's ideas about constructing things emphasize the inseparable relationship between thinking and doing. The one gives rise to the other in an endless cycle of practice: by thinking we do new things and by doing things we can also learn new things. This interplay between thinking and doing, using our hands and bodies, is a cornerstone of the *Thinking from Within* idea and practice. When we think from within, when we imagine and construct together, we have close encounters with uncertainty. As Chapter 7 will further describe and illustrate, when we engage in *Thinking from Within*, we have to welcome the unexpected.

The tale of PrintCo illustrates these ideas in the world of organization and strategic thinking. In this case the leadership team engages in a strategy conversation similar but not identical to that of the leaders of OilCo and ChemCo. They use manual work to construct the world as they see it, together and in public.

Case: Addressing taboos in PrintCo[2]

With high market shares, profits and cash flow, PrintCo is in an enviable situation. Building on its success in a groundbreaking technological innovation 50 years ago, the company is the new leader in a specialized market for printing machines. Because its customer base and market penetration of retailers' products are growing steadily, PrintCo's strategy traditionally has been an exercise in accurate prediction of future sales growth. However, in 2002 things began to change as PrintCo's once innovative printing technology was becoming increasingly challenged by substitute technology.

Although PrintCo's subsidiary in Spain was as profitable as its peers, it faced three strategic issues. First, PrintCo had recently acquired a manufacturer of the substitute technology in the operating area of the subsidiary, which meant for its management team that a former rival had suddenly become a 'sibling'. How should they deal internally and exter nally with this foe now turned friend? How would customers react? How would their sales people react?

There were two other important issues. In the local Spanish market, end-users were trying to bypass PrintCo's direct clients and get machines and specialized printing material straight from PrintCo. Although PrintCo's corporate strategy was clearly to stay loyal to its traditional con stituency, the management of the subsidiary was less clear about that position. How could the subsidiary refuse the large retailers, even though it implied negative effects for a direct client? Could it strike a win–win balance? Finally, the relationship between corporate headquarters and the Spanish subsidiary was relatively constrained, especially regarding product development. There was a feeling within the subsidiary's management that headquarters was monopolizing innovation and holding back information about new initiatives. How could it improve its relationship with the development people at headquarters? Could it continue to experiment with new technology with its own customers?

The leader of PrintCo Spain was not sure its current strategy was enough to guide decisions and actions relative to these challenges. Therefore, he was eager to engage his entire top management team in an open and frank discussion about these strategic issues. The retreat took place in April 2002 and the CEO of the subsidiary stated, in his invitation letter, that its objective was to 'discuss strategy in a new way'. It was the first time that the subsidiary leader was prepared to take this conversation up with his leadership team. From the outset of the retreat he told his people he was open to modifying the strategy based on new insights developed during the day.

What happened?

The eight executives used a variety of materials to build models with their hands that represented their organization in its business landscape. During this process they discussed the three issues, one of which had previously been seen as taboo. The executives collectively built their own organization as a castle with 'strong walls' but 'under attack' from more innovative competitors. To bring this point home, one participant took a big piece and banged it against the supposedly solid walls of the castle, which partially crumbled. This led to much laughter and ironic comments about the new substitute technology and how it would eventually break those walls.

The group portrayed its overall relationship with corporate headquarters as an elephant, which meant it was 'strong' but sometimes too 'slow'; 'friendly in general' but 'dangerous if irritated'. The group did not seem to have made any major new insights, regarding how to collaborate on product development, beyond sending more 'scouts' to corporate headquarters and having them develop better personal relationships with key people.

As they constructed together the overall business landscape, the executives came to discuss the corporate PrintCo's policy in relation to the newly acquired competitor, which was seen by the corporate body as an isolated event not worthy of much attention. They had instructed the Spanish subsidiary leadership to collaborate and be friendly with this new inclusion in the corporate family. Interestingly, the group never built a shared representation of this company, but its many individual models captured the friend-or-foe kind of ambiguity participants felt about it.

They also built and discussed the even more sensitive topic, namely their end-users' (retailers) tendency to contact PrintCo directly. Here they expressed views that PrintCo could not and maybe even should not prevent this from happening. Retailers, it appeared to the workshop participants, were simultaneously supporting and potentially upsetting PrintCo's ways of doing business. This ambivalence was captured in their collective representation of retailers: a construction almost as big as the one representing PrintCo, with a friendly face on the front and a tiger crouching behind a wall. Developing this construction generated a heated discussion about potential pros and cons of actively encouraging, or passively letting this happen, the participants often illustrating their ideas and viewpoints by touching the construction or pointing at its 'face'. The group never reached any decision about what to do, but seemed to feel good about venting its views on the previously taboo subject. The issue, as the executives said, was now on top of their agenda and would be revisited at each and every leadership meeting.

At the following debrief the executives expressed positive views about the depth of their conversations. They were particularly surprised about the open and passionate discussion about the two sensitive topics: how to deal with the newly acquired company in Spain, and how to deal with the retailers, bypassing PrintCo's direct clients. They also highlighted the many new metaphors used to symbolize their organization, customers and headquarters. The executive responsible for strategy held up a thick summary document of their current strategy and said spontaneously, 'Not in these many pages could I have captured the richness of what we built together today.'

Quick reflection

Overall, this tale illustrates many of the points made earlier: the importance of engaging more of the senses (and even moving around) for being creative; the benefits of using hands-on construction work to make sense of existing views and develop new ideas; and what can happen if the communication is based on the philosophy of constructivism.

The PrintCo leaders surprised themselves by doing things and thinking in deep ways that were new to them. These managers had spent years working together so they knew one another reasonably well and as a leadership team they met regularly. Rather than just receiving information from or instructing one another, they here engaged in a practical experience that caused them to tap into their deeper resources – to think from within. By using their hands to manually construct together their view of important issues they came to see the issues in new ways. They also came up with entirely new conceptualizations about important challenges and were able to discuss taboos.

The case also illustrates that they were able to do this on a social level. Whereas Piaget's and Papert's work focuses on the individual level, the literature on what is called 'social constructionism' explains what the PrintCo executives did *together*. As the story illustrates, 'reality' is always interpreted, perceived and negotiated. As Denis Gioia puts it, 'the reality people confront is the reality they construct' (2003: 12).

To know something means using our hands to construct it. Like Piaget posited for children, when the PrintCo managers modelled retailers with a friendly face on the front and a tiger crouching behind a wall, at the same time they developed their own knowledge of their complex and taboo-constrained relationship with a new category of customers. Their experience illustrates that sometimes *we need to construct something in order to understand what we mean*. If we want to understand something together, we need to construct that something together.

The stories also illustrate how constructivism and constructionism are not just ideas relevant to children, but fundamentally help us understand and improve managerial work too. Compared with the usual austere efforts of deductive analysis, which had only involved the manual work of developing a long PowerPoint presentation, fuelling their thinking with the signals that came from engaging their senses was valuable to the PrintCo executives. That day, they were *Thinking from Within*.

Three phases[3]

One of the core practices of *Thinking from Within* is constructing together, but people's mindset is more important than technical skills. The hands-on construction work is not intended to compete with Picasso or Rodin, but is similar to group-based creative arts processes that share many traits with creative arts therapies (see Chapter 2). Like athletes and musicians practise before they go live, so too must managers seeking to think from within.

In principle, *Thinking from Within* should follow the three phases of warm-up, action, and the subsequent sharing of insights and experiences. Although this is not illustrated in detail in previous and subsequent stories in this book, in each and every case the facilitators (in all cases me, and in some cases also one or two others) followed these phases. Over time, my colleagues and I have come to appreciate the tremendous importance of each of these phases for the emerging benefits of *Thinking from Within* – regardless of the setting at hand. To balance the focus on hands-on media and construction work based on the principles of constructivism, the following section describes briefly each of the creative arts phases.

Everybody needs to warm up before any kind of experiential exercise. An athlete would never expose his precious body to hard physical exercise if it were not ready to do so. The same goes for the mind. During the warm-up, verbal and non-verbal exercises are used to create an atmosphere of confidence and security within the group, while also enhancing spontaneity and imagination among participants. In this state the participants will gain increasing access to what is needed for the creative process. This is also the opportunity to familiarize people with the close encounters with uncertainty, which, by definition, is an integral part of the practice. *Thinking from Within* cannot be reduced to a linear sequence of causes, and participants must be prepared to induce and cope with unexpected insights and actions (Chapter 7 expands on this). Moreover, they have to be encouraged to let go of the habits of distancing themselves from the matters at hand and instead be encouraged to be subjective and dare to take a stance. To reduce the risk of embarrassment and fear that might surface later in the thinking and doing that make up *Thinking from Within*, the action phase must not start until people are sufficiently warmed up.

With the participants' minds and bodies warmed up and ready to practise their imagination and, ideally, journey deeper into their inner unconscious resources, the action phase is when they construct individually and together and use drama techniques to enhance authenticity (to be discussed in Chapter 12). This phase assumes openness for emergence and thereby a higher state of vulnerability, which *any facilitator must be conscious of and have the necessary skills to handle.* In an atmosphere of trust and security, vulnerability is a positive quality, which can induce the emergent benefits discussed in Chapters 9–13.

The third phase of debriefing is a conscious and verbal process of completing the project. Participants stop the construction work and, guided by the facilitator, begin systematic conversations to share within the group the experiences and insights gained during the previous activities. Immediate feelings are just as important as the possible implications in a wider meaning of what has been brought forth during the action. The sharing also serves the purpose of winding down and relaxing the heightened state of mind previously experienced. Even though the energy level sinks, the increased level of awareness on the issues just worked on stays with the participants, who often appreciate ending the sharing with a summary of what has been achieved, especially if the issues are of a professional character like, for example, practising strategy (to be discussed more in Chapter 13).

Over the past decade I have learnt first-hand how delicate the process of *Thinking from Within* is, and the vital importance of competent facilitation attitude and skills. Just like insufficiently prepared athletes risk injury when they unleash their inner strengths, we too risk a bad experience of *Thinking from Within* unless we are sufficiently prepared to imagine and be spontaneous.

Conclusion

The starting point of this chapter was to acknowledge the importance of our bodies and hands for creative expression. From a physiological perspective the notion of constructing things with our hands is a fundamentally human one, ever since our ancestors developed the five-finger grip. The hand is a primary tool for manipulating the world, and as such a powerful means to stimulate our thinking. It has been said that ideas are sometimes stuck somewhere between the brain and our hands. In light of the close connection between the hand and mind, this make sense.

Piaget's constructivism idea teaches us that manual activity fuels our thinking in ways pure intellectual reasoning does not. It is the way children learn about the world, but the theory works equally well for adults too, and by implication also for serious managers practising strategy. Thus, as I and my colleagues Peter Bürgi and Claus Jacobs have suggested, crafting something as abstract as strategy is more than a cute metaphor – it implies manual construction work.

The typical approach to managerial problem-solving practices, such as strategy, involves posing a question, reflecting, and then verbally articulating some answers or solutions. In contrast to this essentially mental method, the workshop in PrintCo illustrated how people were 'thinking with their hands', and thereby were able to tap into their own private feelings and emerging ideas. The activity of building models helped the managers to simultaneously develop and represent solutions to the key questions being posed. Compare this with what went on in the RedCo story of Chapter 1, where the CEO denied others the opportunity to think from within and instead prescribed his own meaning upon others. This practice, illustrated in the PrintCo case, shrinks the gap between thought and activity and makes the 'thinking' much more akin to the activity of the potter at her wheel that Mintzberg discussed. Just like potters, the PrintCo managers experienced their strategic issues in a manner that was perceived as real, vivid, and immediate. In *Thinking from Within*, thought and action converge.

Imaginative expressions or spontaneous actions, in the *atelier* or in the boardroom, cannot be planned in advance. To reap the emergent benefits of *Thinking from Within*, we need to prepare our bodies and minds. By warming up we intentionally create the context for our imagination to surprise us and others involved, and reduce the risk of 'injury'.

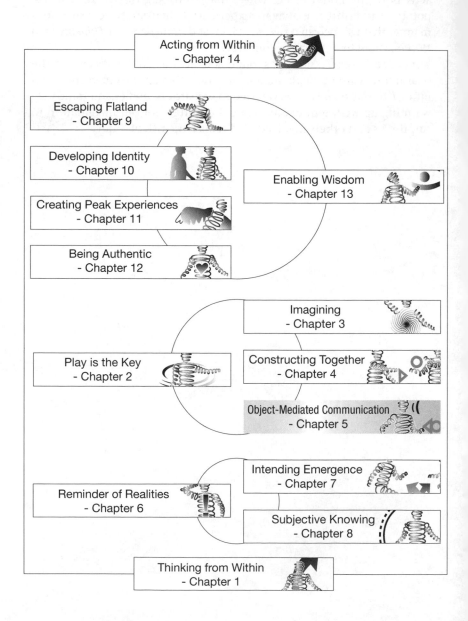

5

Object-Mediated Communication

Johan Roos and Roger Said

Introduction

Whereas in Chapter 4 we focused on the very act of constructing together, in this chapter we focus on how our playful constructions can mediate serious and sincere conversations. Here we focus on the meaning of the objects in the centre of the communication. (The communication itself is here a traditional verbal exchange, but in Chapter 12 we will extend the verbal notion to include dramatic techniques.) Clay, gouache, bricks, watercolour, markers, oil pastels, LEGO bricks, play dough, coloured pencils, paper of different kinds, connecting materials (glue, string, scotch tape, string, chains) and just about any material that we find useful for making hard and soft symbolic representations can be used to mediate communication. Some are more convenient than others, though.

Recall how executives in our case stories thus far (OilCo of Chapter 1, ChemCo in Chapter 3 and PrintCo in Chapter 4) were taken aback by the insights that came from constructing things together and gave the items personal meaning as well as showing how they were interrelated. Insights connected to objects carrying their symbolic meaning affect us more deeply. As an essential part of the practice *Thinking from Within*, in this chapter we suggest that object-mediated communication influences us in three fundamental ways: objects make us *know*, *agree* and *cope* differently. The purpose of this chapter is to reflect on and illustrate *why* objects transform communication in such striking ways.

Due to the explorative nature of this chapter we will not confine ourselves to one particular theoretical framework, but draw on a broad range of thinking, including semiotics and rhetoric, sense-making in organizations, cognitive mapping and psychotherapy.

Adding to the series of case illustrations throughout this book, we illustrate our points with a story of how a cross-functional group of leaders in TelCo came to know, agree and cope differently when, in the context of *Thinking from Within*, they used objects to mediate their serious and sincere communication.

Objects make us know differently

A basic fact of object-mediated communication is that it is not about the objects themselves, which are only standing in for something else. In the language of semiotics (Eco 1976), what the objects signify and the relationship between them is arbitrary – there is no grammar. Somebody who uses objects in a communication can recruit them ad hoc and assign them any meaning that suits the occasion.

If we were to compare objects to anything within natural language, it would be most plausible to see them as *three-dimensional tropes*. Tropes are figurative ways of speaking; metaphor, analogy, metonymy, synecdoche, irony or paradoxes are some of the most common. The term trope is derived from the Greek word *tropos*, turn, and this is very apt: tropes turn around the conventional, dictionary meaning of words to create surprise effects. Tropes lead to insight in two contrary ways: by making the unfamiliar *familiar* or by making the familiar *unfamiliar*. In the first case something that is known too little or is too abstract to be grasped easily is rendered in terms of something that is better known. For example, our 'industry is like a landscape of interconnected villages'. In the second case, a trope highlights an unfamiliar aspect of something that is all too familiar. For instance, 'their group performs like a computer'. Objects in object-mediated communication have the same potential as verbal tropes to turn, twist and tweak conventional understandings and stimulate radical shifts in thinking.

Although any object can be used to signify anything, *in practice* the relation between a three-dimensional trope and its signified object is rarely arbitrary. The cases of previous chapters illustrate how managers used a wide array of cords, tubes, play dough and plastic bricks to freely create and express their meaning of connections, obstacles, resources and so on. In their 'toy box' Doyle and Sims (2002), in contrast, used *ready-made* objects like light bulbs, dice, chains, chess pieces or keys to provide imagery. Usually participants will assign stereotypical meanings to them, but the possibility of using these ready-made objects against convention and have them stand for the opposite of the stereotype is always available.

Artifacts help us stay in control. When we fear losing track of all the entities that we juggle in our mind, we often recruit external elements to reduce the cognitive load and organize our thoughts. As Kirsh said:

The external elements may be our fingers or hands, pencil or paper, movable icons, counters, measuring devices, or other entities in our immediate environment. Typical organizing activities include pointing, arranging the position and orientation of nearby objects, writing things down, manipulating counters, rulers or other artifacts that can encode the state of a process or simplify perception. (1995: 212)

Maps

Human beings are spatial creatures, accustomed from the first days of our lives to moving around and manipulating objects. Concepts like distance or size are so basic for us that even in speech we draw on them constantly ('I am very *close* to her', 'I owe him a *big* favour'). They are concepts we live by in the most fundamental way (Lakoff and Johnson 1980). An extension of this notion is how we typically project information into two-dimensional histograms, tree-diagrams, flow charts, clusters and so on (see Huff 1990; Huff and Jenkins 2002), which are kinds of maps. The central feature of maps is that they put various items in relation to each other by employing relative size and relative position. Our most natural approach to simplify complex or abstract knowledge is, however, to put it in spatial terms – or even into space itself, as an artifact that we can see and touch. Cummings and Wilson added their understanding to the value of maps.

Maps can help people to orient themselves or 'think strategically', by offering a language by which complex options can be simply understood, communicated, bounced around and debated, enabling a group to focus in order to learn about themselves and what they want to achieve, and locate themselves in relation to their environment. They can also foster 'acting strategically' by getting people beyond indecision so as to begin the process of mapping and taking a course. (2003: 1–2)

Landscape metaphors

Landscape metaphors can be particularly valuable (Lissack and Roos 1999; Oliver and Roos 2000). The reason is that humans are very good at envisioning space, especially landscapes. As our ancestors had to hunt and gather on spatial plains, recognizing patterns in space evolved to become a natural ability. From rolling hills, mountain ranges, forests, skylines, ponds, and bridges we can all use the simple notion of landscapes to develop and use effective metaphorical imagery:

Visually, we may *see* rolling hills of grassy fields, or perhaps boiling mud pools and erupting volcanoes in the distance. We can *hear* the sounds of cowbells [the authors do live in Switzerland], the birds chirping in a calm pastoral scene, or thunder and the screech of flying dinosaurs in a primeval landscape world. Similarly, we may *smell* scents from nearby flowers mixed with the freshness of a just-passed thunderstorm or the acrid fumes of sulphur. We can *taste* the fruit of nearby trees or the lava dust gusting in our faces. We can *feel* damp grass, or rumbling gravel, under our feet, its hardness, smoothness or slippery qualities. Each of these landscape features triggers memories for us that we can easily communicate, making landscapes a good sources of metaphoric imagery. (Oliver and Roos 2000: 31)

When we shift our thinking to landscape images we convert our discomfort with time and meaning into the familiar world of geographical space. Landscape images can draw on all our senses and thereby allow us to express ourselves in way that make more sense to others. Let's illustrate this with an anecdote.

In the mid-1990s Johan was asked to help a company to make sense of a new business that seemed to emerge in between several traditional industries. Rather than only presenting traditional 'strategic analysis' types of maps, he also used an image from the Renaissance landscape:

It is like an ever-changing landscape of interconnected villages. In other parts of the world experts reside in one village most of their life. In this landscape experts are wanderers, who offer their services to the highest bidder, then move on to the next village.

Unlike the traditional strategy grids, this story caused the executives immediately to verbally picture what their company looked like in comparison, and how they treated experts who left their company for a competitor. They settled for 'bunker' and 'target practice' respectively.

Three-dimensionality

Thinking from Within takes this notion one step further. By choosing which real-world item is to be represented by an object and by placing the object in a particular spot, participants in object-mediated communication create not only three-dimensional tropes but also three-dimensional maps, thereby profiting from the expressive power of relative size and distance. In Chapter 12 we will take the concept of what is real beyond the traditional into *surplus reality* that we can also see examples of in previous case stories. Recall how the OilCo executives constructed together a map for the 'journey' of their new customer focus concept. The ChemCo Fragrance executives (Chapter 3) mapped their entire organization as a flow of activities, under the increasingly unpredictable influence of the 'winds of change'. The PrintCo leaders (Chapter 4) mapped their relationship with corporate headquarters, and how they perceived retailers.

Maps have a number of advantages over pure text or speech. Because of our preference for spatial terminology and spatial imagery, we usually process maps more easily than texts containing the same information. Whereas the linearity of text (or speech) forces us to focus on one thing at a time, maps allow us to take in a fairly complex state of affairs in one sweep. Maps also facilitate communication: pointing to a particular part of the map only takes a fraction of the time that is required to describe it. The items on the map, furthermore, are contin uously available for sustained talk and interpretation by participants in ways that the contents of conventional speeches or written texts normally are not. If the maps are constructed during the communication they also provide a record of the process, in itself an artifact. Thus they facilitate a sort of communication, where one can easily go back and forth between items, along argumentative and temporal lines. Doyle and Sims (2002) have noticed that such 'loops' prompt less exasperation, such as 'we are going round in circles', in object-mediated communication than in the purely verbal communication. Because all items are available at all times, they can re-enter the communication at just the right moment.

Using objects to create a three-dimensional map we get not only relative size but relative mass too; not only relative distance across length and breadth but also height. As illustrated in previous chapters, three-dimensional constructions can be explored with the hands from more than one angle, from left and right, above and below; not only visually but also with other senses.

Two-dimensional charts or drawings on paper do not have the same materiality as three-dimensional objects, and they cannot afford us the same wealth of haptic, olfactory (if the paper is not scented) and kinaesthetic experiences. Compare the two strategy maps in Exhibit 5.1 and Exhibits 5.2a–c in the plate section. Both types of maps capture certain elements of the business environment. Only one lends itself to the kind of hands-on sensemaking that object-mediated communication enables.

The variety of materials (wood, iron, textiles), consistencies (solid, brittle, liquid, viscous), or *objets trouvés* (toys, fruits, tools) that can be used simultaneously for object-mediated communication add dimensions far

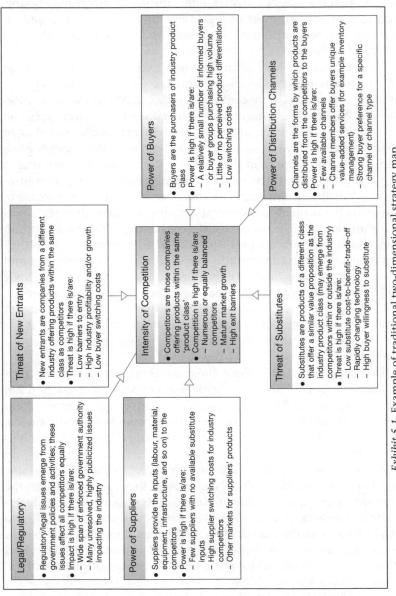

Legal/Regulatory
- Regulatory/legal issues emerge from government policies and activities; these issues affect all competitors equally
- Impact is high if there is/are:
  – Wide span of enforced government authority
  – Many unresolved, highly publicized issues impacting the industry

Threat of New Entrants
- New entrants are companies from a different industry offering products within the same class as competitors
- Threat is high if there is/are:
  – Low barriers to entry
  – High industry profitability and/or growth
  – Low buyer switching costs

Power of Buyers
- Buyers are the purchasers of industry product class
- Power is high if there is/are:
  – A relatively small number of informed buyers or buyer groups purchasing high volume
  – Little or no perceived product differentiation
  – Low switching costs

Power of Suppliers
- Suppliers provide the inputs (labour, material, equipment, infrastructure, and so on) to the competitors
- Power is high if there is/are:
  – Few suppliers with no available substitute inputs
  – High supplier switching costs for industry competitors
  – Other markets for suppliers' products

Intensity of Competition
- Competitors are those companies offering products within the same 'product class'
- Competition is high if there is/are:
  – Numerous or equally balanced competitors
  – Mature market growth
  – High exit barriers

Threat of Substitutes
- Substitutes are products of a different class that offer a similar value proposition as the industry product class (may emerge from competitors within or outside the industry)
- Threat is high if there is/are:
  – Low substitute cost-to-benefit-trade-off
  – Rapidly changing technology
  – High buyer willingness to substitute

Power of Distribution Channels
- Channels are the forms by which products are distributed from the competitors to the buyers
- Power is high if there is/are:
  – Few available channels
  – Channel members offer buyers unique value-added services (for example inventory management)
  – Strong buyer preference for a specific channel or channel type

Exhibit 5.1 Example of traditional two-dimensional strategy map

beyond those that can ever be captured by a two-dimensional map. As such, this three-dimensionality is an emerging benefit of the practice of *Thinking from Within*, which we will discuss further in Chapter 9.

Materiality – colours, textures and consistencies – also comes with conventional associations like 'slick', 'smooth', 'slimy', 'hunky', which tend to be emotionally loaded. By using the cute and fluffy toy instead of the sticky and nondescript thing, we can infuse items in the communication with emotional colouring.

This inclusion of emotions adds a whole new quality to understanding and knowing; it admits the close link between emotion and cognition. Abelson (1963) introduced the concept of 'hot', or affect-driven cognition; Damasio (1994) spoke of emotions as 'somatic markers' that colour available options with varying degrees of urgency, thereby acting as constraints on decision-making. Wartofsky (1979) discussed how we invest artifacts with both cognitive and affective content, and Simon (1996) discussed how artifacts mediate the inner life and the outer world. Recall also how practices in psychotherapy such as play therapies and creative arts therapies, discussed in Chapter 2, have used artifacts for almost a century. Objects thus, by virtue of having a particular material instantiation and being accessible through all senses, allow us to draw on many aspects of our thinking and tap into our emotions.

Objects make us agree differently

Object mediated communication is guided into a shared sense-making. To make sense we select cues – present or past – from the environment, embellish them and construct a story around them. Sense-making is not concerned with accuracy but with *plausibility*. It is what allows us to *act* rather than to be paralysed by the complexity of the world around us (Weick 1995).

Stories

For members of the same organization to act consistently, they need to share their sense-making. This often happens in a very informal way through stories, that is, relatively short, often anecdotal and very subjective, accounts of things that selectively focus attention on certain aspects of the world (recall the role of storytelling in Chapter 3). A story is always told with a purpose, if only to entertain, and its narrator will give it the twist that is consistent with this purpose. They are not expected to get all the details right, but to convey the essence of a matter; they are supposed to be truthful rather than true.

Organizations have been described as 'storytelling systems' and stories as the 'sense-making currency' within organizations (Boje 1991). Stories float around organizations and have sometimes been handed down through generations of employees. They constitute part of the organizational memory, but they are also used to explain, warn, motivate or instigate a rebellion; they are told to cause a certain effect or withheld to prevent that effect. The point is that a story is never finished, nor definitely told, because every retelling will change it again.

Given the central role that stories play in organizations when it comes to sense-making and action, it is remarkable that conventional managerial practices consistently fail to integrate them. Object-mediated communication distinguishes itself by providing a forum for stories to be told and a medium for them to be captured. Recall how the stories, enhanced by drama (discussed fully in Chapter 12), told by each of the OilCo leaders of Chapter 1 defined the very practice of the new 'journey' concept.

By accommodating stories that float around the organization and offering a space for the creation of new stories, object-mediated communication can contribute to the resolution of long-standing problems and conflicts that people avoid addressing. Stories are often the medium through which discontent is expressed, often with ironic ambiguity and paradoxes, and their exclusion from the official discourse results in a suppression of this discontent. Life in each organization unfolds against a background of unwritten and unspoken conventions. Members of organizations know what talk and interpretations are acceptable or not in the context of their organizations.

As illustrated in the PrintCo story of Chapter 4, object-based communication can give voice to repressed taboo issues. The other stories in this book also illustrate how emotions and insecurities, potential conflicts and disagreements or scepticism towards innovative ideas can be unlocked. Constraining and debilitating notions of what is acceptable and what is not can be unhinged, and once the issues are out on the table, they cannot be ignored any more and have to be resolved.

When using the concept of shared sense-making to understand some aspects of object-mediated communication, we have to acknowledge that there is a strong political dimension. Sense-making is about plausibility and not accuracy and to converge on a shared sense, a process of negotiation and persuasion is needed.

The material manifestation of shared sense-making – the convergence of individual viewpoints – is a joint artifact that integrates contributions from individuals and provides the vanishing point towards which the conversation is moving. It is, at the same time, emerging from the process and shaping it in a sort of feedback loop. In its final form, it is a tangible outcome of the communication, exhibiting areas of agreement reached as well as persisting differences. It can capture in memorable imagery what participants need to take away from the communication and can serve as a reference point for further discussion (more on this in Chapter 13). Exhibits 5.3a–c in the plate section exemplifies an object-mediated communication – managers describing their business.

It is helpful to think for a moment of the artifact produced by co-construction once more as a map. As the saying goes, *the map is not the territory* – not even on a different scale – but an abstraction. A map is a political instrument that presents the world according to its maker and each maker uses the map in pursuit of a different interest. When we make a map we are forced to choose what to present and how to present it. Maps are not like transparent windows onto the world, but, 'they get things done ... maps sweat, they strain, they apply themselves' (Wood 1993: 1). This is what the OilCo leaders of Chapter 1 voiced at the end of their retreat.

The aim of object-mediated communication is not to have an unrelated collection of individual objects, but an artifact created jointly by the participants. Thus, there needs to be some convergence of people's views on how that artifact should look, like the picture of the 'journey' in OilCo, or the 'winds of change' in ChemCo. In other words, participants have to convince others of the plausibility of their individual contributions to the joint artifact. This bears some similarity to how Latour (1987) describes scientists enrolling objects to persuade peers and funders. To fashion the map according to their view of the territory, participants in object-mediated communication will marshal the rhetoric force of the objects. Some individual contributions, and the rhetoric accompanying them, will be more articulate and persuasive than others and will be integrated into the joint artifact of the group. Others will disappear or be rearranged. Persuasion in object-mediated communication does not only happen through the force of an analytical argument, but also through the force of an inspiring image that aptly captures the aspirations of the group. In that sense, object-mediated communication not only appeals to reason, but also to aesthetic appreciation: other participants not only have to be *convinced* by a contribution, but have to *like* it too. This follows Kant's (1781/1950) claim that sensual perception and sensual initiation matters for how we know, and come to know.

Objects make us cope differently

From our own and other researchers' experience with organizational interventions that are mediated by objects there is abundant evidence that supports what Case and Dalley (1992) have observed on how the use of objects in group therapies can plunge people into unexpected levels of intensity. When the facilitator has created a safe and secure environment, objects can be used to externalize repressed emotions and issues and help in dealing with them in a proactive manner (see Chapter 2).

Expressions

As is evident from the pictures of serious managers engaged in playful construction, object-mediated communication in organizations looks and feels different compared with the setting of traditional meetings (see Exhibits 5.4 and 5.5 in plate section).

Instead of sitting around a table and gazing at slide projections, participants in object-mediated communication are required to handle play dough or connect plastic strings. They have to get up from the table and move around the room to intervene in the building of the joint artifact. Despite initial resistance, the unconstrained ways of expression that are afforded by an array of objects, or material to manipulate, have subversive qualities all of their own. Providing the facilitator is competent, participants quickly realize that instead of taking the risk of looking ridiculous, the use of objects can be good for illustrating different scenarios and hazarding risky suggestions. Participants often discover that it is difficult to keep one's hands off the construction; and even before they are convinced of the utility of the exercise they cannot resist the fun it provides. Before knowing it, people become attached to what they are building. They 'revel' in their creations and activity rises to 'manic' and 'feverish' levels (see Barry 1994 and Chapter 11). Their actions come from within. In contrast to purely verbal communication, it is much more about the issues and not about who voices them. When responding to a suggestion presented in the shape of a construction, other participants are invited to offer an alternative by rearranging the construction.

Other characteristics of object-mediated communication are the qualities of contradictions and paradoxes. Participants are not required to avoid them at all costs – quite the contrary: the ambiguity inherent in the three-dimensional imagery allows for and even encourages the testing of different scenarios, repeated changes in parameters, and the gradual settling on a collectively embraced vision in a way traditional communication does not. In purely verbal communication it is not acceptable to end our sentences with question marks again and again; in object-mediated communication this is often the norm. In the theories of play, as discussed in Chapter 2, the value of such ambiguous and transitional spaces of exploration has long been recognized.

The emotional aspect is due not only to the imagery, but also to the *three-dimensionality* as sensory experience combines the visual with the haptic and olfactory (see Chapter 4). Objects can give us different interactive experiences depending on their texture, malleability or delicacy. In our own experiments we have tried out materials differing significantly in these respects and have anecdotal evidence for the implications. For instance, we have observed how hard construction materials tend to mediate intellectual communication about details represented by their particular colour, robustness, size and ability to connect with similar pieces. In contrast, we have observed how softer and pliable materials, like clay or soft play materials, mediate more intuitive and emotional communication. Case and Dalley (1992: 99) noticed the same in the context of using clay in art therapy:

> Clay encourages a very physical involvement that aids release of body tension which helps emotional release. For this reason it can be a most powerful medium with which to work.

McNiff (1998: 29) has similar experiences in his work as an artist experimenting with many material and techniques:

> Clay is an excellent medium for experimenting with the ways shapes emerge from the unknown ... what appears to be random movement has a purpose in the process of transformation ... throughout the process clay is a stable partner, always interacting with your eyes and hands.

Although we can share this enthusiasm for clay, in the organizational settings of this book wet clay is less appropriate – it is just too messy. Yet, the benefits of softness are important ones and can be found in other materials, which do not cover our clothes and faces afterwards. The benefit lies in pulling, squeezing and twisting materials in addition to more systematically putting them together.

Each medium makes it special contribution to creation and expression of *Thinking from Within*. Almost any feature of the material impacts our experience. The trick, McNiff (1998: 30) tells us lies in:

experiencing the different physical properties of the media. Explore what they do in response to different kinds of involvements you make. Watch how the spontaneity of your gestures correspond to you ability to feel the medium and what it is capable of doing.

The technical skill that is required to handle materials, and personal inclination, can sometimes set a threshold of entry. Whereas most people will quickly stick their hands into and begin shaping a pile of play dough, some are intimidated by the skills that are supposedly needed to build with small pieces of construction toy materials. The solution is that we let go of our tendency to think in terms of outcomes. Thus, we should intend emergence rather than plan a result (more on this in Chapters 7 and 8).

When objects mediate a communication, they can become the target of projected feelings like, for example, unease, fear, anger, but also relief, joy and pleasure, which then literally can be dumped onto the table. The artifact becomes a sort of talisman, an object that is more than its material self – it assumes special powers. We saw some of this in the PrintCo case in Chapter 4. Not only is it a representation but also an embodiment of all that is wrong or good. If it carries negative feelings, it can take the role of a scapegoat – like the white goat in biblical times, onto which a priest laid the sins of the community – before it was sacrificed for the absolution from sin. As Schaverien (1987) has remarked, transference to objects allows us to safely enact such a process, which would be unethical, if the scapegoat were a living being. Projection of negative issues onto an object or an artifact allows members of organizations 'to come face to face with an often threatening image...', and give it 'substance and endurance' (Mook 2003: 266). In turn, this allows for the issue to be addressed head-on and ultimately, disposed of. Disposal can be understood literally as taking apart or putting away the object; but it can also be understood, more generally, as 'coming to terms with'. Once again we see the vital need for the facilitator to be competent in handling the delicate emotions that are vital and important parts of the experience when practising *Thinking from Within*. But we must also always be aware that professional psychotherapy belongs to the authorized psychotherapists.

Quick Reflection

Far from being a mere embellishment to conversation, mediating objects, by virtue of their three-dimensionality and the sensory experience they provide and when the session is well facilitated, have the power to substantially transform communication. Because the participants in object-mediated communication 'think with their hands', that is, temporarily suspend a pure intellectual mode, they sometimes don't know what to make of their constructions – like waking up from a dream and trying to make sense of it. Object-mediated communication rests on the assumption that no detail of the artifact is accidental. As noted by Barry (1994: 4):

participants are invited to assume that 'every inch of their creations [has] some message, some meaning that [is] waiting to be revealed. Thus, things like color differences, massing, use of space, supportive structures, use of boundaries, and so on, [become] vehicles for inquiry.

Yet, object-mediated communication becomes deeper when the people involved have constructed their objects, rather than just taking on a given meaning assigned by somebody outside the situation. What all the details mean is not always immediately evident. But it is exactly the occasional denseness of the constructions that opens up discursive avenues that the participants would not normally go down. In some ways this process of interpretation can be likened to free association in psychoanalysis; issues that lie at the edges of participants' everyday thinking may suddenly be brought to the foreground. As Oswick et al. (2002) say with respect to metaphor and analogy, there is a movement from the 'cognitive comfort zone' of everyday routine talk to a 'cognitive *discomfort zone*' of semantic dissonances (imagery that resists interpretation). It is the collective resolution of such dissonances that stimulates exploitative non-routine talk.

In sum, the power of object-mediated communication stems from its possibility, when the session is well facilitated, to make use, think (and feel), agree and cope differently. To further illustrate these points we use a case story about how a cross-functional team of managers in a telecommunication company used object-mediated communication to think, feel, agree and cope quite differently than they usually did.

Case: Mediating serious conversations in TelCo[1]

TelCo, a European telecommunications company, was a remarkable success story in its home market, arising as an upstart in a competitive environment dominated by the national public telecoms utility company. A series of innovative tactics, including unit pricing approaches, billing options, non-traditional advertising, highly responsive customer service and avant-garde lifestyle appeals, had rocketed TelCo into the marketplace during the 1990s. However, it then went through a phase where it was acquired and sold by a variety of larger corporations and was ultimately acquired by a very large national telecommunications utility from another country. As part of this latter transition, a key founder figure of TelCo decided to leave the CEO position to an appointee from the new holding company. Also, the company's board of directors was rebuilt, and the new set of board members wrestled with the question of how to respond to the sharpening strategic difficulties facing a more mature TelCo in an increasingly competitive marketplace.

With TelCo's moving into and out of the corporate structure of several larger holding companies, some employees in the corporate strategy department began to worry about dilution of elements they regarded as the core of TelCo's success. For instance, they worried about the well-known entrepreneurial mind-set, close attention to customer service and a set of internally – and externally – directed brand values. The strategic problem they perceived, was the decay of the organizational attributes they felt to be at the core of its successful growth. As part of their efforts to counteract these tendencies, they contacted Johan in late 2000.

In the ensuing months, he had repeated contact with TelCo's strategy planning department and the planning/strategy staff from various businesses. There were several meetings and small-scale experiments with the company's strategy team using experimental and playful techniques, which had enabled these people to move from habits of 'prescribed thinking' towards *Thinking from Within* (see Exhibit 1.1 in Chapter 1). In an internal e-mail, a key member of this team narrated the development of this relationship in the following way:

> [The Corporate Strategy group at TelCo] has been experimenting with new methods to create, communicate, interpret and implement strategy since the group's foundation four years ago ... A key focus over the past 18 months has been our experiments [with Johan] that revealed very promising insights in this neglected area.

Johan agreed with the leaders of the strategy group to stage and facilitate another workshop, this time for a mixed group of senior strategists, brand managers and human resource managers. In preparation for the workshop, eight of the nine individual participants agreed to hour-long, individual interviews. The semi-structured interviews covered individual current position and job history, perceptions of organizational morale, culture and the company's brand. The interviews revealed the organization's strategic needs in terms of four themes pertaining to the question of the TelCo 'brand'.

1. Interviewees emphasized TelCo's history of succeeding despite adverse circumstances with a considerable amount of pride, lending the entire discussion a palpable sense of nostalgia.

2. TelCo's essential distinctiveness as an organizational culture was found to be practically impossible to articulate, although many references to a 'moral' or 'ethical' way of operating were made.

3. The ability of TelCo to be *both* ethical and successful in the past was felt to be under threat and a choice now loomed between 'being ethical' *or* 'being successful'.

4. The challenges of globalization were felt intensely as a need to balance the essence of 'what TelCo is' with the need to adapt to local cultures and contexts.

This suggested to us the enormous significance to employees of TelCo's growth story, coupled with its strong sense of itself as being both a high performing organization and a force for moral improvement in society in general. TelCo's 'brand' was constantly referred to in terms suggesting an icon that fused aspects of history, mission, performance and morality for the organization. Two excerpts from the interviews make this point particularly well. One participant said:

> It was a bad year and I did think about leaving. But it's such a fantas-tic brand – and some of the stuff we come up with here for promoting it – you just couldn't do it anywhere else! Incredible, but I've been here 11 years now.

And another offered:

> The heart of this company is emotional and passionate. It's a very emotive organization, especially because of where it came from, that powerful brand – it relates to a feeling.

The retreat

The retreat followed a similar pattern as already described in the ChemCo case (Chapter 3), where participants used their hands collectively to construct together more or less complex models of their situation. During the two-day retreat participants co-constructed, de-constructed and re-constructed their view of the organization and its business landscape. Johan facilitated the workshop.

Approaching the strategy workshop, participants seemed interested but guarded about what they were to undertake and some scepticism was voiced. In the warm-up exercises, the senior brand manager seemed upset by a comment one of the other participants made about what she was doing and became more tentative in her contributions to the group work for several hours. Eventually they all got involved in constructing a model representing what participants could agree on as a common identity for the many-sided and diverse TelCo organization. The group voiced frustration at its inability to arrive at a representation all participants felt was accurate and yet comprehensive enough and considerable time passed with different ways of representing it presented and then rejected. They seemed to be relieved when several different views of the identity of the organization were combined to show a flotilla of ships of different sizes, shapes and capabilities, scattered over the sea, straggling forwards. Relief then gave way to some excitement and participants' behaviour began to be more positive, instead of the almost moody and pensive demeanour they had shown in the previous hour.

As the end of the first day of the workshop drew near, participants' engagement remained quite intense – there was a constant conversation around the table, and they would frequently lean in, pick up, adjust or add to the now quite complex model on the table in front of them while talking with others about what these adjustment meant.

In the morning of the second day, there were a number of comments about the intensity of the experience they were having. Several individuals complained of feeling 'knackered' by the intensity of the session so far. It was unclear to the researcher-facilitators involved if this sense of being emotionally drained was viewed positively (exhaustion with a sense of accomplishment) or negatively (exhaustion without a sense of accomplishment) at this point. One of them stated quite seriously that she had dreamt of playing with materials last night and another added that he had as well.

In the next phase of the workshop, participants began to populate the area around their flotilla model with different constructions representing aspects of their social, economic and competitive context. One participant, for example, sought to illustrate how a very large competitor with its power base in another part of the world was likely to enter into direct competition with TelCo and she placed the large, blocky figure representing this competitor on a bookshelf on the wall behind the table. The competitor was, as she put it, 'coming in from left field', an assertion made patent by the physical location of the figure at the edge of the space where the group was working. Two of the other participants eagerly began to question the individual who had arrived at this particular contribution – did she really think this competitor was interested? Yes, she responded, 'that's why I've placed them coming right over at the table', and the construction was quite big. 'Do they have the resources to really come in and shake things up?' 'Absolutely', she continued – 'look at how big and threatening I've built this model of them.' In subsequent interviews one participant recollected this dialogue as a powerful episode, which 'hit them in the gut'. Just a few weeks after the workshop she was proved right: the competitor surprised the market and TelCo's leadership by entering Europe at full speed.

Cumulatively, this and several other surprises made for a particularly strong impression on participants about their competitive position. One participant commented; 'I used to think we had maybe three or four competitors. But now the table just isn't big enough to hold all of them!'

The concluding phases of the workshop were characterized by a shared group perception that the holistic panorama and the communication it had mediated was a novel and important experience for them all. One participant stated, 'It's like, once you get all the problems on the table, you can deal with them. And that's what we've done – we've got them all on the table!' This point crystallized for participants in one key event. Up to the morning of the second day, they had placed an icon of their brand in front of the 'flotilla', as if that was what was drawing them further. In a moment of experimentation, one participant placed the icon of the brand at the *rear* of the flotilla. After a moment's hesitation, participants nodded in acceptance of this radical statement of the impor tance of the brand to their present situation, even though the notion that the brand was somehow 'behind' them clearly struck several people as an almost taboo thought. This episode and agreement among partic- ipants remained with them for the rest of the day and almost all of them kept referring to potential implications, including political, of such a radical statement.

Near the end of the second day, the group engaged in a discussion about the interactions among many of the elements it had built and rep- resented on the table. There had been a running commentary among the group throughout the workshop about a surge of emphasis on EBITDA (earnings before interest, tax, depreciations and amortizations) growing among senior management, which was visibly manifested in their flotilla construction. While many among the group recognized the importance of financial issues, they also seemed to think that a focus on EBITDA alone couldn't take precedence over the more fundamental issue of atten- tion to customers and to the brand. There were several cynical refer- ences to the concept, suggesting that it was perhaps not to be taken too seriously. But in ensuing discussions, awareness seemed to dawn on all that a great number of fundamental strategic decisions and opportunities were going to hinge on available cash. One participant muttered 'EBITDA' in a tone that suggested that he had suddenly had an epiphany about the importance of this measurement to organizational success. From that point on, the group discussed the importance of EBITDA in a much less cynical way.

Aftermath

Approximately three weeks after the workshop, Johan and a colleague debriefed the senior strategy member of the participant group about continuing discussions among those who had participated in the workshop. Subsequently, follow-up interviews were conducted with these participants, in which they evaluated the influence that this workshop had on their own activities inside the organization. Some e-mail exchanges among TelCo staff were also made available to the researchers, helping to shed light on the effects of the object-mediated communication, which had unfolded in a playful context a few weeks earlier.

Overall, they all said the workshop had penetrated the shell of objectivity most people had towards their work and created an 'unusual subjective' state. The reports of dreaming of construction work indicated that a uniquely emotional depth was attained in this workshop. This was supported by the lasting feeling of fatigue – 'feeling knackered'– that many reported having had throughout the week, as if some great accomplishment had drained them. One individual had a particularly strong statement about an emotional epiphany he had had:

> I remember reflecting on the workshop content and reaching a moment of clarity that helped develop a framework for looking at the future.

Quick reflections

The case story of TelCo illustrates how, when adequately staged, object-mediated communication makes us think, feel, agree and cope in ways that are different from conventional communication in organizations. The testimonials after the workshop evidence the emotional dimension. The episodes about EBITDA and 'putting the vision behind the flotilla' illustrate the coping aspect. The very shared and constructed model of a flotilla of vessels exemplifies how such objects can make us agree differently than is normally the case.

In object-mediated communication, manipulation of artifacts mirrors

Donald Schön's (1983) well-known account of 'reflection-in-action'. The situation created by the actions of these managers 'talked back' and forced them to modify their actions. In the TelCo case, the artifacts, like the very flotilla image or that of the surprising competitor, talked back to their makers, challenged them and demanded to be acknowledged and dealt with. Talk and artifacts in object-mediated communication are so intimately intertwined, that it is impossible to claim that the artifact explains the talk or the talk explains the artifact – both explain each other. Again, we see how thinking and doing merge into a powerful practice. It is in the interplay of talk and artifacts that an intellectually adventurous and emotionally engaging communication emerges.

Conclusion

The possibility of externalizing mental items and sharing them through rich imagery, like in maps, gives us an overview and facilitates conversations of complex themes. Objects enable us to experience surprising imagery, which can make both the unfamiliar familiar and the familiar unfamiliar, challenge our current notions and stimulate us to explore non-conventional understandings. The emotional subtext that imagery and materials carry unlocks the power of affect driven cognition. Objects make us *know* differently.

A configuration of objects, their relative size and distance, the imagery and the material that are employed offer repositories for rich interpretation of organizational issues that can be captured in stories. Not only numbers can be presented, but likewise idiosyncratic anecdotes that are often very significant for members of an organization; this appeals to our need for meaning in addition to reasons, and for beauty in addition to truth. Objects make us *agree* differently. Agreement is not a purely rational act here, but involves passion, enthusiasm and commitment.

Finally, the exploration of untested ideas becomes less risky, because the focus is taken away from the speaker and directed towards the artifacts that carry the expressions. Contradicting parts of the artifact can easily stand next to each other, at least for a while. Objects also provide a screen onto which to project negative emotions that, after being out on the table, can be owned and faced up to. Thus, objects make us *cope* differently with ambiguity, contradiction and repressed issues.

Overall, our discussion in this chapter has provided us with more awareness and understanding of how objects can be used to mediate communication when practising *Thinking from Within*.

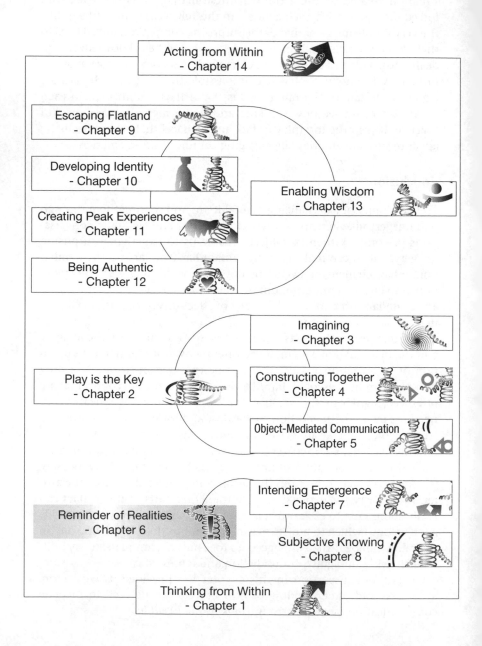

Acting from Within
- Chapter 14

Escaping Flatland
- Chapter 9

Developing Identity
- Chapter 10

Enabling Wisdom
- Chapter 13

Creating Peak Experiences
- Chapter 11

Being Authentic
- Chapter 12

Imagining
- Chapter 3

Play is the Key
- Chapter 2

Constructing Together
- Chapter 4

Object-Mediated Communication
- Chapter 5

Intending Emergence
- Chapter 7

Reminder of Realities
- Chapter 6

Subjective Knowing
- Chapter 8

Thinking from Within
- Chapter 1

6
A Reminder of Realities

Johan Roos

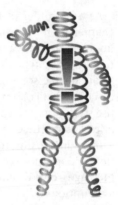

Introduction

So far in this book we have described and illustrated how to practise the conceptual, behavioural and material dimension of our imagination, construct together by manipulating materials with our hands and use these objects to mediate communication – while keeping the emerging benefits of play in mind. The tales of OilCo, ChemCo, PrintCo and TelCo illustrated how these ideas can be played out in real-life strategy practice, broadly defined. In my experience, however, *Thinking from Within* remains the exception and the 'prescribed' way of thinking more of the rule in organized life in general and in strategy practice in particular. Despite the many calls from scholars and gurus in the field, strategy practice remains in many firms an unimaginative and boring routine of deductive analysis that, by definition, rarely tap into the imagination and spontaneity of the people involved. As such, strategy practices risk being more of a waste of time than a valuable investment.

Imagine you have just been invited to participate in the next strategy process of your organization. What do you imagine you will be *doing*? Some of you may look forward to reworking the vision or mission statement or revising the previous Strengths Weaknesses Opportunities Threats analysis. Others may feel less excited about the inevitable project someone with more authority will assign to your current workload. Others may simply feel honoured to be included in such a politically important activity, typically reserved for the managerial elite. After all, strategy practice can be an excellent opportunity to both prove oneself and build useful coalitions for the future. Perhaps all of you will look forward to the first evening's *fois gras chaude*, surrounded with a spoonful of raspberry vinegar sauce and the chilled Chateau d'Yquem? That was what some of the people depicted in Chapter 1's Exhibits 1.2 and 1.3 (plate section) told me at the outset of their strategy retreat.

As a reminder of the perceived realities in many organizations this chapter presents two tales of strategy practices, in which I was deeply involved and thus also co-responsible for. These cases are neither the usual teaching-case type of success story nor hero worship about extraordinary smart people solving problems in brilliant ways. Rather the cases only describe what I observed as groups of experienced executives set out to practise strategy in ways that made sense to them. At the end of the chapter, I briefly relate these to the Chapter 1 models of *Thinking from Within*.

In addition, and to serve as a reminder of conventional strategy practices, the purpose of this chapter is to prepare readers for the ideas and messages of subsequent chapters, which outline two philosophical assumptions of *Thinking from Within*. The two cases in this chapter will feature prominently to illustrate such assumptions.

In the first case, BrassCo, a group of German manufacturing executives reached a dead end after four months of ritualized attempts to develop the next strategic plan. As the external facilitator of the retreats I tried to help these executives and their internal project leader to do what they wanted to do well: lots of 'strategic analyses'. Deep inside I experienced an increasing concern about what unfolded in terms of thinking and doing among the group and also about my own role during these practices.

In the second case, TechCo, a new CEO was brought in to rejuvenate a profitable but stagnating service company in the Dutch telecommunication industry. Together with an academic colleague from a business school, I was deeply engaged in designing and facilitating a retreat-based, cascading strategy process, which the CEO wanted to use to reignite the organization. On the surface, with its beautiful off-site retreats, expert inputs and advanced process facilitation, the strategy practice was different from the experience of both the CEO and the managers. As a participant observer, however, I gradually began to wonder about the growing gap between what the CEO said and did and how this came to influence what people were thinking and what they did during the strategy practice.[1]

Methodology

These case descriptions are based on an inductive research methodology. In terms of research method, I mixed elements of participant observation (Whyte 1991) and action research (Lewin 1949; Eden and Huxham 1996; Eikeland 2001). Rather than following the Glaser and Strauss's (1967) *leitmotif* of enabling prediction and explanation of behaviour, in this study I did not want to explain or predict anything. Instead, I simply wanted to *describe what was going on and present these descriptions to the reader*. In turn, in the remaining part of the book I will reflect over these case

stories both in light of the practices of *Thinking from Within* already discussed in previous chapters, and additionally in terms of deep philosophical assumptions about how we view (Chapter 7) and know (Chapter 8)
the world.

In terms of participant observation to gather data I entered a real-
world, field-based setting, where I subjectively observed and recorded
strategy practices in two companies. In terms of Patton's (2002) definition, my study was a partial rather than full participant observation; I
used *overt* observation during which people in the organizations knew
who I was; I *partly* explained the purpose of doing research; I carried out
several observations of limited durations (from three hours to three and a
half days); and *my focus* of the situation was broad in terms of the setting
and people involved, so that I could be open for emerging insights.

In terms of action research, I kept the three phases suggested by Lewin
(1949) in mind. Firstly, I defined and described the problem to be investi-
gated (that is, strategy practice) and the context in which it was set (preparations for, and the actual retreats and meetings). I also described what the
participants (the members of the design group, liaison persons, leadership
team members, the CEO, and so on) were doing. Secondly, I interpreted
the situation and reflected on what these people were doing, with a special
emphasis on their problems and issues (for example how to motivate
people to contribute during the retreats and meetings). Thirdly, I inter-
vened to help resolve these issues and problems and thought about the
appropriateness and outcome of those actions. Although this action
research 'spiral' never unfolded in such a clear way, I tried to be conscious
about the distinct activities embedded in it. Here is the result.

Case: Strategizing in BrassCo

As I looked at the executives in the conference room I had a hunch we
had approached a breakpoint. The table was covered with copies of the
presentation they had just seen as well as used coffee cups. Jackets rested
on the chairs, ties had been loosened and sleeves rolled up. It was hot
outside and the air conditioner struggled to keep up.

The group was the entire top-management team of a German-based
metals company, BrassCo, all seasoned executives in the industry. At this
time, in 1998, the CEO had more than 20 years of experience with the
firm and had been at the helm for more than ten. His lieutenants were
the five 'heads' of business units in different countries, the CFO and the
HR director. These managers knew each another very well, sometimes
playing golf together at weekends.

Looking at each one of them, I was struck by how similar these eight middle-aged Caucasian men looked. They dressed, moved and talked as if complying with an unwritten script of appropriate corporate behaviour. From my first meeting with this group, I was amused to see how one of them was an almost identical, younger version of the CEO, perfecting the mirror image of his boss, including the haircut and colour.

After a pause the leader of the largest business unit, Ernst, sighed noticeably. 'This doesn't feel right' he said, flipping through the pages before him. Suddenly, he had everybody's attention: 'Our new strategy looks an awful lot like the one we came up with five years ago.' His colleagues seemed uneasy as they changed positions or fixed their stares. He looked at the CEO, who was staring at the pen he was fiddling with, for some sign of agreement. Getting none, he ventured further, this time with his usual smile. 'We know the industry's changing fast, the data show it. All of us feel we've got new business opportunities.' Around the table were seven impassive faces. 'But', he said, his voice unusually slow and now with the distinctive smile gone, 'the way we've been thinking, we'll be stuck for the next five years with our same five business areas – the same old thing.' The others traded nervous glances. Ernst continued, 'I just don't think we're imaginative enough.' The CEO, who looked very uneasy cleared his throat and said, 'Okay ... so what are we supposed to do?' There was more silence.

Delegating responsibilities

Six months earlier the CEO had selected a junior manager, Jan, to lead and facilitate the strategy process. Jan had been called back to headquarters from one of the country operations. He later told me he accepted the job, because he got the offer directly from the CEO, which he considered an honour and because the task came with the prospect of an attractive staff position after a job well done. After organizing himself at the headquarters, Jan approached me for help with facilitating the strategy process.

Jan and I developed a good working relationship and collaborated throughout the process, including visiting some of the production plants for input from the 'front lines' together. During our field trips he shared his mixed view of the company and its leadership with me. On the one hand, the company was doing well, so it was a good place to work and he was proud to be affiliated with it. On the other hand, he considered its leadership stodgy and inflexible, lacking new initiatives and any sense of entrepreneurship from the top. The latter was also evident to me as I interviewed some of the managers in the business units.

As a young professor my contribution was to help Jan with frameworks and tools that could be useful to carry out his preassigned list of analytical tasks. The CEO had already set the agenda for the strategy process to be led and facilitated by Jan. Easily recognized as a traditional top-down planning approach, I soon discovered that the preset agenda was a carbon copy of how they had developed the existing strategic plan.

Jan asked me to be a 'sounding board' for his analytical work to develop summary presentations of the findings, to be reported in subsequent meetings. By briefly revisiting the company vision during each meeting, a new step had been taken towards their ultimate grail – the action plan that would ensure execution of the new strategy. So far the group had covered industry analysis, assessment of competition, review of strengths–weaknesses and opportunities–threats, core competencies appraisal and portfolio analysis. At each step I offered my views on Jan's findings and conclusions, which I found relatively straightforward and non-controversial. Given the data about the company and its industry, the current strategy seemed to be the appropriate one.

A detached exercise

Whereas the previous steps had been taken without much discussion or controversy, Jan's presentation of the portfolio analysis was what the head of the largest business unit, Ernst, reacted against. Jan's overall conclusion was that the portfolio situation was fine and everything should continue the way it was now: the same business units doing the same things lead by the same people (in the room). Clearly, Ernst did not agree.

Jan decided against my suggestion that, although the status quo may have looked like a natural conclusion, he should let the executives draw it themselves. I suspected he did this to look good. He told me beforehand that this was what the CEO implicitly expected of him, though he was never told this directly, and he thought it very unlikely that any of the people around the table would want to change the current organizational structure – much less the location of their current homes.

Throughout the process these eight executives met in the same conference room in a luxurious hotel near their headquarters. The meetings followed a traditional schedule of discussions around a large table, interrupted by mid-morning coffee, shared lunch and mid-afternoon coffee, typically ending at 5 or 6 pm. Yet, Jan scheduled the meetings so that most of them could spend an hour at the office before making the short drive to the hotel. In practice this meant that several of them were always late, typically offering excuses about the need to 'run the business'. This pattern recurred during the breaks, when each one of them walked outside talking on the mobile phone.

Similar patterns of activity were evident after each meeting, where these discussions seemed to follow an invisible script. People appeared to know what to say and not to say, how to behave and what not to do. After morning coffee, the CEO ushered the group into the room, quickly introduced the day's topic and then handed over to Jan, who made his PowerPoint presentation. The other participants would lean back in their seats and occasionally interrupt Jan with comments like 'I agree ... ' or 'No, you are wrong ... ' rather than asking questions. When he had finished they would evaluate what he had said in terms of 'What I really liked was ... ' or 'I am not sure you understand ... '.

Following this, the CEO would mediate a discussion of the content matters and prompt their views and suggestions. This discussion typically unfolded between an executive and the CEO. I rarely observed a longer debate among the executives themselves. Occasionally, one of them had been asked by a peer or the CEO to make an additional presentation to illustrate a particular topic matter, such as competitor analysis or core competence appraisals. These additional inputs rarely led to any deeper or heated debates; only nods of confirmation and the token question. The meetings always ended with the CEO giving Jan a new task, according to the meeting plan, followed by participants hurrying away. Only Jan and I stayed for 'cold talk' afterward, which we used to debrief both the content and the process of the meeting.

Sameness

Early on I was struck by how dull these people seemed during the sessions, in contrast to the attention-grabbing they demonstrated during the three-course lunches when jokes and humour flourished. After Jan had finished answering questions, or rather defending his presentation, he typically withdrew to become an observer of, rather than contributor to the discussions among the more senior people.

Over time I noticed that although the CEO kept a very low profile he seemed to exert tremendous influence on what was said and done throughout the meetings. As soon as he said something everybody else instantaneously went silent and looked at him. He never had to raise his voice to get their attention. As far as I could see during this strategy process, they never challenged him in any way. Early on Jan told me that due to his unmatched experience in the industry, the CEO was considered the most knowledgeable person in the group and as such deserved everybody's respect. After informally poking into these matters with most of the other executives, it became clear to me that despite his low profile style, the CEO kept a firm grip on the operations and not only at headquarters. None of the business unit heads was allowed to make any significant decisions without his informal or formal consent. I also learnt that the only person he made allowances for was the business unit leader, who happened to be his mirror image. It was an official secret that this man was seen as the CEO's crown prince and it became clear to me that the others did not appreciate this informal status.

I also learnt from chats and my observations that the only person who really questioned the CEO was the leader of the largest business units, Ernst, who represented almost 50 per cent of the company's revenue. This perpetually cheerful executive asked questions in a friendly way and what I thought was a genuine smile. Some of his peers, however, privately told me they thought he should 'wipe that grin off his face'.

The breakpoint

Ernst's comment completely changed the dynamics of the meeting and after a seemingly painful silence, I suggested a break for individual reflection. Everybody agreed and got up from their chairs and left the room. During this break I took the CEO aside and shared my views that they needed a radical shift in process to proceed. He asked me to mediate the discussion and report back to him, as he wanted to get back to the office.

What happened afterwards in the meeting room remains a vivid memory. The discussion erupted like a volcano. People spoke out loudly and interrupted one another in ways never seen before during the process. Jan was taken aback and just watched in amazement, while I had to mobilize all my limited facilitation skills to mediate among the six executives. They talked about everything we had done so far, questioned it and offered alternative views. For the first time I saw these people engage with the content they were discussing, but mostly, I saw a group of very frustrated people. As I confronted them with my observations and interpretations of the strategy process, including their interactions with the CEO, they became more reflective and self-critical. They all realized the process must be changed, but they did not have any suggestions as to how. They had always developed strategy this way and likewise, in principle, approached this task in their respective units. Until now they had never even wanted to do things differently. We agreed that I would bring my observations to the CEO and discuss ways to reignite the process with him.

To be continued in Chapter 7.

Case: Rejuvenating TechCo

'Thanks for a job well done' the CEO told the group. As facilitator I had just handed the group of 50 managers back to him and stepped aside for his concluding remarks. Before I even sat down he continued: 'I am delighted you reached the same conclusion about what needs to be done as I did a few weeks ago with the top-management team.' Silence. I could not believe my ears and judging from their raised eyebrows, neither could the people sitting closest to me. While the CEO kept talking about what they had already agreed to do, I observed how the ambience had suddenly changed in the room. Just a few seconds ago the atmosphere was warm and positive and now I saw stiff facial expressions, shoulders down and glances aimed at infinity. Maybe this radical shift happened because it was late Friday afternoon of the last strategy retreat day during the autumn of 2004? I suspected, however, it was because of what the CEO had just said.

Background

TechCo is a Dutch-based, regional company in the telecommunications sector, offering tangible products and related online services. Although the company operates in eight countries, Holland dominated its sales, costs and culture. Almost all top managers were Dutch, as were most of the subsidiary managers and the other 700 employees.

In December 2003, the current CEO presented his company to me as 'very successful' and a 'role model' in its industry. Despite the rosy picture he also identified several problems, as indicated by statements like: 'We have stretched the organization very hard'; 'I am looking for the next big step for the organization that everybody can take part in'; and 'We haven't yet realized synergies from our acquisitions.' To deal with these challenges the CEO had already decided to launch a strategy process during 2004. He wanted this process to (1) 'develop a shared view' among his people, (2) 'make people really understand the strategy', and (3) 'make people speak the same language'.

A few weeks later the CEO was abruptly dismissed by the board for reasons of 'disagreements about the strategic direction of the company'. While the board searched for a new CEO, the chairman became the acting CEO. As the chairman looked for candidates he searched for someone who could 'create a feeling of pride and radiate this throughout the organization'. I learnt from him that in 2003, he had recruited two executives, both with previous CEO experience, as a way to 'contain' the former CEO. During this four-month period, the chairman kept the strategy on hold, made only minor and organizational changes, but encouraged senior executives to continue preparations for the intended strategy process.

At this point my interviews with the entire top-management team revealed an organization that on the surface was very successful and profitable, but below was in deep crisis. People were talking a lot about the former CEO and there were camps both in favour and against him and although aware of the need to make changes, few seemed to want to do anything to change the status quo.

I also found that senior executives took several things for granted about their business, for example that profits were proportional to market share. Moreover, the senior leaders were fully aware that customers considered their sales people arrogant and 'monopolistic'; had incoherent views of the mission and what business they were actually in; and perceived a real need for new inspiration from the leadership.

Getting the new CEO on board

The new CEO was eventually recruited from a CEO position in a consulting firm operating in a related business. When I interviewed him a month before he formally started he said he was: (1)'intrigued by the mess' of the company, (2) wanted to be 'a big fish in a small pond', and (3) wanted 'to have control'. Like his current job, this job would provide those aspects, but on a larger scale. Later in our conversation he said another reason that played a major role in his decision to accept the job was: 'I really want to do a great job here, which will be good both for the company and for me.' He also said he would eventually like to lead a much larger firm once the job with TechCo was completed.

At first he was reluctant to continue the idea of doing a strategy process that involved many people, because he had never done this before. Instead he was used to contracting strategy consulting firms to 'cut through' the organization and present him with what needed to be done, which typically was well aligned with his own hunches. After a few hours of conversation he changed his mind and wanted to see if such an involving process might serve his purposes: 'Now I see it – I can use the strategy process as a tool for change.'

Preparations

As the new CEO took office, he explicitly told the organization that he wanted to pursue the strategy process as a way to help him 'make necessary changes to the strategy and structure' of the company. As the process design was only in draft format when he joined the company, the CEO used his authority to adjust the purpose and timing to his liking. He enlisted a global strategy-consulting firm to 'analyse and present these facts about the organization', which were to become part of the strategy practice. He also spent two months interviewing all top managers to 'get a better feeling' for current strategy, the organization and the people.

Based on discussions with three of his senior colleagues as well as with me, the CEO set the objective for the strategy process to 'develop and implement' a new strategy, which he thought was the mandate from the board. The strategy process was designed to be top-down, but also an invitation for people to be involved in and shape the strategy. The process was set to be anchored in four retreats, which represented layers the CEO sought to achieve during 2004: a few trusted leaders, the corporate top management team, the entire home market management group and the leadership teams of the international operations.

First retreat: Top three people

During a *first* stage the CEO invited the current top three people for an off-site, two-day strategy retreat: the HR, online business and strategy directors. The meeting took place in a small villa converted into a hotel, one hour by boat from the mainland. TechCo had blocked the entire villa and we had a spacious dining room area, several rooms with large fireplaces, as well as a sizeable deck outside with a great view over the ocean at our disposal.

A few days before the retreat the CEO suddenly reinstated the director of strategy, who had been pushed aside by the chairman-acting CEO just one month earlier. This move caused some confusion among his colleagues and gave rise to several rumours about possible organizational changes and rifts with the chairman.

At the outset of the retreat the CEO said that he did not know what changes he would make to the strategy, organization or people. From my perspective, this retreat served primarily to present the CEO to the top people and also for him to listen to their views about the organization.

During this retreat the CEO told his three colleagues that 'we are living on borrowed time'; 'everything starts at the top'; and 'sometime [in two months] I will change the organization'. Throughout the informal conversations he kept referring to how things were (successfully) done in his previous company. He also kept saying how important it was for all of them to think and act in the company's best interests and how he had learnt this from people he respected, like his father.

As facilitator I led a series of exercises designed to engage them in an honest and deep conversation about the organization and its future. For instance, I asked them to list their hopes and fears about the future. The retreat unfolded as planned and the ambience remained informal and pleasant. At the end they agreed on who the CEO should invite to the second retreat, that is, who should be invited to co-develop a new strategy.

Preparing the second retreat

In between the first and second retreat the CEO was busy preparing for his first meeting with investors, enlisting several top-management team members to support and help prepare the story he would deliver to them in a few weeks time. His main concern was how much to say and not say, given the strategy process and the need for his managers to feel involved. He was particularly concerned about the need to reorganize domestic operations and when to do this. He told me: 'What is needed is easy to see, I just do not want to do this before we have developed the strategy.'

As the preparations unfolded the CEO felt an increasing pressure from the board and stock market to communicate what changes he would make to strategy and the organization. Two weeks before the retreat, he agonized about announcing major organizational changes that would influence the jobs of the people at the retreats. After discussing this with the director of HR and me, he didn't. We had both advised against this idea, stressing that it might be counterproductive to the very purpose of the next retreat.

The second retreat: Top 15 people

The second retreat was a four-day session in an old and beautiful mansion converted into a conference hotel, a few hours from the closest airport. The idea was to retain this place for subsequent retreats, which were important to the director of HR. We designed the retreat to deal with four topics that the CEO, the director of HR, and I felt followed on naturally: (1) reflecting on past successes and future challenges; (2) making choices about competing and (3) where; and (4) how to work together in terms of organizing and leadership.

In his welcome statement to the 15 participants the CEO framed the retreat as he saw it:

> This is an important event in our leadership of the company as we go forward. I expect this to be an anchoring event, where we come together and build together where we will take this company. This event is about buying into our future direction of the company, through contributing to and owning it.

Later on the first evening he also said, 'We have to stop flipping strategies, or creating fancy new words.' He made it clear to participants that he did not know what part of the organization he would reorganize. At the outset he did commit to keeping them in various managerial roles, but he left open possible changes of responsibilities.

In broad terms the retreat process followed the plan. Yet, the first evening, which was supposed to include a short talk by the CEO, turned into a long and deep question and answer session, which continued after dinner. The CEO was seated in front of 15 executives who kept asking him a range of questions, but mainly about the new organization. In the beginning the CEO followed our agreed plan, namely to avoid elaborating on organizational changes. Yet, later that evening he did just that. Although evasively, he nevertheless kept talking about the future organization, reassuring them about their future roles. The remaining time followed the flow we had set out and during these days they addressed and resolved many of the issues on the agenda.

Throughout this time, I facilitated a series of sequential sessions following the plan. In the large plenary room the CEO kicked off each day with a short introduction, which I had drafted for him. I immediately followed by introducing the next exercise in terms of anticipated content and process. Typically, we split the group into small groups and sent them to resolve the same or different challenges. Most groups went outside to gather around small tables and flipcharts. We had prepared poster-sized templates for each individual task for each session. We asked the groups to fill them in and bring them back to the plenary room, where we displayed them on the increasingly cluttered walls. Following this routine, groups took turns in presenting their content and a discussion pursued. The discussions were typically relatively light in terms of content and it was rare that people disagreed or challenged each other. During these presentations participants showed signs of gaining some insights, manifested by 'aha' or similar expressions. For the most part, however, they confirmed each other's hunches about the market, competition, investors' and analysts' views, and so on. At each presentation, we took digital pictures of this content and organized a report, which we gave to the CEO immediately after the retreat.

With the CEO, we organized the overall outcome into three categories: industry definition, mission and financial guiding principles. Each of these emerged after significant discussion and comparison, with conclusions offered by the strategy consulting firm, hanging in PowerPoint format on the wall.

The evenings were used to create favourable conditions for informal interaction, around dinners of different kinds. Overall, people showed signs of being very much at ease and used the occasions to meet colleagues and nurture friendships. On the final evening the CEO became increasingly concerned and even irritated by the numerous questions he was asked regarding the upcoming organization, many of which were a follow-up to what he had said and revealed the first evening. Later on he approached me to say that he had changed his mind about even discussing this matter during the last day and instead he wanted to abandon this part of the programme (the last afternoon). The following morning he told the group: 'As your CEO, I need to take your great input back home and figure out an appropriate organization to go with this strategy.'

Preparing the third retreat

In between the second and third retreat the CEO announced a new organization. The major change was to merge the corporate and operational levels of the domestic organization. This was by far the largest part of the corporation and in great need of improved performance. The corporate level CEO thus also became CEO of the domestic organization, which meant that several senior executives were made redundant. Thus, he did not keep his promise, made at the second retreat, to retain all people.

Another structural change was related to how he intended to lead the company overall. He had decided to set up a new governance structure with two parallel leadership forums; one for domestic operations and one for international. The CEO and a few functional, corporate directors would be members of both. This way he could keep these two groups of leaders focused on their task, while minimizing 'disturbances' across both operations. As he thought the time wasn't necessary, on several occasions the CEO told colleagues and me that the retreat should be cut short. The HR director was eventually able to persuade him to agree to run the retreat as planned.

The third retreat: Top 50 people

The third stage of the process focused entirely on dealing with the home country organization. Labelled '*Step-Up* [the home country]' this retreat totalled 50 people, including all the home country leaders and corporate level participants from the second retreat, with the exception of the international country managers. It was scheduled to take place three weeks before the board meeting, at which the CEO would present the new strategy. Designed to follow a similar flow of topics and activities to the second retreat, it put particular emphasis on three areas he felt were particularly critical to improve: sales, product development and operations.

The CEO made a welcome statement similar to that of the previous retreat, which I sketched for him, and stressed the need for participants to put their personal agendas aside and focus instead on 'what is best for the company'. He also encouraged them to be 'brave' and try to generate new ideas. Without getting into the details, he shared with the group what he and his 15 colleagues had been doing during the previous retreat and their overall outcome (mission, guiding principles and industry definition). The difference, this time, he stressed, was that now they would focus on the domestic rather than the corporate strategy and agenda. He made a particularly strong point about the need to 'spend time, discuss and decide together'.

Overall, the third retreat unfolded as planned and the conversations oscillated between the overall and specific choices within the three critical areas. In terms of process, we followed the same process as the first retreat. However, as facilitator, I had to intervene several times to urge the CEO to engage with the group more than he was doing. Too often I caught him sitting and watching passively, making phone calls outside or taking people aside for ad hoc meetings. As in the first retreat people did not argue or discuss a lot. Several participants praised the very fact that they were invited in the first place and also showed appreciation that the CEO did not 'lecture them', which obviously had been the case during the old regime. In terms of topics, the retreat content outcome was similar to the first retreat, this time focused on the home country operations.

After thanking them for their contributions during the past days, in his closing statement the CEO uttered the words I began this case with: 'I am delighted you reached the same conclusion about what needs to be done as I did a few weeks ago with the top-management team [participants on the second retreat].' Immediately, I noticed how many participants looked down or puzzled. In follow-up chats after the closure, I learnt that several executives felt 'cheated' by this statement. As one of them said, 'was the retreat just a show?' The HR director told me he was very unhappy about that ending and promised to bring up this unfortunate episode with the CEO first thing the following day. In a follow-up interview the HR director told me that despite his intervention he was not sure the CEO understood he had done something less appropriate.

Preparing the fourth retreat

After he announced the reorganization of the corporate and domestic organization, the CEO's attention focused on improving the diverse international operations. When he started a few months earlier, he told me that some of these operations would inevitably have to be divested, a conclusion that many of his managers shared. As his thinking evolved he let me know that geographical proximity was an overarching consideration, which he had also used to include and exclude country managers in the second retreat.

While planning the fourth retreat, the CEO supported the idea of gathering these teams and, in principle, do what we had done with the group from domestic operations. The country managers' interest in the (fourth) retreat for their leadership teams was mixed. From my interviews with them, it was evident that some wanted more cross-country collaboration on the highest levels and saw the retreat as a great way to go beyond the existing 'hub and spokes' type relationships with the CEO. Others sought to remain as autonomous as possible and considered the upcoming retreat as a total waste of time. One of them even said that he was unaware of the dates and that it was impossible to get his team to agree to come.

During the preparations phase for this retreat the CEO finalized plans for divesting some of these operations and forming alliances in others. His divestiture plans made it difficult for him and his team to come up with a clear and simple definition of their geographical market. In particular, one attractive country was geographically separated and distant and as such disrupted the current formulation of their 'home region'.

In the midst of preparing for the fourth retreat the CEO surprised his colleagues and me by announcing by e-mail that he had cancelled it. The reason, he said, was that the strategy had been developed and just approved by the Board, after which, the formal strategy process should dissipate. From my interviews and informal conversations with several executives this was a controversial decision that few appreciated. The most enthusiastic country manager was very frustrated, as he too had learnt about this decision by e-mail.

Quick reflection

The *Thinking from Within* practices discussed in Chapters 3–5 look far from what was going on during these two strategy practices. In BrassCo the routine-like presentation and assessment of analysis after analysis did not enact much of the participants' imagination. The way they behaved, what they did and what they used remained the same as during normal, 'work'-like conditions. Moreover, they were not constructing together more than in their minds and the only objects used to mediate communication were stacks of paper.

The situation was not much better in TechCo. On the surface, the milieu was probably more prone to engage their imagination but the paper-based process constrained them, or rather did not unlock their normal habits. With one exception, when they took the role of analysts and investors, they remained with routine-like and deductive analytical thinking throughout these days. In both cases the only time these people engaged their bodies in what could have been 'creative expressions' was during breaks, lunches and dinners.

Moreover, in both cases the process was not sufficiently safe for participants. In BrassCo, the CEO kept a firm grip on what was going on until the breakpoint. In TechCo, the CEO kept everybody guessing about his real intentions about what mattered most to them, which was the new organizational structure. When he finally revealed this, the process seems to have become obsolete, at least for the CEO. From this brief analysis, it is striking that these tales of strategy practices have little to do with the emerging benefits of play discussed in Chapter 2.

Chapters 7–8 will take this superficial deliberation much deeper and demonstrate how the practices of these firms and others in this book rest on certain assumptions about how we see the world and what we know about it that influence how we practise strategy – both the thinking and doing.

Conclusion

The dual purpose of this chapter was to serve as a reminder about the (perceived) realities of practising strategy in organizations and to offer a contrast to the previous, somewhat more positive illustrations in this book. Of course, I do not in any way claim that these two tales depict what happens in all organizations all the time. Far from searching for some kind of objective, generalizable truth I do not offer any conclusions more than this: these two cases illustrate the 'prescribed' thinking that, in my experience, dominates strategy practices in organizations for better and for worse.

In terms of the framework of Chapter 1, and depicted in Exhibit 6.1, both stories illustrate a routinized way of doing strategy and an analytical way of thinking strategy. Still, there are some differences between these two cases and Exhibit 6.1 depicts my subjective assessment of the extent they are prescribed. The point is, however, that in the world of prescribed strategy the comfort zone is where thinking is prescribed

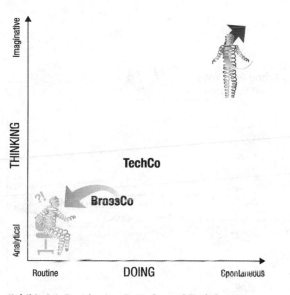

Exhibit 6.1 Positioning BrassCo and TechCo

from outside ourselves, and we deal with the knowable and the doable. Even with the best of intentions to develop original ideas for rethinking or shaping the business, when we practise 'prescribed strategy' our communication tends to focus on ways to just adapt efficiently to given circumstances. Even with the best of intentions to move the time scale years ahead and abstract on the future, our strategy communication tends to easily revert to the daily and operational (for more stories about this see Roos and von Krogh 1996).

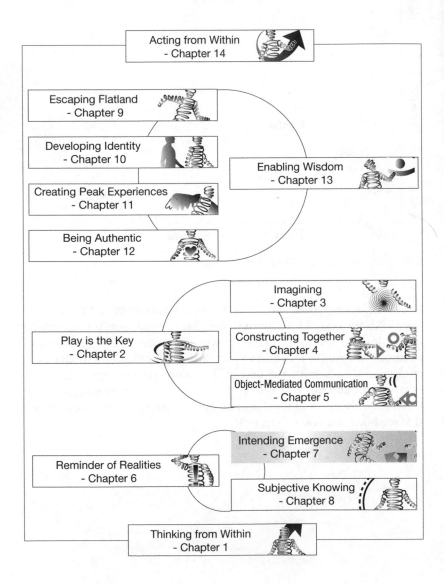

7
Intending Emergence

Johan Roos

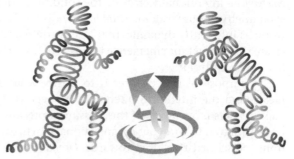

Introduction

As already suggested in previous chapters the way we think about the world influences what we do, like how we practise strategy. Chapter 2 identified and described the possibility of 'intending emergence' as one of the distinguishing characteristics of play not found in work. As such, this ambiguous notion is a cornerstone for practising *Thinking from Within*. The concept of intending emergence is a deep one as it touches how we view the world and what is possible to control. In philosophy this is called ontology, which is the study of existence and the nature of reality. Ontology is a systematic account of existence, of what it is that makes up or defines reality, that is, the objects, concepts and other entities that are assumed to exist. To examine ontology is to examine the often unspoken, unrealized assumptions that comprise our understanding of what it is that exists. In its simplest form, which is the focus of this chapter, the ontological discussion is relatively uncomplicated since the choice is simple: either we view the world as inherently static, with occasional fluctuation, or we view the world as inherently dynamic, with occasional episodes of stability.

We can make it more complicated by saying that there are three options: the world is static, can change and change inherently. We can also add that each of these pertains to our view about the environment and ourselves. For the purpose of this chapter we will simplify the choice to the one above: *either* we think the world is inherently static *or* we think of it as inherently dynamic. Pick one or the other and your thinking and doing will change dramatically. From the former worldview, practising strategy is about uncovering causality, predicting and controlling. In the dynamic ontology, the world is vibrantly interconnected across many levels of scales, that is, complex,[1] and strategy practice implies *intending emergence* – intentionally creating the conditions for imagination and the spontaneity of our wisdom. *Thinking from Within* requires us to view the world as inherently dynamic, that is, uncertain and ambiguous. We can create the context for emergence to possibly take its unpredictable route, but never control it.

The purpose of this chapter is to clarify what a dynamic ontology means and the intending emergence it suggests. Its purpose is also to make readers more aware of these assumptions and their consequences. If we want to transform our organizational practices, for example strategy, from 'prescribed thinking' towards *Thinking from Within* (see Exhibit 1.1), understanding these assumptions is a must.

First I briefly summarize the Enlightenment-inspired, static ontology alluded to in Chapter 1, and what it means in practice. Then I briefly review the intellectual advancements that led even natural scientists to question the static ontology. From here I summarize the main ideas of the dynamic ontology as these have evolved in the field of 'complexity theory'. Armed with the ideas and concepts of the dynamic ontology, I reflect on the BrassCo and TechCo cases of Chapter 6, and the contrasts these make with the other cases presented so far, in particular the ChemCo case of Chapter 3. Finally, I will conclude that ontology matters, a great deal, and that the practice of *Thinking from Within* calls for a dynamic one.

A static world

Chapter 1 described the ideals of rationality and objectivity which, combined with the primacy of pure intellectual reasoning, have dominated our worldview since the Age of Enlightenment. This was a description of a static ontology in which people viewed the world as a stable system abiding by fixed laws. Parker and Stacey (1994) summarized the cornerstones of the static ontology:

1. *Linearity:* In linear systems, any given effect will have one cause, which leads to one and only one effect. Linear equations thus have only one solution. Small changes to a system can be expected to lead to small effects. Because of these clear-cut, cause–effect relationships, actions can be expected to lead to predictable outcomes.

2. *Reductionism:* Systems can be reduced into component parts and any system can be understood by studying its parts. Reductionism implies that the whole consists of the sum of its components (additivity).

3. *Equilibrium*: Systems exist in equilibrium and are driven by negative feedback processes towards predictable states of adaptation to their environments. Successful systems tend towards equilibrium, stability, regularity and predictability.

Together, these three assumptions say that the world has a stable configuration, which has been the underlying idea in the natural science since Isaac Newton et al. Yet, these cornerstones have also formed an important intellectual heritage of much organizational theory, from Frederick Taylor's (1911) 'scientific management' principles of the early 20th century, to the strategy practices illustrated in BrassCo and TechCo. Just as the great scientists of the Age of Enlightenment described Mother Nature, social scientists have come to think successful organizations are those best able to achieve equilibrium with their environments. This idea of equilibrium is dominant in classical and neoclassical economics, for example the meeting between supply and demand. In strategic management the basic idea of 'fit' between the company and environment is an analogous, theoretical equilibrium.

Reductionism is an essential ingredient in decision-making theory and practice – we break down the problem into smaller elements, consider these separately, put things back together and then make a choice. Max Weber's well-known bureaucratic model, with its notions of specialization, clear lines of authority and rule-based procedures, beautifully manifests the static ontology. In a bureaucracy, the manager predicts where the environment and the company are going and moves the company to where it achieves the best fit (read: equilibrium) with its environment. Hence the prominent notion of 'strategic fit' and the corresponding plethora of 'gap' analyses, for example SWOT, used in strategy practice. It is this static ontology that underlies the deductive analyses of 'prescribed' thinking in strategy discussed in Chapter 1.

Questioning the equilibrium[2]

Oscar II, King of Sweden and Norway, initiated a mathematical competition in 1887 to celebrate his sixtieth birthday in 1889. One of the questions in this contest was to show that the solar system as modelled by Newton's equations is dynamically *stable*. The question was nothing more than a generalization of the famous three-body problem, considered one of the most difficult problems in mathematical physics. Consisting of nine simultaneous differential equations, the difficulty was in showing that a solution, in terms of invariants, converges.

French scientist-mathematician Henri Poincaré won the prize, and his solution surprised his contemporaries. He claimed that the orbits of three or more interacting celestial bodies exhibited unstable and unpredictable behaviour and did not necessarily converge. While Poincaré did not succeed in giving a complete solution, his work was so impressive that he was awarded the prize anyway. In addition to shocking his contemporaries into disbelief, Poincaré's work demonstrated that some systems are inherently unpredictable, even ones that are as deterministically 'simple' as three celestial bodies interacting. In his own words:

> If we knew exactly the laws of nature and the situation of the universe at the initial moment, we could predict exactly the situation of that same universe at a succeeding moment. But even if it were the case that the natural laws had no longer any secret for us, we could still only know the initial situation approximately. If that enabled us to predict the succeeding situation with the same approximation that is all we require, and we should say that the phenomenon had been predicted, that it is governed by laws. But it is not always so; it may happen that small differences in the initial conditions produce very great ones in the final phenomena. A small error in the former will produce an enormous error in the latter. Prediction becomes impossible, and we have the fortuitous phenomenon. (excerpt from a 1903 essay 'Science and Method')[3]

By implication, what were thought to be stable and even non-living systems turned out to be, in principle, impacted by everything. Although such systems may be roughly predictable in the short run, miniscule differences in initial conditions can over time, lead to huge, unexpected effects, making such systems unpredictable in the medium to long run. It took 60 years for the scientific community to recognize the enormous implication of his insight and this is why our weather forecasts are only reliable a few days ahead.

Systems thinking

The founder of the general systems theory is widely acknowledged to be Austrian biologist Ludwig von Bertalanffy who, in the 1940s, made the useful observation that while the world of physics focuses on the study of closed systems, the universe consists largely of open systems. He distinguished between closed systems, which are closed to the transfer of mass (although not energy) over their boundaries (such as computers) and open systems, which exchange both matter and energy across their boundaries, such as living organisms, which take in food and expel waste (von Bertalanffy 1968).

Because physicists focused on closed systems, they were able to calculate future states with perfect accuracy, as all masses, particles and forces that impact the system were included in their models. Closed systems are also deterministic, meaning the final state is always determined unequivocally by the initial conditions. The dream of the Enlightenment was realized and manifested in, for instance, the second law of thermodynamics (that entropy will increase to a maximum at which equilibrium is attained).

Von Bertalanffy noted, however, that no biological systems are closed, since organisms must exchange energy and matter with their environments. Because living things are engaged in a continuous inflow and outflow in which components are built up and broken down and are never in a chemical and thermodynamic equilibrium, but maintain a 'steady state', they are invariably open systems. Von Bertalanffy proposed that qualitatively new properties could be developed through 'emergence', to be discussed below. He called for greater study of the input, 'throughput' and output of systems. Determining the boundary between the system and its environment became extremely important from this perspective.

A great deal of effort in the literature on systems theory has been devoted to defining exactly what is meant by the term 'system'. Von Bertalanffy (1968:19) defined systems as 'parts in interaction'. Most authors make reference to the importance of the 'parts' of a system being linked together in some form of bounded 'whole'. As Andrew (1989:13) described: 'One essential feature of a system is that it has internal cohesion. There must be some sense in which its variables are more tightly bound to one another than they are to others not belonging to it.' The point is that systems cannot be fully understood through reductionism because their properties are not intrinsic, but depend on context. Such an approach focuses on the arrangement and organization of relations between the parts that connect them into a whole. A major tenet of systems thinking is that the whole, one way or another, is more than the sum of the parts, which assumes a pre-given whole. Over time, general systems theory became highly transdisciplinary and attracted physicists, biologists, mathematicians, sociologists and philosophers.

A small error with huge consequences

In 1963, MIT meteorologist Edward Lorenz noticed some significant variations in the results he generated when running weather simulations on a computer, even though they were based on the same set of input of various parameters (for example temperature, humidity and atmospheric pressure). It appeared that although the simulation generated the same results in the short run, over time, different runs of the same experiment produced very different results. He discovered that minuscule differences in rounding off numbers used in setting the initial parameter values (millionths of one decimal place) led to these huge variations. Since computers rounded off all real numbers, it was not possible to perfectly duplicate the same medium or long-term results twice. The implications pointed straight back to Henri Poincaré. Lorenz's work on deterministic non-periodic flow related to weather (Lorenz 1963), and other research within the growing field of non-linear systems presented a major challenge to the dominant, static ontology. In fact, the apparent inability of linear thinking to account for macroscopic behaviour resulted in a review of the accepted scientific doctrine.

Scientists in many different disciplines are now increasingly impatient with the kind of linear, reductionist thinking that has dominated science since Newton. Instead they are considering and applying ideas about interconnectedness, co-evolution, chaos and order, which lead to entirely new ways of thinking about both nature and human behaviour (in organizations).

The assumptions underlying the static ontology are difficult to sustain, as is apparent in organizational science. Disorder, unintended consequences of actions and turbulence followed by calmer periods are part of our everyday experience at work and at home, when we are thinking and when we are acting.

A dynamic ontology

Consider how a nice and orderly meeting, for instance, can suddenly turn messy or even nasty. Perhaps someone just left, or joined the discussion. Maybe someone just said something that upset somebody else. Recall what happened in the BrassCo case when the CEO left the meeting, when the CEO of TechCo thanked the group at the end of the third retreat (both described in Chapter 6), or the sudden unplanned discussion of taboos in PrintCo. In the dynamic ontology, systems can be both orderly and disorderly and flip between the two states in an unpredictable way. Systems do not follow clear rules, that is, they are not 'deterministic' and as such, can only be predicted in the short term. A given cause can have more than one effect, equations can have multiple solutions and the whole can give rise to synergies and become more than the sum of the parts. Normal family dinners, strategy practice, or the Internet, are all systems highly sensitive to initial conditions and some tiny error or 'noise' can escalate to have major implications on the outcome. In the dynamic ontology change is constant, systems are not reducible to their parts, components are mutually dependent, and systems behave in unpredictable ways.

Complex *adaptive* systems theory more than 'chaos theory' is the intellectual foundation of the dynamic ontology. While chaos theory focuses on how simple systems can generate complicated behaviours, complex adaptive systems theory describes how complicated systems can generate simple behaviour. As Oliver (2002) summarized, complex adaptive systems theory explores and describes the self-organizing cohesiveness of complex systems, which is beyond the scope of chaos theory. It is concerned with studying the forces that appear to bring order to chaotic systems, which spontaneously enter new stable states and higher levels of organizational complexity.

In the dynamic ontology, systems may appear random when looked at from moment-to-moment, but in the longer term, they feature distinctive patterns, or 'hidden order', or 'order for free' (Kauffman 1995). Take a look at an anthill from a few metres away and then move closer until you see the structured paths of the busy ants. Recall the 'messy' strategy meeting depicted in Exhibit 1.2 (plate section). On closer inspection, it may not be so messy after all and we see the orderly patterns of traditional strategy practice and even one person taking a nap. Nature is full of such regularities, including cloud formations and the flowing of rivers. More interestingly for our purposes, such Islands of order are commonplace in social systems too. How else can we work?

Characteristics of the dynamic ontology

In the dynamic ontology, systems are very sensitive and dependent on initial conditions. Tiny errors or disturbances can hurl an entire (chaotic) system into a different trajectory. This is what happened to Edward Lorenz when his computer rounded off his starting numbers and this is what happens when we miss the deal, because we missed the flight, because of the guy in front, who forgot his passport, because he hid it from his two year old the previous evening, because ... , and so on. This so called 'butterfly effect' has fascinated people, including movie-makers, for decades. Just imagine what could have happened if a few years ago you had/had not ... (please fill in any choice you made when you were

18). If we share the dynamic ontology we need to *pay careful attention to the initial conditions of what we do and participate in.*

One of the factors accelerating the rate of change in the dynamic ontology is 'positive feedback'. Positive feedback is one of two forms of feedback that can impact a system. If a system deviates slightly from its expected path, *negative* feedback processes can bring it back into equilibrium, by shrinking the gap until it eventually disappears. A classic example in systems theory, this is what we do when we use the thermostat to reduce the heat in our hotel room. This is also the purpose of my instinct to remove the hand from fire and this is the purpose of an organizational incentive system (recall the story of RedCo in Chapter 1).

In the dynamic ontology, however, a small deviation can lead the system to move further and further away from its expected path so that things can escalate out of hand. This phenomenon is called *positive* feedback and it describes one way in which systems can become even more destabilized and distanced from equilibrium. It describes the high-pitched sound that occurs when a loudspeaker is placed next to a microphone: the sound from the speaker is picked up by the microphone, which plays back through the speaker and is picked up by the microphone, in a spiral of amplification. Other examples of positive feedback include avalanches, mob behaviour at a soccer match, rumours, and other chain reactions in social life. Economist Brian Arthur (1996) has argued many industries should be described in terms of positive feedback. When we take on a dynamic ontology, we are particularly observant of *potential positive feedback effects.*

In the dynamic ontology, patterns exist on multiple levels of scale (see von Krogh and Roos 1995). Quarks, atoms, molecules, DNA, cells, organs, bodies, families, cultures and the global community are levels of scales, which are intertwined into sub-systems and eventually an entire, living, interconnected system of people. A *system* at one level of scale operates as an *agent* at a higher level of scale, which has been called 'aggregation' (Holland 1995). Also, characteristics of the whole can be indicative of important characteristics in the parts. In the static ontology, the same rules apply on all levels. In the dynamic ontology the *standpoint of the observer and how we measure things matters tremendously.* Ideally, we want to focus on the correct level of aggregation at the right time.

Emergence

In the dynamic ontology, we expect sudden radically new patterns and behaviours all the time. The classic example of emergence is birds flocking. No matter how complicated their acrobatic path, the birds always stay close together but never collide. The computer-based model explaining emergent flocking behaviour consists of three simple steering behaviours (Reynolds 1987):

- Separation: steer to avoid crowding local flock mates.
- Alignment: steer towards the average heading of local flock mates.
- Cohesion: steer to move towards the average position of local flock mates.

These three 'simple rules' seem to generate complex, emergent behaviour, at least in computer animations and among animals. Just as birds suddenly flock, or fish suddenly form shoals, people interacting also give rise to new, surprising behaviour without formally coordinating their activities, or following the instructions of a leader. It is not possible to predict how people collaborate by studying the individuals. This is called *emergence*, and this concept and phenomena lie at the heart of the dynamic ontology. Exhibit 7.1 seeks to depict the intricacy of emergence.

Although scholars have studied the concept of emergence, scholars are far from a full understanding of the mechanisms by which it occurs. Definitions of emergence abound (see Exhibit 7.2).

The emergence of properties appears particularly mysterious, because it is impossible to predict the form of emergence simply by studying the

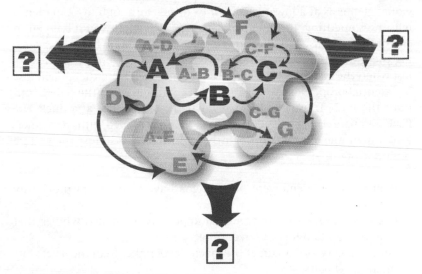

Exhibit 7.1 The intricacy of emergence

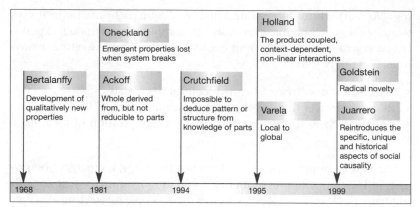

Exhibit 7.2 Definition of emergence
Source: Oliver (2002).

individual parts. The basic idea is that everything is potentially impacted by everything, that is, similar to the problem Poincaré tackled a century ago. In the field of strategy, the concept is more than the 'emergent' strategy idea suggested by Mintzberg and Waters (1985). An emergent property is not simply an aggregation of individual actions, but has unique properties not possessed by individuals (Drazin and Sandelands 1992). It is difficult to identify overall patterns or structures that will emerge at a higher level of analysis simply from understanding the individual elements at a lower level. For example, although my experience tells me something, in principle, I had no idea what would happen in any of the cases used to illustrate the ideas of this book from interviewing the individuals beforehand. Moreover, the emergent properties are lost when the system is broken and a part removed from the set will lose its essential properties (Ackoff 1981), for example, when the police confront the mob, it usually dissipates; when I take a shot at a duck, the flock dissipates as such. As Goldstein (1999) has argued, although emergent phenomena appear differently in different systems, they share certain properties:

- Radical novelty: emergent phenomena have features not previously observed.
- Coherence: emergent phenomena appear as integrated wholes that tend to maintain identity over time.
- Global: emergence occurs at the macro-level rather than the level of its micro-level parts.

Note that interaction among parts (including people) alone is not enough for emergence. Interaction must result in novel patterns not found among the interacting agents alone.

As humans we can express our intentionality in ways birds seemingly cannot, we can choose what rules to follow and what to bend. More importantly, together we can develop, articulate and share the meaning of the rules we think make sense. What some co-researchers and I have called 'simple guiding principles' (Lissack and Roos 1999; Oliver and Roos 2003; 2005) may be a more appropriate term for the emotionally laden, shared, narrative headlines that create the context for emerging actions and decisions in organizations (in Chapter 13 I will revisit this concept in the context of the emergent benefits of *Thinking from Within*). In the dynamic ontology, to help people deal with the unexpected (emergence), we use *simple guiding principles*, not just rules.

In the dynamic ontology self-organizing emerges all the time. Self-organizing systems change their basic structures as a reaction to their experience and environment (Yocits et al. 1962; Jantsch 1980; Parker and Stacey 1994). It is the members, not a 'leader' who contribute to the unfolding future of a self-organizing system, for example, people spontaneously help each other out when a member of a group is absent. In the dynamic ontology, actions and decisions emerge spontaneously from the self-organizing processes among people, and within individual brains.

In summary, emergence fundamentally prevents prediction, and this attribute distinguishes the static from the dynamic ontology. In the static ontology we consciously or unconsciously expect things to unfold according to the plan, in dynamic ontology we expect, and ideally *intend emergence* by carefully creating an appropriate context. The dynamic nature of emergence teaches us to abandon the notion that 'the whole is greater than the sum of the part' because emergence does not assume pre-given wholes (Holland 1998; Goldstein 1999, 2000).

So far I have claimed that in the dynamic ontology we pay careful attention to the initial conditions of what we do and participate in; we are sensitized to potential positive feedback effects; we have levels of scale and potential interconnectedness in mind; we know that our standpoint as an observer matters tremendously (since we want to focus on the correct level of aggregation at the right time); and we realize actions and decisions emerge spontaneously from the interaction and sometimes even from self-organizing processes among people in organizations. In the dynamic ontology, to be prepared for the unexpected, we complement rules with simple guiding principles.

Practising strategy with a dynamic ontology

What are the consequences of the dynamic ontology for strategy practices? Let us now apply what we have outlined in three longer cases presented so far in the book: BrassCo, TechCo and ChemCo.

Consider the practices described in the BrassCo tale. These leaders appeared to know what the business was all about and what the result of their actions would be. They also seemed to be comfortable with the picture portrayed by the strategic analyses; familiar stakeholders competing in their industry and equally recognized resources in their organization and predictions about financial performance. Initial conditions were not an issue and the only feedback they had in mind (and offered Jan, the internal facilitator) was negative. Levels of scale discussions focused on the traditional hierarchical levels of the organization, from a top-down mindset and what could be portrayed in the two-dimensional strategic analyses. They seemed to neither expect nor desire spontaneous self-organization in any way whatsoever. So, what ontology underlies the BrassCo practices? We can now confidently answer: a *static* one.

To make the point that ontology matters, I will now describe what happened when I proposed that the BrassCo leaders should try out an unusual workshop, intended to stimulate them to think from within. After all, I had carefully observed how they were totally able to do this during the last meeting, when the leader of the largest business unit confronted their outcome and when the CEO left.[4]

To revitalize the strategy process I suggested to the CEO that they tried out a playful and experiential method. After some discussion about how much time would be involved and the best place for doing this, the CEO agreed to add to the planned process an extra retreat to take place two months later in a different off-site location.

What happened? A colleague and I divided the executives into two groups of six and instructed them to build a representation of the company as they saw it in the future using a range of construction materials available in the room. The group that included the CEO spent 30 minutes building a representation of the current businesses, carefully building their relative *size*. Despite the radically different context the modus operandi of these managers did not appear to be significantly different from the previous strategy meetings. The conversations were heavily steered and directed by the CEO. In the group without the CEO, after an initial discussion without constructions, participants each began to build only their own parts of the organization's future, typically something close to their current responsibilities.

Overall these managers were not willing to be playful, as manifested by closed body language and seeming lack of enthusiasm. In both groups they continually referred, in their constructions and explanations of them, to the dominant opinions of the CEO. And yet, the representations appeared to result in a lengthy discussion about the company's core attributes, as the participants, in comparison with the company's official vision, mission and core value statements, had constructed them. But even as they began to recognize a certain lack of coherence, the conversation eventually focused on what was the 'right' description of their business. Not surprisingly, the view of the CEO prevailed.

This continuation of the BrassCo case further illustrates the point. From the lens of previous chapters, it is obvious that the context was not sufficiently playful and hence, we were unable to bring the emergent benefit of play to bear on their challenge. Specifically, these leaders were not practising much of their imagination as they were not taking on the metaphorical roles discussed in Chapter 3. Although they were constructing together using their hands, they were reluctant to do this because it really did not make sense to them and they were visibly uncomfortable playing along. The degree of object-mediated communication was surprisingly low, but they tried. As is evident from the description, the psychological milieu was not very safe for these managers, as the CEO dominated the process and they let themselves be dominated by him.

If I now take on the deeper, ontological lens and once again look at the continued story, I see the consequences of a firmly rooted static ontology. It is all there, the assumptions about prediction and control and this, I will argue, is why the playful practice did not work very well. The static ontology prevented them from *Thinking from Within* and they were stuck in their normal, prescribed way of thinking – seemingly no matter what. Of course, I may have been lacking too. In retrospect (this happened eight years ago), the requirement of 'intending emergence' was not fulfilled.

What about TechCo's strategy practices as portrayed in the case description? The starting point for the strategy practice was the previous CEO's realization that the organization needed rejuvenation. When the new CEO came on board, he was persuaded to use the already planned, retreat-based strategy practice as a way to transform the entire leadership layer. The first retreat, involving only three people and the CEO, appeared to be a great context for emergence. They were offsite, in a relaxed and informal atmosphere and the CEO declared he did not yet know what to do with the organization. In fact, he also framed the conversations with what looked like a simple guiding principle, 'think about what is good for the company'. Yet, certain unresolved political issues seem to hamper the emergence of any radical novelty.

In between the first and second retreat it looked as though the CEO's ontology oscillated between a dynamic and a static one. He indicated that he had already figured out what the situation was and what needed to be done. The external consultancy work appeared to have been carried out in order to verify what he already thought he knew. Yet, during his opening speech at the second retreat (involving 15 people), he actually claimed that he had intended emergence, by inviting them to co-create the future strategy with him and this began to unfold during the first evening. Given the sequential and planned process used to facilitate the practice, there was limited place for spontaneous self-organizing. Yet, in some of the exercises, participants took different standpoints, like that of investors and customers, which led to new insights and awareness.

In between the second and third retreat, the previous 'ontological oscillation' became increasingly biased towards a static worldview. Given the pressure from outside stakeholders, the CEO appeared to have already made up his mind. Despite the well-intended facilitation process, exercises and informal interaction, the retreat (involving 50 people) did not result in anything resembling emergence. In fact, that is what the CEO unconsciously verified with his notorious concluding remark.

So, what ontology was underlying the practices of TechCo, as described? Taking the standpoint of the CEO I suggest a *static* one, which due to pressure from people he respected, was temporarily pushed towards a dynamic one. Beyond the initial retreat, when he was very new to the job, he did not seem to have intended any emergence.

The ChemCo case (Chapter 3) illustrates what may happen when people shift their ontology from a static to a dynamic one. The very reason for trying out an experiential strategy retreat was a static ontology. Recall how the corporate director of strategy complained that their strategy plans looked too similar to previous ones and, given the changing circumstances, how this was not right. As described in the case story, the playfulness (both by label and practice) of the session as such, created the conditions for emergence, which they testified had not happened in the previous strategy sessions. The facilitators and the corporate director all intended emergence. When participants had been sufficiently prepared in terms of psychological dimensions (see Chapter 2), they began to interact in new ways and this created the conditions for disagreement, ideas and relationships to be aired openly. Emergence stemmed from people interacting, which is described in the ChemCo tale. Thus, the case illustrates several of the characteristics of the dynamic ontology, such as the impact of initial conditions (for example the corporate director's initiative), levels of scale (for example who was involved and what level or function these represented), positive feedback effect (for example one thing leading to another), and awareness of standpoints (for example by means of three-dimensional models). Therefore, I conclude that a dynamic ontology underlay ChemCo's strategy practice, that day.

To further illustrate the ontology of intending emergence, consider the case of PackCo. In this case a small group of leaders set out to talk about one thing and ended up covering a series of adjacent issues. Eventually, they returned to the initial focus and decided to take unexpected actions. The story is riddled with emerging topics and the group is open enough and the context playful enough for fruitful, object-mediated communication.

Case: Intending emergence in PackCo[5]

A few years ago the CEO of a major packaging firm approached me for insights about a potentially serious challenge for the company's after-sales technical service business. The CEO had solicited both internal and external assistance to identify and analyse the most important issues. In his view, two camps of opinion had emerged from within the company. One group of managers considered the challenge a non-issue not worthy of executive attention, because the firm already dominated the industry and the technical support business did not represent a significant part of its revenue or profits. The opposing camp saw many more worrying aspects, which they believed could pose a threat to their customer relationships. They argued that the technical support people had very strong relationships deep inside customer organizations, which arguably played a significant, indirect role for repurchasing decisions.

Moreover, although the firm's competitive position was solid, the CEO was concerned with the potential threat from small firms to its business system. Although he had not yet made up his mind about a course of action, the CEO believed he had all the facts worth knowing. However, he complained that the process of discussing these matters had become routine and he jumped at the opportunity to reframe the conversation in a way that might generate new insights and perspectives.

Accordingly, a research colleague and I gave the corporate boardroom a more playful appearance. Now hands-on construction materials in many colours shared the boardroom with the dark oil paintings of the company's founding fathers and employees passing by the open door stopped in their tracks to stare in silence as the room took shape. In order to familiarize the workshop participants with the method, we asked each of the four executives to make a small construction prior to the meeting and to bring their models along with them.

On the morning of the workshop, as the four participants entered, they expressed amazement at the radically different atmosphere of the room. We began the meeting by asking the participants to use the materials to build a representation of their company in the context of its industry sector, taking care to also represent the competition in their after-sales service business. Despite this intended focus on the downstream part of their value chain, the participants' discussions kept drifting back towards how they viewed their own organization in comparison with competitors. They constructed their company as a well-defended fortress with elaborate yet inflexible, large and expensive connections with the outside world (see Exhibit 7.3 in the plate section). Their castle was full of gold and heavily guarded with canons pointing in all directions. In contrast, the competitor was portrayed as a small pirates' nest with a great diversity of people with very flexible connection points.

The conversation eventually focused on the sources of the company's competitive advantage today and in the future, which, in turn, sparked a discussion of their own core competencies. Although they all knew the official line about what these competencies were supposed to be, they did not appear to have a shared view of what they looked like. One participant had placed a sarcophagus, taken from a retail set of adventures in Egypt, in a larger solid box that had been placed within the centre of the fortress. As the conversation continued, he pulled out the larger box from within the group's construction, slowly opened it, pulled out the sarcophagus, blew off the imagined dust, and opened it saying: 'This is our core competency.' The box was empty.

This dramatic moment shifted participants into an elaborate discussion of the business environment where they explored how different players, manufacturers, customers, retailers and consumers as well as the firm's numerous subsidiaries were connected and the nature of those interrelationships. After trying to summarize their thinking on a flipchart (see Exhibit 7.4 in the plate section), they returned to the models they built on the table.

In their representation of the company in its landscape, the participants had portrayed some connections as straightforward and based on common sense, whereas other connections were seen as ill defined or even 'ridiculous'. In the process, participants made statements like: 'This is absurd! We have to change this.' The emotional intensity of the conversation about contradictions and absurdities sparked by the model the four had built led the CEO to ask the group: 'Are we just like the dance band on the Titanic, trying to keep spirits high after the ship has hit the iceberg?'

One of them suggested that the company could form an alliance that would enable collaboration with, rather than competition against, other organizations that were positioned to supplant their after-sales service business. No one had dared to explore such a radical idea in previous strategy conversations. They agreed to try this approach.

Quick reflection

Among the many elements of the dynamic ontology illustrated in this case, I would like to highlight the importance of standpoints and scale. The notion that 'what we see depends on where we stand' is apparent in the story. When the executives step back from what they have built they are struck by the 'insanity' of their business. Clearly, this three-dimensional, metaphorical imagery strikes them as entirely different from what they have previously seen and written in text format. As they move back and forth around the table they are able to scale and see new things. By stepping back they see how strikingly different they have portrayed their own company compared with the competition. When they move closer they see the details of different customer connections. This ability to scale is important when practising in the dynamic ontology, and highlights again the importance of *who* is looking and from *where*.

Conclusion

Our assumptions about the world matter for what we do. What makes sense to one person may drive another crazy. In this chapter I have described and reflected on two different worldviews: the world is stable and the world is dynamic. I have outlined the intellectual foundation of the former, using complexity theory and variations thereof to describe the latter. Then, I used the basic ideas of the dynamic ontology to revisit three cases from previous chapters. Looking at the strategy practices described in the book, I hope it is now easier to both see and understand what they did and what unfolded because of their actions. I hope it is equally easy to see the problems facing the groups in BrassCo and TechCo and why things unfolded in certain ways in PackCo. That is the value of taking seriously ontological assumptions.

This will be increasingly clear as we progress through the remaining chapters of this book: *Thinking from Within* calls for a dynamic rather than a static ontology. The static ontology will work against the idea of *Thinking from Within*, no matter how hard we try. In the case examples that manifest in the *Thinking from Within* idea of this book, we will be able to follow how our ontology supports or hampers our strategy practices. But, there is one more set of assumptions we need to bring to the surface, that of how we know, which has a similar impact on our practices and is the topic of the next chapter.

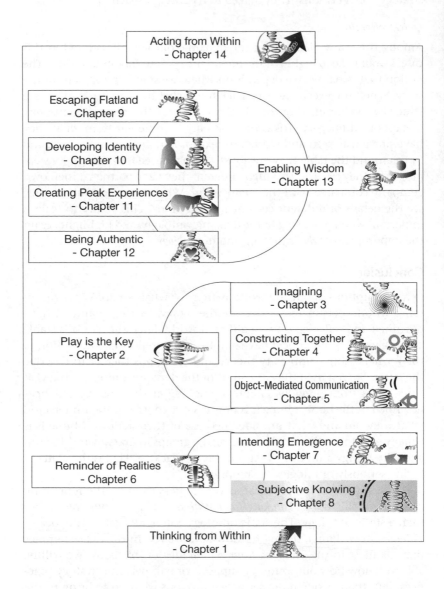

8
Subjective Knowing

Johan Roos

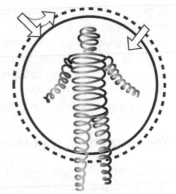

Introduction

In this chapter I take on the second of the philosophical assumptions, epistemology, which influences how we think and do things. Epistemology is about our views on knowledge and knowing or, as I will refer to it in this chapter, 'ways of knowing'.

Recall how the strategy practice of BrassCo centred on a series of more or less 'strategic', deductive analyses of the business and the company, which we now know was firmly grounded in a static worldview (see Chapter 7). Drawing from my limited repertoire, I helped the leadership team apply the most prominent set of thinking tools available to 'cut to the chase' of their business. In TechCo the three groups of leaders framed their conversation by the analytical results, posted on the walls, developed by a major strategy consulting firm and the company's internal strategy group. When we met the people in ChemCo, the divisional leadership teams had already pursued similar routinized analytical practice, which made up most pages of the strategic plan. To the surprise of the ChemCo leaders involved, during the workshop they saw the existing situation in new ways and they developed entirely new insights about their business. They were *Thinking from Within*. These tales illustrate the importance of being aware of our assumptions about knowledge and knowing, that is, epistemology.

The purpose of this chapter is to enhance readers' awareness and understanding of what epistemology is required when we seek to be *Thinking from Within*. To this end I will first describe three views of knowledge and knowing that underlie strategy practices – the Computer, Networked and Subjective ways of knowing. The message of this chapter is that *Thinking from Within* calls for the Subjective way of knowing. The Subjective way of knowing forces us to recognize that what we perceive, think and do, depends on who we are. From this perspective, which is hinted at in the ChemCo story and illustrated throughout this book, strategy practice is inherently people and context dependent. It also helps us appreciate the various practices of *Thinking from Within* discussed so far, that is, to imagine (Chapter 3), construct together (Chapter 4) and use objects to mediate communication (Chapter 5) in the context of the human activity we call play (Chapter 2).

The Computer way of knowing

In his seminal article about the use of knowledge in society, Friedrich Hayek claimed: 'If we possess all the relevant information, if we can start out from a given system of preferences and if we command complete knowledge of available means, the problem which remains is purely one of logic' (1945: 519).

Despite Hayek's deliberation, about the problems society faced, his observation captures the problem of the strategy practice illustrated in BrassCo, TechCo and ChemCo. Strategy, for many people, is framed as a problem of logics. Just as Hayek questioned this approach, I doubt that strategy-as-logics is an appropriate assumption for the problem-setting and problem-solving involved in strategy practice. Given the complexity of any business, with its inherent emergent behaviour, having all the relevant information and complete knowledge seems a mirage. Consider the reactions of surprise among the ChemCo executives when they realized their precious strategic plan, completed with the help of all possible strategic analyses, downplayed 'the winds of change' and ignored how the organization informally functioned. Their vivid three-dimensional image of their organization in its landscape had little in common with the sterile dots in the logical two-by-two matrices that framed the action plans and budget.

The strategy-as-logic idea stems from neo-classical economics, in particular, the kind of micro-economics called industrial organization (Caves 1980; Porter 1980), or IO. In turn, and as I discussed in Chapter 1, the roots of these ideas are the combined Cartesian and Enlightenment historical ideals of pure, rational thinking. Over the past few decades the powerful insights from theoretical and empirical IO research helped generate a language and tools to, as IO guru Michael Porter once told me, 'worship the outside'. The natural unit of analysis is the 'industry' and clearly defined players and the challenge of strategists is to uncover the optimal position within that space, given power relations among stakeholders. Although the focus changed to also include the inside, the so called 'resource-based' (for example Wernefeldt 1984; Barney 1991), and subsequent more knowledge-based views of the firm remain anchored in the idea of strategy as simple, deductive logics.

An assumption underlying this practice pertains to ways of knowing, or its philosophical connotation, epistemology. In short, the assumption is that the world is out there (for example a pre-given industry or a set of resources) and the challenge for strategy practice is to uncover a given truth (for example the optimal, competitive position and resource combination). Because the world is pre-given, as long as strategists are armed with appropriate analytical tools, people will eventually see how things really are, that is, the truthful picture of the industry or the firm. Consequently, it doesn't matter *who* is looking. Armed with the same tools for mapping, for example core competencies, we assume people will see basically the same thing. Recall that in BrassCo the leaders put their faith in Jan and me to tell them the 'truth' about the business, which they typically evaluated against their own sense. In TechCo different groups of analysts used different tools to present the truth about the company and its environment, which became the very foundation of the strategy conversations.

As useful and necessary as such analyses are for knowing what is going on in the business, the underlying assumption of strategy-as-logics is to view thinking as a representation of a pre-given world (March and Simon 1958; Minsky 1975; Simon 1989). This view of knowledge and knowing implies that reality, be it events, processes and things, is *outside* the thinking person and objectively *given* for everyone. The mind has the ability to create inner representations of this reality and the more these images correspond to reality, the more we know about it. From this perspective *knowledge is a mirror of an objective, outside world*. Knowledge is abstract, task-specific and oriented towards problem-solving. Consequently, quality of knowledge has to do with accuracy, adequacy and truth in itself (Lyotard 1984).

How do we gain such knowledge? The answer is straightforward: *thinking is information processing and sequential, rule-based manipulation of symbols* (March and Simon 1958; Varela et al. 1992; von Krogh and Roos 1995a), like words and two-by-two matrices. From this way of knowing human intelligence is comparable with computation and gained from visual object recognition through perception, memory and rule-based reasoning. Like a computer, humans take input from the outside world, process this information according to some explicit rules (logics) to build mental representations, which they store in their minds. On a social level, it makes sense to think of the stored repertoire of such representations, for example databases and filing cabinets, as a form of 'organizational memory' (Walsh and Ungson 1991). In turn, this assumes that our brains and organizations are open systems.

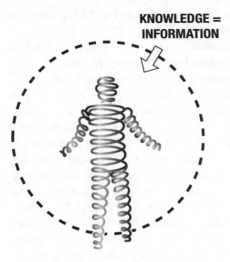

KNOWLEDGE = INFORMATION

Exhibit 8.1 The Computer way of knowing

In summary, and illustrated in Exhibit 8.1, the Computer way of knowing information is more or less transparent; knowledge represents a pre-given world, is universal and objective, results from information processing, is easily transferable (stored and accessed), and enables problem solving.

The Networked way of knowing

A variation of the Computer way of knowing is the Networked way of knowing. This perspective grew out of two deficiencies of the former view. Some scholars were not pleased with the assumption about information processing as a sequential, rule-based manipulation of symbols. Others critiqued the assumption that information processing is localized so that if one part (rule) breaks down the entire system is threatened (Varela et al. 1992). Instead, the brain appears to have dynamic and global properties in a network of neurons. The Networked view holds that learning is an emergent process that depends on interactions and history, but is always based on specific rules of interaction.

Scaling to the level of people rather than neurons, in its infancy the networked way of knowing was used to explain self-organizing of social systems and processes (Jantsch 1980); how information technology facilitated connections among people (Sproull and Kiesler 1991); and the emergence of 'collective mind' among people interacting (Weick and Roberts 1993). The overall idea embedded in this way of knowing is that organizational members contribute to and within a network of other people so that their actions are interrelated within the organization. Knowledge emerges and resides not only in the brains of individuals of the network, but also in the connections among network members, governed by rules of interrelating. Still, the basic assumptions of an objective reality and knowledge-as-accurate-representations remain in this way of knowing.

From the Networked way of knowing it is absolutely critical to facilitate connectivity among the people. The more and better connections among people, the more and better information can be processed and knowledge shared. The objective is to break down walls among the people involved, turning people into an ever-changing and thriving knowledge network.

One of the basic assumptions of knowledge in the Networked way of knowing is that knowledge resides in the network and is only considered *organizational* knowledge if it has been stored and is accessible to others. To ensure and facilitate that everybody involved in the network has access to knowledge throughout it, we need an open storage and retrieval of information in databases and other forms of organizational memory.

From the networked perspective we should balance the use of electronic communication with the rich, multi-sensuous experiences of face-to-face meetings. PC monitors screen out all the smells, sounds and textures of the environment that we normally pick up in a face-to-face meeting. From the Networked way of knowing face-to-face interaction develops richer information exchange.

In summary, and illustrated in Exhibit 8.2, the main difference between

KNOWLEDGE =
INFORMATION

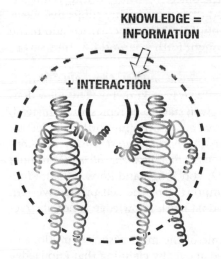

Exhibit 8.2 The Networked way of knowing

the Computer and Networked ways of knowing is that in the latter, the emphasis is on people interacting and that knowledge resides not only in objects, like documents, but in the interactions among people.

The Subjective way of knowing

Consider now the fundamental shift described in the ChemCo case. When these managers were freed of their existing representations about the world, as captured in the strategic plan already completed, by using different shapes, sizes, distances, textures and colours they created a new picture. Each one of them contributed a personal view of the outer and inner world of the organization, as he or she perceived it in that room on that day and there was much variation in these views. When given the possibility to bring forth a world of their own they all described different things. Eventually, they negotiated to gradually develop a reasonable, coherent view of what they discussed and its implications. In doing so, they seemed to see the familiar in a new light and also created entirely new insights.

This practice does not seem to follow the assumptions of either the Computer or the Networked ways of knowing. The former view concerns how representations of the world are created by information processing and in turn stored in individual knowledge structures and organizational 'memory'. While resting on the basic assumptions, the latter view highlights the inherent need for connectivity among people and with information to uncover the objective 'truth'. During our intervention these executives expressed their own, highly subjective views rather than trying to mirror an objective, pre-given truth about the business or the company. They brought forth 'the world' as they saw it, there and then.

What these managers did linger on was a way of knowing distinct from the previous ones, the Subjective way of knowing. This view does not assume that the world is a pre-given state to be represented. Instead, it assumes that thinking is a creative act of bringing forth a subjective world. *Knowledge is personal, history-dependent, context sensitive, and oriented towards problem-identification more than problem solving* (Maturana and Varela 1987; Varela et al. 1992; von Krogh and Roos 1995a). More theoretically, knowledge is a component of the self-productive (Gr. *autopoietic*) process. On the individual level, knowledge is not abstract but embodied in each one of us.[1]

This idea implies rethinking some of the most basic assumptions of the two ways of knowing discussed above. By claiming that knowledge is 'self-produced', our view of managerial thinking changes in two ways. First, everything known is known by somebody, thus, knowledge depends on our point of observation. Consequently, what you see depends on who you are. Through norms and distinctions each one of us consciously or unconsciously selects what we observe and consider relevant and/or legitimate. Knowledge is what makes us able to make distinctions in what we observe and our personal norms determine what we see. In the subjective way of knowing, observation and knowledge are closely intertwined – the distinctions we make reveal our knowledge. In this way we develop new knowledge by referring to both past and potential future knowledge. We use what we know to determine what we see and use what we already know to choose what to look for in our environment. Our personal knowledge is therefore very dynamic, changing as we perceive the world in our own ways, talk or write about what we see, or imagine how things might be, and when we identify and solve specific problems.

The second implication is that we need to differentiate between information and knowledge (von Krogh and Vicari 1991; von Krogh and Roos 1995a). Distinct from the Computer and Networked ways of knowing, in the subjective way of knowing information is a process of interpretation by which (personal) knowledge is developed (von Foerster 1984). Information is not a thing. When we read a report the text is just raw data to us, which we have to take in and put into our own personal 'form'. By using our norms and distinctions, we convert some of this data into our own personal knowledge. When we chose to write down what we know in a report, or engage in a conversation with colleagues, our words or utterances become, in turn, only raw data for the people listening to or reading what we say.

Recall that in the previously described ways of knowing, information is synonymous with knowledge and seen as a thing to be stored and retrieved in our personal or organizational memory. For this to work, people and organizations must be open systems (of information processing). From the Subjective way of knowing, people and organizations are simultaneously open and closed systems – open to raw data from the outside but closed to knowledge. The self producing perspective teaches us that knowledge is the end result of a value-creation beginning with raw data, which is converted into information, which, in turn, is converted into knowledge. Already we see here a distinction from the other two ways of knowing: knowledge is not objective information, rather *knowledge is something private, and residing within each one of us.*

An important facet of this way of knowing pertains to what organizational knowledge is. Such knowledge is not what is stored in the memory, like a database, but knowledge of the organization shared among its members. From this perspective, organizational knowledge allows for shared distinctions in observations, created and maintained through conversations and shared reflection. The key concept to understanding development of organizational knowledge is languaging, as it is through languaging that knowledge brings forth a world (Maturana and Varela 1987; Becker 1991; von Krogh and Roos 1995b, 1997).

Languaging is the process by which language is constantly created based on previous language, through making new distinctions, using old distinctions on new situations and developing new words. In this process of languaging some distinctions are preserved, and others discharged as less useful. The process will gradually form the basis for organizational knowledge and even finer, or new, or fewer distinctions. Organizational knowledge is, thus, shared among organizational members and connected to the organization's history, and both allow for and require languaging.

In this delicate process existing 'knowledge' must be seen to connect with new or future 'knowledge'. People must be able to convey their observations (for others to use) so as to allow the development of a more detailed understanding. This may be viewed as a self-producing process to develop (future) knowledge. If this communication stops so does the knowledge development process.

Just like the Networked way of knowing, this is a living process that relies on both formal and informal relationships between members of the organization. The process requires a clear understanding of the organization's role and culture (a self-description) so that the relevance of individual observations can be evaluated and accepted or rejected as appropriate.

The self-description in effect defines what the organization regards as relevant information. Through it the actions of organizational members are judged legitimate or not. The absence of such an understanding leads to a risk of both incoherent understanding and incoherent actions. (Chapter 10 will further expand on this topic.)

In summary, and illustrated in Exhibit 8.3, from the Subjective way of knowing there is no objective reality, or world, to be represented in our brain. Relating signals to previous experience develops knowledge and our knowledge is developed in language. Organizational knowledge development requires a shared and coherent view of the organization, identity, and connections between people.

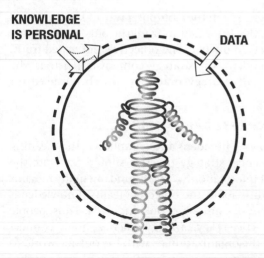

KNOWLEDGE
IS PERSONAL

DATA

Exhibit 8.3 The Subjective way of knowing

Ways of knowing in use

Although the distinctions between the three ways of knowing may seem to be clear-cut, in practice each one of us is always activating all three – at home and at work. The distinction is nevertheless important, because the three ways of knowing naturally suggest different strategy practices, as these unfold naturally from the underlying assumptions discussed above.

Strategy practice from the Computer way of knowing

The implication for strategy practice is similar to the problem of logic Hayek (1945) mused over. The BrassCo story illustrates well how strategy was about trying to possess all relevant, more or less transparent information, in order to gain 'complete knowledge' about 'all available means'. Strategy practice should effectively and efficiently produce accurate and reliable representations of reality, like the industry. Just as in BrassCo, the practice naturally becomes a computation-like, analytical exercise of information processing based on logical rules, such as a particular type of industry analysis to create accurate representation of the company and its environment. Given the 'computer' assumptions, who does the job (inputting and processing information) is, in principle, not important.[2] In the case of BrassCo it was Jan and I, but it could equally have been anybody else.

In summary, strategy practice from the Computer way of knowing is an exercise of processing objective information from the outside. The practice involves analysis of facts to uncover the objective, but veiled truth. Inherently observer-independent, the strategy content rather than the process is at the forefront of strategy practices, which are used for problem solving.

Strategy practice from the Networked way of knowing

The Networked way of knowing broadens and complicates the meaning of strategy practice. In essence, strategy practice should facilitate the exchange and processing of information. While it fundamentally remains an effort to uncover the truth about the objective reality, knowledge is what comes out of the *interaction* among people involved. Thus, people involvement in strategy practice is key. Strategy practice should connect people with people within the organization or with the outside world to stimulate them to share existing company information with one another and to access, and store new information more effectively.

The strategy practice of TechCo, described in Chapter 6, shows signs of the Networked way of knowing. Recall that the CEO endorsed a practice that involved 4, 15 and 50 people, respectively. The idea was to create the best conditions for people to interact formally and informally. TechCo's leadership seemed to recognize that knowledge did not only reside in the documents posted on the wall but also, more subtly, among the people involved. To mix the processing of documents, which were distributed beforehand, during group discussions with more open-ended, informal chats makes much sense from the Networked way of knowing. Compare this with the approach used in BrassCo, where interaction beyond what they did in the leadership team was a non-issue. Even so, these leaders did not really interact in ways that promoted 'even more accurate representations' of the objective and given reality they sought to uncover.

Additionally, the TechCo story illustrates how rules implicitly and explicitly guide interactions among people, which is an essential feature of the Networked way of knowing. For instance, in TechCo primarily outside consultants provided the accurate ('truthful') representations of the company's reality, which was in line with the new CEO's implicit rule about how to practise strategy. Similarly, as facilitator, I set certain rules about time, topics and deliverables for each and every group discussion during the strategy retreats, which was in line with my implicit rules about adult pedagogy.

To develop knowledge, the network of people involved in the strategy practice needs a shared understanding of the problem. Such shared understanding gradually evolved among TechCo leaders, but not really among their BrassCo peers. The courageous comment about 'lacking imagination' by one of the BrassCo participants (Ernst), did not only cause the strategy practice to break down, it brought the incoherent view among these leaders from the aft to the forefront of their strategy practice.

Although this way of knowing highlights the human dimension of strategy practice much more than its Computer way of knowing cousin, people are still seen as nodes in a knowledge network. *Who* gets involved in the strategy practice is still a non-issue. The strategy practice of TechCo engaged some 50 people, but it could equally have been another set of 50 individuals.

In summary, strategy practice from the Networked way of knowing remains an exercise to process objective information from the outside, which calls for people to interact. The practice involves connecting people and information to help the network process information in order to more efficiently uncover the objective truth. Inherently observer-independent, the strategy content rather than the process is at the forefront of strategy practices, which are used for problem solving.

Practise Subjective ways of knowing

The Subjective way of knowing forces us to radically rethink traditional strategy practice. Maybe the most obvious implication is that strategy practice is an inherently human activity that involves thinking, sentient people developing and sometimes even sharing private knowledge. As trite as this may sound at first, in my experience much of the computational and logical 'strategic analyses' could eventually be done by software and probably with more 'accurate' outcomes. The Subjective way of knowing suggests that based on their shared experiences, culture or identity, all strategists develop their own knowledge over time.

This particular view of how knowledge comes about leads naturally to quite different strategy practices than in the previous two ways of knowing. The subjective way of knowing forces us to embrace the inherent humanism of strategy practice, that strategy content depends on *who is part of the process.* In the ChemCo case, we described how we turned the traditional mechanistic practice (based on Computer and Networked ways of knowing) on its head and how the process used invited all participants to bring forth their own, subjective world and that this was desirable.

Strategy practice should, thus, be personal, history-dependent, context sensitive and also oriented towards problem-identification rather than only problem solving. It also suggests that organizations or groups of strategists develop an ever-changing organizational knowledge that is connected to previous experiences, which enables them to perceive and act tomorrow. What knowledge the people involved consider legitimate, depends on who they are. The analysis also matters tremendously. Consequently, each strategist is a value creator who has the potential to creatively differentiate the strategy content and also the entire organization. From this perspective, *strategy is a living, creative and human practice rather than a computer-like way of thinking and doing.*

Specifically, during strategy practice it is important to recognize that everything known (and imagined) is known (and imagined) by *somebody* and then design the practice accordingly. All people involved should feel that they have the potential to develop new knowledge throughout the strategy practice (and all the time), just like the leaders in ChemCo gradually came to appreciate the variation in views represented around the table. Perhaps the OilCo tale from Chapter 1 illustrates this 'egalitarian' view even better, and the BrassCo case (and the RedCo anecdote from Chapter 1) shows the opposite, that is, the boss always knows best.

To successfully stimulate strategists to bring forth and share their own views about, say, the competitive landscape, the strategy practice should make explicit the norms, beliefs, values and worldviews of people involved and other relevant units of analysis, such as the strategy group, the divisional leadership, or the CEO. This suggests that identity (self-description; Luhmann 1990) is an essential part of and perhaps even an outcome of strategy practice and in turn, that the people involved should develop and understand who they are and who the company is. There has been much research about identity of organizations from a wealth of theoretical perspectives, yet few theories link identity with strategy. Based on the maxim 'what we see depends on who we are', the implication is that *identity (self-description) is an integral part of strategy practice.*

This was not the case in BrassCo and TelCo nor was it so during the first part of the strategy practice in ChemCo. Of course identity issues are often part of strategic analyses, but often in an abstract way and in terms of pre-given categories, like 'strengths', 'weaknesses,' or 'core competencies', which is far from the self-descriptions discussed above. Sometimes leaders like to express identity in term of external image, or more aspirational, visionary statements, which are more or less detached from coherent self-descriptions (identity) about the organization as it is today, seen by the people involved. The ChemCo case hints at how this may profoundly influence both the practice and the content of the strategy (Chapter 10 expands on this topic).

Taking one step further, from this way of knowing, strategy practice

Exhibit 1.2 Illustrating
effects of prescribed thinking

Exhibit 1.3 Illustrating effects
of *Thinking from Within*

Exhibit 3.5 Practising
imagination in
ChemCo

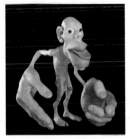

Exhibit 4.1 Statuette of motor homunculus
Used with permission from Foundation Claude
Verdan, Lausanne, Switzerland.

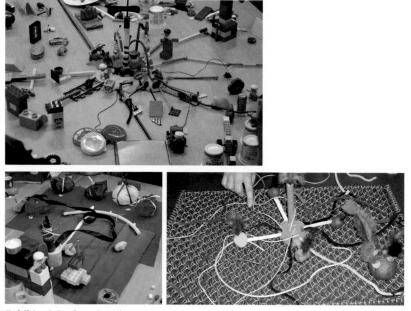

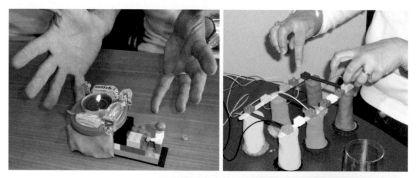

Exhibits 5.2a, b and c Three-dimensional strategy maps

Exhibits 5.3a, b and c
Exemplifying object-
mediated communication

Exhibit 5.4 Context for paper-based communication

Exhibit 5.5 Context for object-mediated communication

Exhibit 7.3 The metaphorical landscape of PackCo

Exhibit 7.4 Flipchart summary (later abandoned)

Exhibit 9.1 Metaphorical landscape imagery in HandyCo

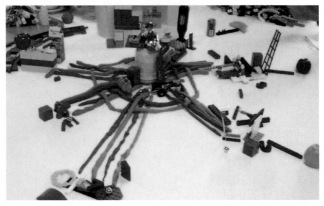

Exhibit 10.1 Identifying InfCo

Exhibit 10.2 Mediating a personal story in DiscCo

Exhibit 12.1 Constructing
meaning in GadgetCo

Exhibit 12.2 Drama in
Nebuchadnezzar (amphitheatre of
Avanche, Switzerland, 22 July 2005)

Exhibit 12.3 UtilityCo, Group 1's construction

Exhibit 12.4 UtilityCo, Group 2's construction

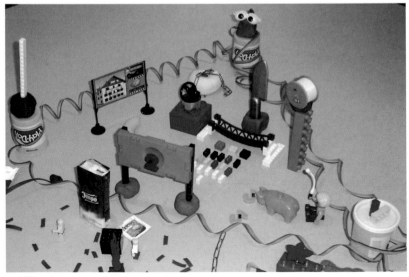

Exhibit 13.3 Representing BancCo

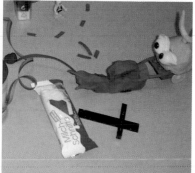

Exhibits 13.4a and b Representing BancCo customers

Exhibit 13.5 Capturing potential wisdom

Exhibit 14.1 From prescribed thinking ...

... to *Thinking from Within*

should create the context in which strategists' distinctions made during the strategy practice are taken into account, and cared for. Because of self-referencing, we all have a unique set of experiences that helps us to make *our* own personal distinctions in life. So, the more knowledgeable we are, the more distinctions we can make. The more knowledgeable I am about the media business the finer distinctions I can make regarding the development, production and distribution of media products and services. Contrary to this implication, in the BrassCo case I described how the leaders used their knowledge to mostly critique, or evaluate the content presented by Jan. In the TechCo case I described how we attached on the walls the 'facts' (read: truths) about the business in the form of long PowerPoint presentations and strict rules about conversation format. In this way, we did not care much for the distinctions made by participants. One could also say that it is unclear how much the CEO cared about distinctions made by others, as it appears he had already made up his mind early on in the process.

Another implication for strategy practice is the need to stimulate people to challenge assumptions already made by others and often taken for granted in the company. This is about challenging tradition acquired from and handed down by experience and practice (Roos 1996). In the language of distinction making, tradition means making increasingly finer distinctions resting on the same basic assumptions. In other words, we add another twig onto the same branch of the tree we are currently operating within. Yet, following tradition means that assumptions are *not* questioned – they might not even be known to the people involved. Breaking tradition is a painstaking approach that requires identification and examination of assumptions previously made by oneself or others and seeking out possible new branches of knowledge. It is about creatively going beyond the knowable and doable, which, from the Subjective way of knowing, should be an important part of strategy practice.

The BrassCo story illustrates well how tradition constrains strategy practices. The way they set out to practise strategy was to do again what they had done previously. In that respect, the TechCo case illustrates how the strategy practice was new to both the CEO and to the rest of the managers. The CEO used to contract a specific global strategy consulting firm to do the job for him and the managers were used to being lectured about a fait accompli prescribed by the former CEO. Yet, when it came to the actual retreat practice, my co-facilitator and I only modestly challenged our own tradition. The most visible break with tradition is what unfolded in ChemCo, where strategy practice changed from abstract to concrete and from detached to engaging.

From the Subjective way of knowing, a climate for respectful conversation needs to be a central concern of strategy practice. Every organization has its own unique set of concepts and phrases, its own language, which cannot be easily translated or adopted elsewhere. Unless a person is part of the conversations that made the language, and continually remake it, important meanings can be totally missed. Consider how the divisional teams in ChemCo created a new concept that made sense to them, such as 'winds of change', or 'love relationships with customers', which would not have had the same meaning to people who were not part of the conversation. This way of knowing teaches us that an important part of strategy practice is to give meaning to new and old words, concepts and phrases, as well as to innovate appropriate concepts and phrases to make sense of new phenomena.

If the people involved in strategy practice find themselves using only tired words and phrases, they clearly deal only with the knowable and doable (see von Krogh and Roos 1995b). To develop knowledge and new strategy content, strategists should move into new and unfamiliar territory, stretching what is thinkable and doable by talking about things that have never been talked about before. This conversation did not occur during the strategy practices described in Chapter 6 and, in my experience, this is symptomatic of strategy processes in most firms.

In summary, strategy practice from the Subjective way of knowing is a delicate human process to bring forth a new, subjective view of the world. The practice involves conversations about identity, reflective distinction making and languaging. Because knowledge is assumed to reside within

	Computer	Networked	Subjective
Strategy practice is fundamentally:	About processing information from the outside	... and connecting people and information	A creative process of thinking and doing
Goal:	Uncover the objective 'truth'	... shared by people involved	Bring forth a subjective world
Primary activities:	Analysis of the facts	... Connecting people	Conversations about identity, distinction making, and languaging
Orientation:	Strategy is driven from the outside	... and processed by networks of people	Strategy comes from within the people involved
Knowledge resides:	In things, like documents and databases	... and in the network among people	In people, to respectfully be shared in conversations
Used for:	Problem-solving	Problem-solving	Problem-setting
Focus:	Strategy content	Strategy content and interactions among people	Thinking and doing

Exhibit 8.4 Summary of strategy practices from three ways of knowing

each human and only shared in safe conversations, strategy content comes from within people rather than from the outside. Inherently observer-dependent, the strategy process rather than the content is at the forefront of strategy practices. Strategy practice is used for problem-setting, as much as for problem solving.

Conclusion

In this chapter I have described three ways of knowing and used these ways of knowing to deliberate about strategy practices in general and in the three cases (BrassCo and TechCo of Chapter 6 and ChemCo of Chapter 3) in particular. If we want to abandon, or at least complement the strategy practices illustrated in the first two cases, the implication is that *we need to fundamentally shift the way we view knowledge and knowing*. We need to break traditions, which is difficult.

At this stage the emerging message is straightforward: the radical change from the observer-independent and detached practice of BrassCo to the observer-dependent and engaged practice described in ChemCo can have tremendous benefits. Facts and figures should always be an important part of strategy practice, but there is more to strategy practice than detached, impersonal and deductive 'strategic analyses'. The Subjective way of knowing calls for strategy practices that embrace humanism more than the 'physics envy' of economics-rooted tradition. This inherent humanism suggests that we need to understand the intricate and fragile thinking, sensing, and doing that unfolds within and between the people involved. In other words, *Thinking from Within*.

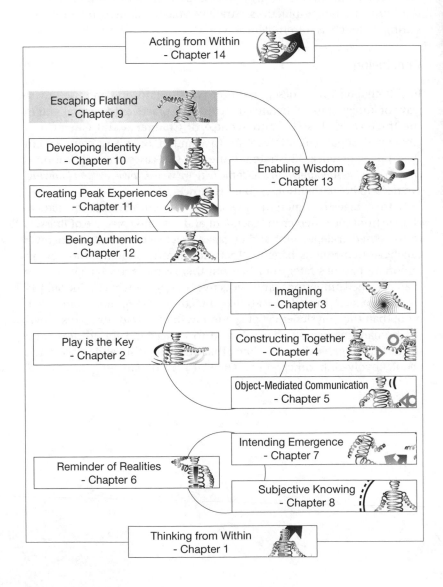

Acting from Within
- Chapter 14

Escaping Flatland
- Chapter 9

Developing Identity
- Chapter 10

Creating Peak Experiences
- Chapter 11

Being Authentic
- Chapter 12

Enabling Wisdom
- Chapter 13

Imagining
- Chapter 3

Play is the Key
- Chapter 2

Constructing Together
- Chapter 4

Object-Mediated Communication
- Chapter 5

Intending Emergence
- Chapter 7

Reminder of Realities
- Chapter 6

Subjective Knowing
- Chapter 8

Thinking from Within
- Chapter 1

9

Escaping Flatland

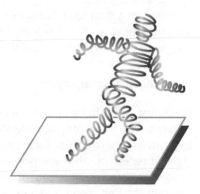

Johan Roos and Peter Bürgi

Introduction

This chapter focuses on an inherent more than an emergent benefit of the practice of *Thinking from Within*: namely, that it yields concrete representation of the rich world we experience. This benefit is inherent since *Thinking from Within*, as defined in Chapter 1, entails constructing physical representations of important matters in three spatial dimensions (see Chapter 4). This benefit is framed in terms of *imagery*, and, as a visualization of this strong view, we use the metaphor of 'escaping flatland'.[1]

The typical, abstract strategy imagery described in the BrassCo and TechCo cases (Chapter 6) is the legacy of the static view of the world (Chapter 7) and the Computer way of knowing (Chapter 8). The problem is that, rather than being supportive 'thinking tools', such abstraction may actually ill serve strategy practice. This problem can be mitigated if we pay attention to what a variety of different theories tell us about the complexity of human experience, and about the role of metaphorical imagery in shaping how that experience is understood, mobilized, and deployed in purposeful action.

This message rests on the ideas already developed in earlier chapters, concerning the practice of conceptual, behavioural and material imagination, co-construction, and the use of objects to mediate communication – all in the context of play. Our purpose now is to describe and further illustrate the benefits to strategy practice of co-constructed, three-dimensional metaphorical imagery.

In the first section we reflect on the role of imagery in our lives in general and in organizations in particular. Agreeing with others that we need a broader set of strategy images, the following sections advocate two key ideas: to use landscape metaphors, and to escape 'flatland' by engaging more of our senses in imagery construction. A case study of how members of a strategy team spent a day escaping the flatland they had long inhabited, and how this experience profoundly influenced the way they view the world, illustrates these arguments.

Metaphorical imagery

Metaphor and other tropes, understood broadly, are devices of comparison, whereby something is understood in terms of something else, seemingly an unrelated thing. Sometimes metaphors are regarded negatively: (1) as a defect in what are presumed to be 'naturally' logical thought processes; (2) as a violation of norms of cooperative conversation in communication, based on an expectation of strict objectivism; or (3) as an ornamental linguistic device that is logically flawed, even though it may have aesthetic value. But while these assumptions suggest that metaphors are at odds with the development and implementation of 'objective' scientific approaches (firmly grounded in the Computer way of knowing discussed in Chapter 8) they ignore evidence showing how fundamental and substantive metaphors are to discourse itself.

In Chapters 4 and 5 we referred to George Lakoff and Mark Johnson who, in their 1980 book, claimed that metaphors are pervasive in everyday life, not just in language but also in thought and action. Metaphors structure how we perceive, how we interact with others, and what we decide to do. The tradition of using metaphors is long and deep, as Gibbs notes in his review of historical views of metaphor:

> Various scholars throughout history ... beginning with Quintillian, Ramus and Vico, have argued that a great deal of our conceptualization of experience, even the foundation of human consciousness, is based on figurative schemes of thought which include not only metaphor, but also metonymy, synecdoche and irony. These tropes do not merely provide a way for us to talk about how we think, reason and imagine, they are also constitutive of our experience. (Gibbs 1993: 253)

Donald Schön has dramatically argued that metaphors often *generate* a radically new understanding in organizational settings and therefore have a crucially practical, constructive role in contemporary human action and interaction (Schön 1963, 1993). He gives the example of a group of product development researchers trying to make a new artificial bristle paintbrush that would mimic the properties of natural bristle paintbrushes. They had been repeatedly stymied until one of their group proposed the metaphor that 'a paintbrush is kind of a pump'; this provided a new way of conceptualizing paint flow in the paintbrush, which led to ultimate success in their development efforts. From examples such as this, which illustrate how behaviour and thought can be fundamentally structured by metaphors, it is a short step to see that analogy and metaphor are intrinsic to the way we think about and know organizations.

The language of business strategy is full of metaphors, still primarily from warfare. The process is 'planned', authority is 'hierarchical', communication is 'top-down', competition is the 'enemy', and people are on the 'front line'. These examples illustrate that the very shaping effect of metaphors sometimes constrains us, so that all metaphors are, by definition, partial. Every metaphor sheds light on an angle of a whole reality, but it never provides the entire picture. For example, using the analogy of high-energy physics, Gareth Morgan (1997) points out that when scientists study light as if it were a wave, they detect wave-like phenomena; but when they study light as if it were a particle, they detect particle-like phenomena. Each of these two 'metaphoring' approaches sheds light on the nature of light, despite the fundamentally differing assumptions about of 'what light is like' that are built into them.

Morgan's contribution to the conceptualization of organizations was to describe and illustrate how our habitual images of organizations influence the way we think and act in and around them. According to Morgan, almost all management theories are based on metaphors of the organization – as a machine, brain, organism, culture, political system, psychic prison, as flux and turbulence, or as an instrument of domination. The message from his work is clear. If we view a company as a *machine*, several cognitively associated images co-occur with this metaphor in our mind, such as the notion that the organization is a closed system, with clear command and control structures, and clearly segregated and non-redundant division of labour, all of it diagrammable as organigram with boxes and lines. If we think of the same company as a *political system*, however, other associated images emerge. For example, conflicts of interests, distribution of power, constituencies and brokers, manoeuvering for advantage, and so on. If we hold the *culture* image in our mind, we see national cultures, belief systems, rituals, symbols, norms, and so on. Each such image reveals the organization in its own set of associated terms, but each is also necessarily incomplete. The message that Morgan derives is that managers should *adopt multiple points of view* in order to see new things in their organizations: otherwise,'much of the richness and complexity of organizational life is passing them by. They are simply not seeing what is really going on' (Morgan 1997: 350).

'In the increasingly paradoxical and uncertain world what use are traditional images of strategy?' ask Stephen Cummings and David Wilson (2003: 25). Some argue that much of the traditional imagery is too trite or is even the sort of pure nonsense that managers should let go of. Cummings and Wilson disagree, and they claim that simple strategy imagery has never been more useful than in these uncertain times. Defending Michael Porter's famous two-by-two matrix of competitive strategy, they argue that one of the main reasons that Porter's images are so popular is that ' their simplicity enables people to interpret them in different ways, work their own thinking into them and express their ideas in ways to which people can quickly relate' (ibid. p. 29). They also find that the more complex and technical imagery is, the more it tends to alienate people and prevent them from incorporating their own ideas. They conclude that useful strategy imagery must have some 'sympathy with' or connection to the specific situation, so that it can be used to guide and support our thinking. The metaphorical image Howard Thomas (Thomas and Hafsi 2005) uses to visualize strategy models makes a similar point: they should be our supportive 'walking stick', available when we need it.

In the language of the Subjective way of knowing (Chapter 8), strategy imagery should not seek to be all-inclusive, a single, monolithic representation of a 'truthful' world. This much we wholeheartedly endorse. Yet, despite their apparent usefulness-as-simplicity, *in practice* value chains, business systems, portfolio matrices and other such conventional strategy imagery remain abstract and frankly rather difficult to connect with, at least if you lack an MBA. In the BrassCo and TechCo cases, certainly, we did not see that people regarded the many such images which surrounded them as an invitation to remake or form them into a shape they could live with. They definitely didn't get excited about them either. So, like Cummings and Wilson, we believe that managers should use a much broader and more eclectic range of strategy images than is typically the case. But we are sceptical whether the simplistic abstractions of matrices, like the one described in Exhibit 1.1 (Chapter 1) really mobilize the richness potentially available to us for understanding the world in our own particular way.

Improving strategy imagery

The question is then how, in strategy images, we can strike a balance between simplicity – which allows people to connect to the image – and complexity – which allows people to capture more of the depth of experience? Contributors to the text edited by Cummings and Wilson (2003) provide a range of sources for new strategy imagery, including ethos and ethics, linguistics, physics, game theory, economics, technology interface, theatre and arts, historical geography, cognitive and biological theories, politics, shareholder value, numbers and decision-making. But, beyond these sources of useful strategy imagery, we claim that people can strike better balances by escaping the two-dimensional flatness implied in *all* of the above, and indeed also Exhibit 1.1 (Chapter 1).

Flatland

Recall some of the metaphors in preceding case examples of *Thinking from Within*: the 'journey' image of the Customer Service Champion of Chapter 1; the 'two-faced' tiger' image of the retailers and the 'elephant' image of the corporate R&D function of Chapter 3; and the 'flotilla' image of many vessels making up TelCo, described in Chapter 5. Put in its particular context, each of these images is in some sense a landscape image. More importantly, the striking difference from normal practice is that these images are not captured on a piece of flat paper, but co-constructed in three dimensions by the people involved – and that is a very significant element.

'The world is complex, dynamic, multidimensional: the paper is static, flat. How are we to represent the rich visual world of experience and measurement on mere flatland?' wonders Edward Tufte (Tufte 1990: 9). An 'information design guru', Tufte has described the dramatic effects to accuracy, fidelity, and persuasiveness that stem from the way that information is presented. His examples, ranging from Galileo's plotting of sunspots to maps of contemporary dance, illustrate his point. When such design is done poorly, it is awkward to pull even the smallest amount of data together into meaningful and useful patterns. Symptoms include 'information overload' or seeing clutter. But when we carefully design how to capture and represent information, a compelling story can be read with a swift glance. His point is that even the most boring, statistical data can be presented in effective and beautiful ways.

Tufte's ideas are relevant for more than timetable designers attempting to squeeze as much information as possible onto a tiny piece of paper. The way data are presented in organizations in general, and in strategy practice in particular, seems rather poor when seen through Tufte's lens – despite the many advantages of simple imagery discussed above. Are two-two-matrices or even PowerPoint presentations up to the standards that Tufte advocates? Even flattened out world maps seem to contain more information and represent it in more compelling ways than the meagre visualizations of graphs and tables, boxes connected by swooping feedback curves and arrows of causality – not to mention spreadsheets and bullet lists in slide presentations. From a distance, analytics in strategy seems to have missed out on how information design has evolved during the past 500 years. Landscape imagery, however, is one step ahead.

Tufte uses the term 'flatland', borrowed from Edwin Abbot's 1884 novel *Flatland: A Romance of Many Dimensions*, to capture in one word the problem we all face:

Even though we navigate daily through a perceptual world of three spatial dimensions and reason occasionally about higher dimensional arenas with mathematical ease, the world portrayed on our information displays is caught up in the two-dimensionality of the endless flatlands of paper and video screen. All communication between the readers of an image and the makers of an image must now take place on a two-dimensional surface. Escaping this flatland is the essential task of envisioning information – for all the interesting worlds (physical, biological, imaginary, human) that we seek to understand are inevitably and happily multivariate in nature. Not flatlands. (1990: 12).

The final point he makes is consistent with the ideas advocated in this book: we live, he asserts, in a richly multivariate world, and we can comprehend it better when we experience it using the remarkable capacities of our senses. For Tufte, careful design is the way to overcome the limitations of the flat surface of paper as a medium and a means of dealing with the problems of 'flatland'.

As much as Tufte's ideas and attempts to bring more sense into a flat surface merit support, we can benefit tremendously from adding still another dimension and stretching our thinking not just *out of flatland*, but *into space*. Like Mintzberg's (1987) crafting image (Chapter 4), Tufte's metaphorical imagery of 'escaping flatland' can be seen as a sort of practice. Previous chapters have already alluded to such three-dimensional images and their benefits. The next section digs further into the intrinsic value of such multimodal imagery.

A multimodal experience

All of the powerful strategy imagery discussed above, including those proposed by Cummings and Wilson and the example of the 'Renaissance villages', (Chapter 5) are verbal. Thus, the experience is a narrative one based on a linguistic, verbal context. We have previously pointed out the underlying assumption is that cognition/understanding and verbalization are one and the same (Bürgi and Roos 2003). Although verbalized metaphors are important for interaction and thought, metaphoring occurs in other dimensions of experience and behaviour. These other modes of human sense-making can therefore also be used to practise strategy, so that the metaphorical imagery of strategy can become multimodal. Moreover, when the imagery is connected to landscapes, we enhance the potential benefits even more.

The argument is summarized in previous chapters, in particular the material dimension of our imagination (see Chapter 3), why construction work is beneficial (Chapter 4), and why object-mediated communication can be very useful (Chapter 5). By superimposing and layering different modes of experience – pictorial-visual, verbal-narrative, spatial-kinaesthetic or haptic – we enrich the overall knowledge that people have of complex situations. As discussed in Chapter 2, play enables the process *but the process can be a sensitive one.* When we engage our senses in ways illustrated in previous chapters we can *experience* rather than just *express* abstractions, analogies, literal similarities, appearances and anomalies and other forms of similarities discussed by scholars as solely verbal phenomena (see Tsoukas 1993). 'Irony' and 'paradox', which stresses difference, take on a different meaning and have potentially more impact when you get a plastic brick thrown at you, or when you suddenly flatten a structure that has carefully been constructed with modelling clay. Imagery which is developed by humans engaging their senses in practice is much more likely to provide the basis for the 'generative, transformative, and frame-breaking insights' that Oswick et al. (2002: 301) hope for using words alone.

All preceding case illustrations in this book, in their special way, illustrate the points made above. The benefits of multimodal imagery, ideally in terms of landscapes, were apparent for the OilCo, ChemCo and PrintCo managers – and, in some cases, such multimodal imagery even broke the limiting frames around their current thinking. To complement the previous examples, though, the story of HandyCo shows how even the most hard-nosed group of strategists, devoted to conventional verbal and flat strategy imagery, can reap the benefits of engaging in a day's worth of multimodal, co-constructed new landscape images of strategy. This way we can extend Abbot's and Tufte's metaphor of escaping flatland. Instead of simply meaning ways of stuffing more and more data into a sheet of paper, it can mean literally lifting out of the length and width of a surface into the third dimension of space.

Case: Escaping flatland in HandyCo[2]

HandyCo was regarded as a benchmark for good corporate strategy practices in its industry and has often been held up as a model for a disciplined and thorough approach to strategizing. But top management also fully endorsed that strategists try out new approaches in their practice, in the hope that it might help them solve difficulties in understanding their current situation.

In this spirit we facilitated an experiential workshop with this group, similar in process and content to the ones described in previous chapters. Prior to the workshop we conducted telephone interviews with all the members of the group, in order to gather information about their understanding of strategy practices at their firm. During the workshop itself, we took extensive notes and still photos of imagery being generated, and videotaped the entire proceedings. Some two months later, we conducted telephone interviews with the participants again, in order to gather data concerning the effect of the workshop on them and their understanding of the strategy process in their organization.

Background

Having emerged as a global leader in telecommunications technology in the early 1990s from a long history as a diversified conglomerate, HandyCo had enjoyed tremendous success with the explosion of the global mobile telephone market at the end of the 20th century. Then, in the first years of the 21st century, HandyCo was facing decisions about technology and market tactics that if realized bore tremendous implications for deployment of its assets.

A core team that follows two primary streams carries out the strategy development process at HandyCo. The first is the stream defined by an annual cycle, beginning in autumn, of visioning, strategic planning, and reviewing, culminating in the cascading of the plan in the following summer. The second stream is defined by regular monthly reviews or checks on key assumptions, forecasts, competitor activity and position, and so on. Interviewees referred to this as a 'continuous planning process'.

Individual interviewees tended to emphasize the overall sweep of the annual cycle, stressing that the phase of analysis of the data was the key part of it. The most important dimension of this analytical phase was the fact that it was highly consensual and discussion-driven. Said one of them: 'We have so many kinds of people in this company that we look at issues from every different point of view – it's always a conversation.'

Overall, the strategy practice at HandyCo seemed both premeditated and systematic, opportunistic and ad hoc. The overlapping of two process streams, one with a long wavelength, the other with a rapid, short and choppy wavelength, seemed designed expressly to balance the demands of manufacturing and production against the enormously rapid changes in the marketplace. Alternatively, it could also be said that the strategy practice at HandyCo was highly abstract, appearing differently to individuals at different levels of the organization, with a marked emphasis on hierarchy. Tellingly, when we asked a junior member of the group what parts of the process could be improved, he responded: 'I am not the best person to criticize the strategy process because I'm junior.'

In summary, the imagery which interviewees used when referring to their strategy-making activities was in many ways as abstract as the more widely used ones we reviewed earlier. Metaphorical imagery for strategy used by interviewees at HandyCo included the following: 'process', 'bottlenecks', 'filtering' of data, discussions and meetings, and the annual cycle of seasons. The emphasis throughout was the calendrical, formulaic, analytical and conversational nature of what they did in strategy. In no way what so ever did we see traces of landscape metaphors. In many ways, as well, organizational norms like the strong expression of hierarchical levels may even have produced a tendency for individuals to be detached from strategizing. A generally high level of abstract imagery among strategists at HandyCo was thus reinforced by their organizational culture.

The workshop

We facilitated and observed a total of nine participants during an intensive, one-day workshop. Initially, the group at HandyCo developed a rather static image of its organization, tightly integrated on a single board, with simple symbols to represent different organizational capacities. This was a rather haphazard configuration of elements, some large and some small, representing their importance to the overall flow of organizational activities, but all locked together onto a single base. However, as the group began, midway through the process, to construct what its competitive landscape looked like, several members realized that they had failed to capture the essential dimensions of its organization. The participants regrouped and lifted several of the complicated constructions of the surrounding landscape out of the way.

They then completely dismantled the haphazard organizational image they had originally created and rebuilt it instead as a highly distilled set of resources clustered around a tower, flying a national flag and dominated by a single leader figure. Instead of rigidly locking this cluster of resource elements to one another, they contained them within a porous, dotted line. They explained that this was because they were in fact not locked together, but rather there was considerable flexibility for determining the internal arrangement of resources in the organization. What held them together was simply the 'brand' of the firm, which they indicated in the form of the 'dotted line' that encircled them all. They had constructed a basic landscape that brought their various understandings together into a unified image.

Next, they arrayed in this landscape a set of different 'gates' to the future that confronted them, suggesting that their organization was essentially fluid and adaptable to whatever future possibility presented itself. For example, to be a strong competitor it could move through any one or more of these gates, beyond which stood a great variety of different competitors and alliance partners, some of them connected to each other in ways that made it difficult to distinguish the adversarial from the beneficial. They had just constructed a complex, metaphorical landscape (see Exhibit 9.1 in plate section).

Follow-up

Afterwards, interviews with the workshop participants indicated that the experience of building, visualizing, and narrating a representation of their own strategic situation had had considerable effect on them. As we reviewed these interview data, several key themes appeared: (1) the analytical clarity of understanding their strategic situation came from imagining and acknowledging the complexity of reality, not from reducing it; (2) there were dominant and unifying visual, metaphorical images that had been constructed by hand and that, when narrated, helped participants make sense of their strategic situation; and (3) these images seem to make sense of the strategy in new ways.

Post workshop interview data indicated that participants felt that the multimodal approach mitigated a tendency towards abstraction in the existing strategy practice. One individual went so far as to evaluate the entire strategy practice in a negative light compared with what they went through that day:

> On a personal level, I experienced a way of understanding what were the demotivating and frustrating factors of previous strategy development efforts. The way we are doing strategy so far is wrong. The way we perform the process and the way we drive it just doesn't get things done. So it was very, very therapeutic because we could really understand our current state.

And, in yet another comment on the effect of a multimodal approach, two participants commented (separately) on what they called the 'crystallizing' effects of the technique:

Our thinking seemed good as we looked at what we were building, so it was motivating the see the thinking actually materializing. It was helpful in providing real motivation for action. It crystallized, and now we had the feeling that the strategy was something that people will buy.

The strategy team leader suggested the experience ' creates crystallization, and I used it afterwards for telling the story of our strategy.'

The 'gates', which represented the different technology options the company would have to pass through, loomed very large in participants' memories. These images continued to influence how they thought about and communicated strategy in the organization, for example 'The gates representing the different alternatives for our strategic choices – that's a big memory for me.' Said another: 'The really good thing was the concept of the multiple gates into the future. It was new not just for me but for many of the others.' The team leader was affected by this concept as well: 'I've been using the gate metaphor quite actively', he noted. In terms of the effects on the organization, one participant drew a direct link to the experience of the workshop: 'What's changed is really not my role in the process, but I now pay more attention to issues like the multiple gates.'

There was a widespread impression among the strategy team that as a means of conveying important information about strategy content, the multimodal constructionist approach was effective. In the words of one: 'It was helpful to see many aspects of the strategy in a different light from the traditional ways like a PowerPoint presentation approach. We could get a real cumulative understanding.' The strategy team leader commented: 'I was surprised at how well it went using this building language. It was very good from an individual perspective and the building with your hands and telling a story was very good.' For many, therefore, a significant takeaway from the workshop was a deep ability to understand and communicate different levels of the strategy concerns in the organization – from high to low level. Said one participant:

When I talk about all the different players in our competitive landscape now, it all comes very easily to me in my mind to see the different things and pieces that we built. I know that the big picture is now influencing me unconsciously.

Quick reflections

The case story illustrates the points discussed earlier. Unlike their habitual approaches to developing strategy, which closely resemble the 'pure reasoning' and deductively analytical approach discussed in Chapter 1, the workshop experience engaged more of their senses and made the experience a multimodal and inductive one. The three modes of metaphorical imagery in the workshop – verbal, visual and kinaesthetic were all used to develop knowledge and to represent this knowledge to others.

Recall the argument above about the value of simple strategy images, which are uni- rather than multimodal in their experience. In HandyCo, clarity and 'crystallization' arose not from a highly reductive simplicity, but from the multimodal overlay of experience(s), from the broadening rather than the narrowing of information. This seems somewhat contradictory to the 'cut to the chase' argument, since the HandyCo strategists tried to pull together the complexity of their situation rather than reduce it. When they completed the picture, in their view, they stepped back and saw patterns they had not seen previously. Thus, sometimes adding, not subtracting data can bring clarity to important questions, at least, if captured in the multimodal ways expressed in landscape imagery. The implication of this is that, it is not so much the quality of the model we should be looking at, to help strategists do their job, but the quality of the *imagery* they are working with.

The visual construction of the strategy relates to the insights of Tsoukas, Oswick and others. Recall how participants first built a static, interlocked representation of their organization, before revising it to better depict themselves. In that latter phase, they built it as a set of resources contained by a dotted line. This second version represents a sort of visual trope on the idea of a collective identity, a visual formulation that captures something paradoxical about reality and offers, therefore, a valuable insight. That is, the imagery of a dotted line paradoxically suggests that the organization is unitary, but that it has malleable boundaries, configuration and constitution – it suggests both 'existence' and 'evolution' at the same time. In fact, just as Oswick et al. claim that such speech tropes may offer qualitatively different insights, it seems that such a visual trope gave participants a new insight into their strategic situation: the construction of organizational identity in this fashion led them to see that the organization might have to move through not one, but several 'gates' to the future.

In this light, Morgan's (1997) argument for the importance of metaphorical imagery to managers is strengthened when managers are given opportunities to multiply and overlay the 'metaphors' available to them. As our interview data show, the convergence of verbal, visual and kinaesthetic metaphors in the strategy workshop seemed to generate the dominant and unifying metaphorical image of 'the gate' that all interviewees, in independent interviews, mentioned as a key takeaway. This may have stemmed from the multiple modes in which the understanding of these images are developed, experienced and understood – creating a super rich image of 'the gate' that became highly effective for making sense of organizational strategy.

The metaphorical imagery from the workshops is enhanced or enriched with dimensions that are not often acknowledged in the life of organizations. The hands of several participants were simultaneously engaged in constructing the collective representation of the organization. They therefore all had the common, shared experience of creating a three-dimensional, complex and sometimes even fragile representation of the essence of their organization. Thus, by focusing not just on a single individual's imagery of the organization and its strategy, but instead on the pooled experiences of several individuals, the workshop is not distilling the information about strategy for individuals so much as it is enhancing it for all involved. Building collectively, therefore, constitutes a straightforward multiplication of the modes in which strategy imagery is experienced (as already discussed in Chapter 4).

But, more importantly, the experience for any one individual is also literally multimodal. This imagery is experienced as:

1. Pictorial/visual information, in which the figures and structures show spatial relationships, colours, textures and symbolic associations that all convey meaning.

2. Verbal/narrative information, with verbal description, linguistic metaphors and story-making techniques all serving to cast meaning in words and speech.

3. Haptic/kinaesthetic information, with participants moving around one another in a shifting group, grabbing handfuls of materials, leaning over the table to press an element into position in the model; thereby constructing images by using their hands to manipulate the great variety of shapes and sizes of different materials.

Finally, the evolving construction in HandyCo formed a landscape in itself. The various objects of different shapes, sizes, colours and textures in combination formed a pattern of thinking and doing, which made sense to the group of strategists. This model became a unique landscape of things, people, events, processes and aspirations that, in some sense, defined their view of the organization at that point in time. The dotted line between the organization and its environment made it clearer than ever that in this landscape traditional distinctions were not necessarily as clear as they used to be. It gave form to the idea that, from a knowledge perspective, the border between the company and other players was shifting and amorphous. The 'gates' became the most prominent spatial features within their landscape, but the image of the complex landscape as such remained with participants too. This is similar to what happened in the previous cases. Recall how the journey landscape of OilCo, the 'information network' and 'the winds of change' landscapes of ChemCo, the overall 'flotilla' landscape of TelCo. All were forcefully constructed by the people involved using their hands while moving their bodies, not just verbalized while comfortably leaning back in their chairs.

Conclusion

The purpose of this chapter was to describe and further illustrate the benefits to strategy practice of co-constructed, three-dimensional metaphorical imagery. It has built on the arguments of previous chapters that, for instance, our imagination has an important material and behavioural dimension, that construction work enhances our ability to access ideas and feeling and express these, and objects can fruitfully be used to mediate communication.

The conventional imagery associated with strategy can be a deadening 'flatland' in Tufte's words. Although this flatland is necessary in many situations, if we work *only* in a flatland we deny ourselves the opportunity of experiencing the wealth of signals that come from engaging our senses, and a variety of modalities, in new ways to generate, transmit and grasp imagery. Although simple models serve an important purpose in strategy practice, this chapter has argued that we should complement these with the metaphorical imagery from multimodal experience of the kind described and illustrated throughout this book. In other words, by *Thinking from Within*.

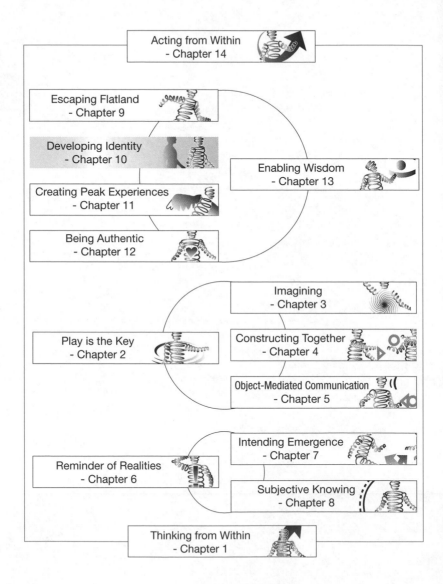

10
Developing Identity
Johan Roos

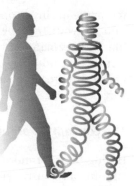

Introduction

Some of the case examples in preceding chapters illustrated how managers entered into deep conversations about what their organization or certain business concepts really mean to them. Because it is grounded in play (see Chapter 2) *Thinking from Within* helps frame and adapt relationships among people, enables people to understand and change their situations and self descriptions, practise and make ethical judgements, and even reach and express more of their inner resources. These questions relate to who we think we are in a broader environment, that is, issues of identity. Thus, one of the emergent benefits of *Thinking from Within* is to both better understand and develop our identities. Although not mainstream thinking in strategy, issues relating to identity are usually, if not always, present in strategy practice. This may be in the guise of other concepts, such as mission, brand values, core competencies or culture. In this chapter I expand on the notion of organizational identity and also, when it comes to images of identity, what makes it important for strategy practice to escape the flatland.

The emergent benefits for organizational identity of *Thinking from Within* are twofold. First, the practice as such can be used to shed new light on such an abstract concept as organizational identity. On a deeper level, because of its roots in play, *Thinking from Within* has an intrinsic link with issues of identity. The purpose of this chapter is to describe and illustrate both benefits.

I begin by reviewing how scholars have defined the concept of organizational identity, in ever disparate ways, and declare my view that identity is socially constructed and related to strategy practice. Then, I discuss and illustrate how organizational identity evolves, and use a shorter case to illustrate the difficulties involved in forcing such evolution. Then I revisit the intrinsic connection between identity and play and, by definition also with *Thinking from Within*, to closer examine how previous case illustrations manifest this link, and emergent benefits of it. My conclusion is that not only does organizational identity matter for strategy practice; approaching it from the *Thinking from Within* perspective can be very beneficial.

The concept of organizational identity[1]

Having lived for more than a decade in Switzerland I have consciously and unconsciously taken up certain ways of thinking and doing, like enjoying a proper *raclette*. These life experiences and others I've gained since leaving my native country in 1988 have surely influenced my self-descriptions and perhaps also how others see me as 'Swedish'. That is, over the past decade my identity has evolved.

The word identity comes from the Latin *idem*, which translates as 'the same' and implies the parts of us that do not change. From a biological perspective this is somewhat tricky as most of our cells are changed every so often. Perhaps only the DNA remains reasonably the same, but then again on that level of scale a token gamma ray or a nicotine molecule may knock out sensitive parts of our gene sequence. From more humanistic perspectives our individual identity can be seen as what makes us the unique individuals we are. What we think, feel, do and how we interact are all part of who we are.

Our biological identities are one thing, and our social identities another. When we move beyond the individual, the notion of identity becomes more difficult. Are we talking about the building, the people who work there, dress code, or certain book-keeping habits? What about group identity? Are we talking about a certain functional identity, like being an engineer or a nurse? Does the informal network among personal assistants have its own identity? If so, how does that relate to the identity of the larger organization? Such questions have caused much debate among scholars from a variety of fields, and the discourse continues. Regardless of definitions most people tend to agree that issues of identity in general, and organizational ones in particular, are important for organizational practice.

The concept of *organizational* identity can be defined in a variety of conflicting ways (Albert et al. 1998). Albert and Whetten (1985) defined it as that which members believe to be central, lasting, and distinctive about their organization. Others suggest identity reflects an organization's culture or ways of working (Elsbach and Kramer 1996). Others talk of an organization's distinctive values and characteristics (Hatch and Schultz 1997). Yet others have argued that instead of an imperfect organization-as-person metaphor, organizational identity describes a social reality of organizational life (Haslam et al. 2003). Scholars taking a postmodern stance (for example Sveningsson and Alvesson 2003) consider identity to be an illusion, an ever-changing collage created by the people in power. In the words of Hatch, 'there can be no stable, steady point, no central essence that could be described as identity, [identity] is impermanent; it is subject to being continuously deconstructed and reconstructed' (Hatch 1998: 39–40).

Organizational identity is related to the notion of organizational 'image', seen as how others view the organization (Hatch and Schultz 2002), including 'reputation', defined as stakeholders' esteem of the organization (Fombrun 1996). 'Corporate identity' is another related term that alludes to how organizations represent themselves to the world (Hatch and Schultz 2000). Some scholars have studied the relationships between organizational identity and image (for example Gioia and Thomas 1996). Others have studied the intricate cognitive and social process we use to identify ourselves with a particular organization (Tajfel and Turner 1985), and how this influences our commitment to it (Ashforth and Mael 1989).

Socially constructed

Identity is socially constructed because it emerges when we interact with others. As we co-evolve with people around us, our image of the organization and ourselves evolves too. As continual 'work in progress', organizational identity is difficult to capture in a few sentences, let alone in a tag line.

The manner in which organizational identity is seen as socially constructed varies. For instance, Fiol (1991: 200) views social construction of organizational identity as a firm-specific form of sense-making, proposing that identity 'serves as a critical link between people's particular behavioural contexts and the underlying values that give them meaning'. Scholars taking a postmodern approach point out that shifting loyalties and differential assertions of allegiance, positional claims and counter claims makes a single identity impossible.

David Oliver and I have previously claimed that the only way we effectively can grasp the socially constructed element of organizational identity is through dialogue (Oliver and Roos 2000). It is in dialogue we make connections, generate new insight and change our behaviour. *Thinking from Within* comes with the possibility not only to socially construct but, by definition, also to *physically construct* a meaningful and rich image of organizational identity (Oliver and Roos 2004). In this case organizational attributes or characteristics stem from subjective and embodied processes of meaning creation, not only from intellectualizing about pre-given 'objective' declarations, such as a list of brand values. To describe specific characteristics of a particular organization, we practise our imagination (Chapter 3), construct together metaphors in space (Chapters 4 and 9) and associated physical media to mediate communication (Chapter 5). The resulting insights guide the essentially strategic practice of, for instance, selecting and applying resources, or decisions about who should be where in the organization. This process of identifying and expressing organizational identity by *Thinking from Within* may implicitly subsume the sorts of decisions otherwise arrived at through consciously performed operations or organizational routines through the very act of defining the meaningful (and fluid) qualities of the organization.

The case of InfCo illustrates the potential benefits of taking the time to describe and reflect over organizational identity in general, and through *Thinking from Within* in particular.

Case: Clarifying identity in InfCo[2]

In early 2000 it became increasingly clear to both the InfCo leadership and industry observers that the technology market was becoming far more difficult after the burst of the 'Internet bubble' earlier that year. High growth and high margins had previously led InfCo to focus purely on growing revenues, and on product sales.

Prompted by these real problems and perceived needs, in late 2001 the CEO decided to launch a new distribution strategy as a way to drive some form of profit and loss responsibility (P&L) throughout the organization, and at the same time create a single point from which to coordinate functions to deliver solutions. One of the major implications of the new strategy was a radically changed role for the country managers. At the time country managers remained 'glorified sales persons' without P&L responsibility or power to influence other functions locally, and InfCo's leadership wanted to change this situation. The desired outcome of the strategy shift and corresponding structural changes was a fundamentally new country management role, a change from a sales person to more of a general manager. Given the history and culture of InfCo the proposed changes were dramatic both in scale and scope.

To support the strategy implementation the CEO selected the corporate HR function. One of the reasons was that the corporate leadership needed a group of people that was seen as reasonably neutral of the sales function and the engineering function. The HR function was 'neither hated nor loved' by either camp. In addition, the corporate HR director, Joe, was well regarded throughout the organization.

Joe asked me to help him get the process moving. After some discussion they agreed to start by developing a more shared view *within the HR team* about what was actually going on inside InfCo to better understand what must be done by them and others. To this end we agreed to an initial two-day, off-site strategy retreat by the end March 2002, for the entire corporate HR team of 12 people. A colleague and I were to facilitate it. This way Joe hoped that the abstract go-to-market strategy and its consequences would become more concrete to all of them.

Pre-retreat interviews revealed that there seemed to be a relative lack of collective identity as a group. But, people saw the retreat as a possibility to move towards a shared sense of collective identity. The HR managers displayed a sense of pride that so much had been accomplished recently by the HR group, while at the same time showing a sense of anxiety about the (unknown) HR group's role in upcoming organizational transformation.

The retreat

What happened? Joe immediately engaged in the process and started to use and seemingly enjoy the physical materials, which set a tone that allowed for collaborative exploration and discovery throughout the two days. In summary, the variety of self-descriptions about the HR function included: (1) an efficient input-output machine; (2) a group of experienced people willing to face line management; (3) change agents; (4) a walled in unit in a hostile environment used to catch casualties; (5) an operational silo; (6) a tireless effort aimed at $ growth; (7) a powerful and strong bear; (8) a beautiful work horse; (9) something underpinning the company, but that is not sufficiently strong yet; (10) a group of people picking up directions ('messages from high above') but not interacting enough; (11) a group of people putting out fires; and (12) a unit brought together by mutual interests in personal gains. From what they individually constructed the variation in views surprised them.

Shared identity

After several hours the group has together constructed an elaborate model, depicted in Exhibit 10.1 in the plate section. Although they converged on a few key characteristics, as a group they were unable to translate this 3D construction into a shared verbal expression describing the

HR function. One of the reasons for this, as suggested by several people, was that the HR function and group of people in itself was split geographically between the home country operation and those of the many operations abroad. The more they tried to come to a unified verbal description, the more it became watered down and politically correct, for example: 'HR is a group of highly trained professionals, specializing in process, systems, tools and high impact activities to support InfCo's strategic business objective.' This was far from the individual, subjective and authentic expressions of their group and function expressed a few hours earlier. Because total convergence was not an objective for this exercise, we instead asked each one of them to translate the model into a single paragraph about the HR function, which we copied and distributed for everybody else to share.

The leader of the international HR managers was very engaged throughout the day. He was particularly excited that several people had engaged with him to portray the international group as detached and distant from the corporate HR group, reflecting the situation for the entire international operations of InfCo. Looking at the model this sense of separation was manifestly evident and cased much discussion throughout the remaining part of the retreat.

During the next phase of the process we asked Joe and his colleagues to look outside the HR function to the rest of the InfCo organization. This resulted in a rather complex construction spread out over the surface of an entire conference table and reaching a height of more than two feet. Encircling their HR function, they included representations of other parts of the InfCo organizations and how these were interconnected, including the CEO and internal projects.

Debriefing

After encouraging them to walk around the table a few times to carefully observe the intricacies of their model, we gave them a chance to revisit how they earlier had described the HR group. With the perspective gained from also looking outside their immediate world, several of them now emphasized HR's critical role in providing channels of communication between and bridging different parts of the InfCo organization. One of them publicly summarized much of the underlying sentiments in the group at this stage: 'We are at the centre of all change within the organization.' Other comments included 'we can't be better positioned', 'we are prepared to sacrifice sacred cows', 'this is better than I thought'. Beyond such self-praise, they expressed concern about the challenges that were evident in the model they had built, as expressed by comments like: 'we are required to be very focused and strategic', 'we must not be married to our structure', 'expect more complexity', 'there is much to be done with less', 'I am worried about timing' and 'there will be enormous pressure on people here and throughout the corporation'. Visibly pleased with what they collectively had achieved so far, they called it a day.

Quick reflection

The spontaneous comment 'We are at the centre of all change within the organization' manifests the emerging sense of organizational identity felt by the HR function, which took these managers by surprise. In turn, this shared identity caused them to consider in new ways the opportunities and challenges ahead. Specifically, the perceived distance between the corporate and the international parts of the function, clearly visible in their construction, caused immediate and deep reflection about how to improve the situation.

Why identity is important

Organizational identity is important because it influences what people think, feel and do. To revert to the landscape metaphor David Oliver and I have previously proposed (see Chapter 5), our identity is like a backpack we carry around when climbing peaks in knowledge landscapes. On the one hand, its content keeps us going. On the other hand, the luggage can be heavy. In that sense organizational identity both enables and constrains the daily life in organizations. For example, consider the variety of answers we can give to the questions of the classic Strengths, Weaknesses, Opportunities, and Threat model when we redefine 'who' we are as an organization. Using Theodore Leavitt's (1960) classic idea to make the point, consider the alternative identities: a manufacturer of roll bearings, or a provider of 'anti-friction' services. What in one case is a strength (for example manufacturing skills) may in the other case be a weakness (for example 'we are in services, stupid'). What in one case may be seen as an opportunity (for example 'the marriage counselling business is anti-friction too, right?') will in another case probably make the board dismiss the CEO.

Beyond the irony of the last example, organizational identity often provides the institutional legitimacy necessary to attract, prioritize and deploy resources (Brown 2001), and even prevent organizations from falling apart (Taylor 1999). For example, if a new project is seen to be close to its core identity claims, the more likely it is that the resource request will be approved. As a shared image held by people, organizational identity can be used to either hide or emphasise both emotions and actions, like in InfCo, or even rebound from crises. In our own research we have found that a strong and shared sense of identity helps management teams handle critical, surprising incidents (Oliver and Roos 2003, 2005).

Because organizational identity has such a profound impact on organized life, it is perhaps not surprising the topic in some form (vision, mission, purpose, core values, guiding principles, and so on) is an integral part of the content and practice of strategy. Organizational identity often serves as an orienting framework for strategic discussions, because you have to know who you are before you can take action (Albert et al. 1998). Some have argued that identity is a source of competitive advantage because it constrains our thinking in the first place. Knowledge of 'what an organization is' (consistent with the Subjective way of knowing discussed in Chapter 8) seems to be a reasonable precondition for strategy practice, not in only in situations of crisis reaction but also when strategy is proactively crafted.

Organizational identity is, thus, not a static 'thing' or something 'pre-given' by others. In that respect, organizational identity emerges from the process of interaction between the people involved. Organizational identity is the answer to the question about 'who' the organization is according to the observer. As such, 'identity' can be a topic among others to which we can apply the concepts and practices described in this book.

Evolving organizational identity

Recall how the ChemCo managers in both divisions (Chapter 3) viewed their organization as a value creating, 'work-flow' and 'network of information'. These metaphorical self-descriptions represent ChemCo's identity, as seen by these particular individuals at that point in time. Another group of leaders would almost certainly have used different metaphors if they too had socially and physically constructed a representation of ChemCo. Even in BrassCo, the leadership's view of 'who' the company is bound to change depending on whom we ask. Perhaps there will be less variation in this company than some of the other examples provided in the book, but the principle remains: organizational identity is not a rigid and enduring 'thing', but a more changeable, contingent and context-dependent set of meanings, and that is why it is so important to continually develop it, perhaps by 'constructing' it.

There are examples of organizations with more rigid identity, which can help them attract and retain members. The Catholic Church, for example, is often used an example of a successful organization, at least in terms of longevity, with a strong identity (the Christian faith). Collins and Porras (1994) argue that successful organizations that have been around for many years have 'cult-like' cultures and that this is good. Yet, to me cults have authoritarian power structures with a leader who is regarded as a supreme authority with no way out or appeal process available. Cult members tend to be very submissive and give up most of their own identities to subordinate themselves to that of the organization. Legitimate knowledge (distinctions, language and so on; see Chapter 7) stems solely from the leader.

On the one hand, the metaphor of 'cult-like' identity is illustrative since it clearly points out the tremendous impact identity can have. On the other hand, I find it a rather disturbing metaphor as it suggests a totalitarian system incompatible with the ideas and practices advocated in this book. In our previous work David Oliver and I took this stance by using a landscape metaphor: 'organizations with cult-like cultures have extremely narrow knowledge landscapes ... It is like pursuing just one trail in the landscape' (Oliver and Roos 2000: 173). For good or ill, such rigid identities imply it takes a very strong signal from the environment to change them.

Far from such a cult-like identity, consider the case of DiscCo, a regional provider of licensed software products in Northern Europe, which illustrates that it is often difficult to change identity, even just a tiny bit.

Case: Leadership challenges in DiscCo[3]

The CEO of DiscCo was not happy about the identity of his organization, at least not the identity perceived from his vantage point. Instead of being a 'network of peers' the six country managers and three functional managers remained mostly independent 'hubs' with limited direct interaction, each having separate profit and loss responsibility. To explore new ways to change their habits we agreed to gather the entire leadership group for a one-day retreat. The CEO kept the agenda open and his people did not really know what to expect other than a team-building experience. First, a facilitator colleague and I asked them to individually build a representation of DiscCo, as they subjectively perceived it that day. Second, we invited them to construct together a common metaphorical construction, which ought to make sense to all of them.

What happened?

The individual identity constructions were quite diverse, including people with 'road construction' between them, animals surrounding a farmer, and a circle of countries surrounding Germany (the CEO was German). Each construction was unique and pointed at a successful company consisting of distinct parts scattered around a leader. When building a shared identity representation, each member of the group continued to modify his or her own operations, and eventually pushed these into the middle of the table to be connected with the others. The final group construction showed six independent country operations with the key feature of individuals linked through 'antenna relationships'. Analogous to radio waves, the meaning was that they could call each other to talk while remaining physically distant.

The process of constructing together the identity of DiscCo was very difficult, and began only when the CEO told a very personal story concerning his position and relationship with his chairman, as briefly captured in Exhibit 10.2 in the plate section.

The discussion became highly animated when the team focused on how the organization was perceived from outsiders such as customers. None of the other participants came even close to such apparent authenticity. Overall, country managers from the less developed market operations expressed the most interest in forming a network. In contrast, the managers from larger, more established markets remained sceptical. This pattern was manifestly obvious in the overall construction, which from a distance displayed a clear hub and spokes pattern.

Reflecting on the experience immediately afterwards, the CEO acknowledged that, on the one hand, he was disappointed that his group did not want to become more of a team. On the other hand, he was now convinced the construction represented their 'true' identity – at least as long the leadership group included these people.

Quick reflection

Organizational identity is a set of socially constructed meanings, shared perceptions and distinctions about the organization and its environment. In DiscCo's case the meaning was 'group' rather than 'team,' and 'remain independent' more than the 'peer-to-peer network' desired by the CEO. On the level of being a leadership team, the story illustrates that although the group's identity is fluid, it is also relatively stable as long as the group remains intact.

Intrinsic link with play

Using the language of Chapter 2, from a sociological view the two illustrations used in this chapter show how managers frame and adapt the social contexts and relationships necessary for their task ahead. From an anthropological view we have demonstrated how they develop and adapt their description of the organization, within which the purpose and value of their work will be determined. And from the philosophical perspective their playful imagination prepared them to make ethical judgements, about what must be done to implement the new strategy, or just work even better as a group rather than team. Taking a psychological view, the managers involved seem to have authentically shared their inner thoughts and feelings about the function and leadership team respectively. They learnt something new and in some instances these people also changed their feelings towards the matters at hand. On the highest level of scale, all these considerations relate to 'organizational identity', which sprung from playful and hands-on interaction among the people involved.

Following the discussion in Chapter 2 the practices illustrated in these and previous cases should, by definition, come with intrinsic, emergent benefits relating to identity. This paradoxical statement builds on the idea of intending emergence, discussed in Chapter 9, where we can intend things to happen, but never be sure they will. Thus, because it is grounded in play when we think from within we cannot avoid touching upon issues of identity, broadly defined. To illustrate this we will briefly reframe what unfolded in the DiscCo and InfCo cases seen through the lens of organizational identity.

Value judgements are always parts of decisions about what to do. The retreat experiences were in many ways intended to focus on identity, but not solely. The InfCo HR leaders had an opportunity to practise their judgements about who they should be, as a group and as 'change agents' for the new initiative. They also revealed problems they had to deal with, such as closing the gap with the international part, or how best to interact with the corporate leadership. In their case they developed a narrative about their group, at first individual and powerful and subsequently more collective and diluted, which formed the basis for the positive realization about being in the 'centre of everything'. In terms of social relationships, during the episode reported here these managers seem to have interacted in ways that brought them closer together than ever previously achieved. They seemed to thoroughly enjoy themselves and 'let go' in ways that were not common practice during InfCo management meetings. Also unusual, they seemed to reach deep inside, articulate and share their personal, subjective views in ways previously not experienced.

The DiscCo experience was somewhat different but points in the same direction. Recall that the CEO wanted to change the way they worked as a group, seeking more peer-to-peer interaction. This was not the first time he pushed this agenda but few things had changed so far. The experience of constructing their organization, individually and together, gave them the opportunity to articulate and share their value judgements about this matter. Only when the CEO could first hear then see the explicit judgements of his people displayed in the construction, that is, 'we want to remain independent', did he give up. From a slightly different angle, the same message was all over the narrative embedded in the construction in terms of their wish for informal connections rather than formal meetings. This story says less about what happened with their social relationships during the exercise, but as a participant observer I can report that these moved from somewhat tentative and formal to positive and informal over the day. As far as we can tell, this evolution made them contribute their authentic views and feelings about the heart of the matter, namely how to work together.

Overall, when we apply the four theoretical lenses of Chapter 2 (philosophy, anthropology, sociology and philosophy) we see a wealth of identity related benefits. In both cases the intended emergence pertained to organizational identity, but for analytical purposes this does not really matter. Recall how managers in OilCo, ChemCo, PrintCo, TelCo, PackCo, and HandyCo (of previous chapters) experienced similar emerging benefits while not necessarily discussing organizational identity as such. The message is clear, when *Thinking from Within* expect 'identity' to be an intrinsic part of the thinking, feeling, talking and doing. This is the case in strategy practice, but we do not see that as the limit. Identity matters in most aspects of organized life, all the time.

Why is this kind of identity development beneficial for strategy practice? In stable circumstances it matters less. In uncertain and ambiguous circumstances, *while* intentionally seeking new outcomes *what* we perceive as important and legitimate (see Chapter 8) matters. Because we all see different things, *who* is involved in developing images and maps of the organization and its business landscape matters tremendously. Unless we have a reasonable shared sense of who we are, as a group, business unit and organization, how can we expect a group of people to act coherently? In short, identity matters and should be an integral part of strategy practice. When we think from within we implicitly or explicitly deal with and develop our organizational identity.

Conclusion

The concept of organizational identity is ambiguous and some will even argue an oxymoron. It is important because it influences what we think, feel and do. Just like 'strategy' can be dealt with on a more concrete level, *Thinking from Within* can be used to make identity more 'real' than a few written sentences. More than this, the *playful* practice it comes with has an *intrinsic* link with matters of identity. When we practise *Thinking from Within*, one way or another, we inevitably develop 'who we are'; we act according to ethical principles, we transform ourselves, we develop social relationships, and we benefit from the process, especially if we can connect with our deeper thoughts and feelings.

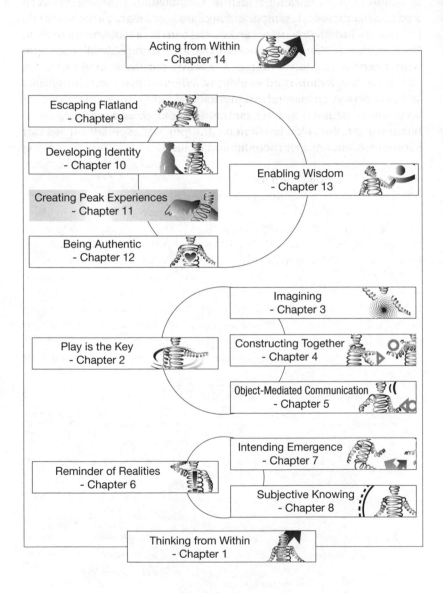

Acting from Within
- Chapter 14

Escaping Flatland
- Chapter 9

Developing Identity
- Chapter 10

Enabling Wisdom
- Chapter 13

Creating Peak Experiences
- Chapter 11

Being Authentic
- Chapter 12

Imagining
- Chapter 3

Play is the Key
- Chapter 2

Constructing Together
- Chapter 4

Object-Mediated Communication
- Chapter 5

Intending Emergence
- Chapter 7

Reminder of Realities
- Chapter 6

Subjective Knowing
- Chapter 8

Thinking from Within
- Chapter 1

11
Creating Peak Experiences
Mark Marotto and Johan Roos

Introduction

Some of the cases in previous chapters illustrate how managers, under certain circumstances, seemed to be transformed by their own thinking and doing. Far from how they described their former routine-like strategic planning process, the ChemCo managers of Chapter 3 seemed to have experienced a sense of transcendence about their 'second opinion' on their strategies. The PrintCo leaders in Chapter 4 displayed intensive concentration when they addressed taboos. Some of the TelCo strategists of Chapter 5 witnessed a sense of wholeness never previously felt in their understanding of the company as a flotilla. The examples throughout this book illustrate how *Thinking from Within* can result in a loss of sense of time and engrossment in the task as well as increased creativity. Given the ground covered in earlier chapters, play and creative arts processes, imagination, construction, object-mediated communication and three-dimensionality, it is perhaps not surprising that *Thinking from Within* can captivate a person's mind and heart. We are not talking about a purely intellectual reasoning, like the ones indicated in the RedCo tale in Chapter 1 or in the BrassCo and TechCo tales in Chapter 6, but an immersed, embodied experience, that sends new and often unusual signals to our mind. The purpose of this chapter is to reflect on the theoretical explanations of such phenomena, seen as emergent benefits of *Thinking from Within*.

To this end, we review three streams of literature on flow, timelessness and aesthetic experience, and relate these to the cases discussed in this book and to other, anecdotal evidence of peak experience we have observed when people think from within. The message of this chapter is that the embodied experience of *Thinking from Within* creates the conditions under which peak experience may emerge. But first let us illustrate this kind of immersion with an anecdote from a group experience at an educational programme.

Case: Coping in ConglomerateCo

At the end of the 1990s Johan directed a two-week consortia programme for groups of senior executives from a handful of non-competing companies. Because of the length of the programme, which included a weekend, participants got to know one another quite well and, gradually, began to share more about their hopes and fears. During the first week it became increasingly apparent that one team – five leaders of business units in a multinational manufacturing company – did not have the same positive dynamic as the others.

During the first day of the second week, he invited the group to try out an early prototype version of the method illustrated in this book in order to work through its problem. He arranged a special room, blocked two hours, introduced the participants to the experiential process and encouraged them to try it (the other groups followed the regular programme).

Three hours later, or one hour more than set aside, to respect the schedule, Johan interrupted their conversation, which they did not appreciate. He had been listening to parts of the conversations, and for research purposes, was capturing the entire session with a video camera, which they had agreed to. During these three hours they articulated, visualized and debated their primary concern, which none of them had openly aired before the session: their divisions were all on the CEO's short-list to be divested. The two tables they initially used as a 'workbench' were now separated and materials covered the floor underneath. Parts of their joint construction had been tossed all over the room; other parts remained on the tables. They were gathered around their 'construction site', using various bits and pieces while talking about how they individually saw things. The conversation was visibly and audibly intense and Johan had to raise his voice to be heard (though he did not want to interrupt such an intense discussion).

What happened? Together the group members built a model that illustrated delicate connections between the parent company and their respective divisions and among their own divisions (as this was a very large company, of which their divisions were few among many). Following this construction phase was a deconstruction phase. They ripped apart these linkages one by one and erected walls in between some of the units. On a few occasions one of them became very emotional, sharing with the others what he felt, that divestiture was wrong and stupid. Frequently used words included 'loss', 'relationships', and 'more than profits' to express their feelings, while materials were used to visualize what they meant. During this time they rarely sat still but instead constructed, moved around the room, shifting places, sitting on the table, and so on.

After about two hours one of them suddenly grabbed one of the two tables that made up their construction site, quickly turned it over so that the construction and surplus materials fell to the floor dramatically. The others looked terrified but after a few seconds got the message. The likely divestiture would 'destroy' important relationships among them and between each one of them and people in the corporate division. They would be 'tossed away' from the group and 'damaged'. He had simply illustrated symbolically what they had been talking about. A colleague begun to laugh, another applauded and cheered, and another went up to kick parts and trample hard on pieces on the floor.

Following this episode they calmed down, picked up some parts and raised the table back up again, but kept it at a few decimetres from the other one. The 'chasm' was wide and visible. From here on, the conversation was about how they could help one another to prepare for such a divestiture, which might not be a bad thing, after all. 'It depends on how we look at it,' one of them said, while connecting representations of two units.

After the session, they expressed gratitude for the opportunity to engage with one another in this unusual way. They testified in the plenary about the perceived depth of the conversation previously not experienced during the programme, or in their organization. Three of them said they had changed their view about the 'risk' of divestiture, which they now saw as a possibility they should be prepared for. They all said they had developed 'real friendships', which they subsequently nurtured by spending the remaining evenings together (which was less good for the dynamics of the consortium programme).

Types of experience[1]

American psychologist and philosopher Abraham H. Maslow coined the term 'peak experiences' to describe non-religious, quasi-mystical experiences. They are characterized by brief and transient moments of bliss, rapture, ecstasy, great happiness, or joy as well as the temporary disorientation with respect to time and space. Psychological healthy, mature people, whose basic needs are met, have the greatest potential to transcend the ordinary and mundane and have peak experiences (Maslow 1968). Others have claimed that people who have 'full focus' and 'clear sense of self' are more prone to have such experiences (Thornton et al.

1999). Although one can question if all managers practising strategy fall into this category, we assume the examples of this book involve reasonably self-actualized people.

Peak experiences are transitory, but their consequences, which can include a deepened understanding of self and the relationship of one's self to the world, may be enduring. Maslow argued that these moments were a key to our unrealized, inner potential (Chapter 12 expands this topic in terms of authenticity).

Peak experiences occur spontaneously and naturally (as opposed to supernatural), triggered by aesthetic perceptions ('it is so beautiful'), moments of inspiration or discovery ('wow'), to unity with nature ('I'm in seventh heaven'). They have been known to occur in a wide variety of circumstances, including, sports (McInman and Grove 1991; Privette 1982; Privette and Bundrick 1997), music (Lowis 1998), and even occasionally, but not too often, the business world (Thornton et al. 1999; Boynton and Fisher 2006). We will now describe and illustrate three concepts that fall within the overall category of peak experiences.

Flow

Csikszentmihalyi (1990) and Csikszentmihalyi and Robinson (1990) made Maslow's notion of peak experience operational in the term 'flow', defined as: 'the state in which people are so involved in an activity that nothing else seems to matter; the experience itself is so enjoyable that people will do it even at great cost, for the sheer sake of doing it' (ibid. p. 4). By engaging in tasks that we could complete if we have clear goals, immediate feedback and concentrate on them, to the exclusion of worries and frustrations of everyday life, we have the possibility of entering 'flow'. Flow experiences can result in a sense of discovery, push us to higher levels of performance and lead to a new consciousness. Among the activities in which flow can emerge, Csikszentmihalyi cites play, which Chapter 2 has already mentioned.

The ConglomerateCo story illustrates the sense of discovery, higher levels of performance and a new consciousness that characterize 'flow.' In these situations, people felt sufficiently comfortable to seize the opportunity to think from within and when they did this, they experienced at least fleeting moments of flow. We suggest that *Thinking from Within* creates conditions for emergent, flow-like experiences.

Timelessness

Without entering into a tricky philosophical discussion about time, we want to make the point that how we experience time is subjective and very much dependent on what we do. Somebody's time (past, present, and future) is time experienced by that person. Timelessness is about how we experience a *loss of time*.

Integrating studies on flow with the literature on time experience, Mainemelis (2001) proposes a model for the experience of timelessness in organizations. The feelings of immersion, recognition of time distortion, sense of mastery and transcendence rest upon a latent state of engrossment, whereby one is completely affectively, cognitively and physically involved in an activity. As a result people feel completely absorbed and consumed by the activity so that they forget themselves and their surroundings. They lose track of time, like in the above story of the five business unit leaders, or feel that it has passed in a different way than usual, also described in previous chapters where participants immersed themselves in strategy practices to the extent that time seemed to pass quickly. In terms of mastery, people experience such a heightened competence, with regard to their task, that they have a peak performance (Thornton et al. 1999). By transcending their boundaries of ordinary performance, they feel as if they are stepping temporarily outside of normal life.

We see traces of such perceptions of timelessness in previously presented tales of strategy practices. For example, one the TelCo managers of Chapter 5, Sean, was known to have some difficulties putting his ideas into words. During the retreat (not described in Chapter 5) he gradually became increasingly involved and engaged in the conversations, which surprised his colleagues. As some stage, he literally jumped up, hurried around the table, sank to his knees and carefully studied the evolving, panoramic construction on the large table in front of him. After an initial pause others continued their own conversations, leaving Sean to his own thoughts, as he seemingly did not have anything to say. After a few minutes, and apparently unaware of the other conversation around him, Sean interrupted by calling everybody over to his side of the table to look at their construction 'from the customers' vantage point'. It was as if he has been lost in his own deliberations and suddenly returned to the others unaware of the time lapsed.

Another anecdote from the same session illustrates a similar point. During the most intensive, object-mediated communication one person felt an urgent need for a bio-break, but did not want to interrupt the flow. She rushed to the door and almost momentarily returned at high speed and while crashing the door open exclaimed 'What did I miss?'

Contrast this with the example of BrassCo in Chapter 7, where they felt the strategy conversations were necessary rather than enjoyable. They could not wait to leave the room for a different kind of (embodied) experience, the three-course lunch, or using their mobile phones 'to get things done'. We suggest that *Thinking from Within* can give rise to a sense of timelessness.

Aesthetic experience

Timelessness and flow describe a latent state that occurs when people are actively involved in a task. Another category of peak experiences belongs to the realm of art and occurs when people are transformed by beauty. It shares many of the manifest characteristics already discussed and has been described by philosophers as the 'aesthetic experience'. Schopenhauer (1969:17–9), suggested we 'lose ourselves entirely in this object ... we forget our individuality, our will, and continue to exist only as pure subject.'

Scholars of aesthetics starting with Baumgarten in the 19th century and continuing through contemporary accounts by philosophers like Dewey (1958) and Beardsley (1982) have identified salient characteristics and functions of the aesthetic experience:

- Object focus: the person willingly invests attention in a visual stimulus.
- Perceived freedom: he or she feels a sense of harmony that preempts everyday concerns and is experienced as freedom.
- Detached affect: the experience is not taken literally, so that the aesthetic presentation of a disaster might move the viewer to reflection but not to panic.
- Active discovery: the person becomes cognitively involved in the challenges presented by the stimulus and derives a sense of exhilaration from the involvement.
- Wholeness: a sense of integration follows from the experience, giving the person a feeling of self-acceptance and self-expansion.

Even if an aesthetic experience is temporarily broken off we are typically capable of picking up with remarkable speed, almost as if there has been no interruption (Beardsley 1969).

We recognize these descriptions of aesthetic experiences in some of the case illustrations of previous chapters and what we have experienced elsewhere. People constructing objects with their hands often say their creations are 'beautiful', 'captivating', or convey a holistic meaning never before seen. When we ask people to break apart what they have built, typically during the warm-up phases, many tend to spontaneously say 'oh no' or 'do we have to, really?' and sometimes they even drag their feet or try to hide from the facilitator what they had constructed. In our experience, people often feel attached to what they constructed. Recall how the entire leadership team in one of the ChemCo Divisions (Chapter 3) carefully took apart their construction, wanting to rebuild and display it to others elsewhere. We have yet to see that happen with a stack of PowerPoint slides.

These people's personal and shared sense of beauty definitely had something to do with it. A reason for this may be that their co-constructed objects and the communication they mediate resemble 'art'. Using the definition suggested by Sandelands and Buckner (1989), like art the process of playfully constructing together and engaging in object-mediated communication has *boundaries* (the retreat; the construction), *dynamic tensions* (the intricate meaning given to the objects), *record of growth* (the communication the construction mediates), and *unresolved possibility* (the ambiguity and potential that remains).

Perhaps the aesthetic experience in the examples in this book is not surprising since anything we experience through the five senses aesthetically in any aspect of life can, potentially, lead to the aesthetic experience. In summary, we suggest *Thinking from Within* creates the conditions for an emergent, aesthetic experience.

Peak experiences in groups

There are striking similarities, both in the literature and in our practical experience of staging *Thinking from Within*, between descriptions of the aesthetic, flow and timelessness experiences. Like others, we also think the experiences are essentially *the same state of mind* (for example, Csikszentmihalyi and Robinson 1990). In the literature these experiences are assumed to occur on the individual level, but in our examples, as already indicated, it may be a group level experience too. Let us take a closer look at what has been written about *groups* experiencing peaks.

Hot groups

An example of a group-level peak experience is the notion of 'hot groups' (Leavitt and Lipman-Blumen 1995). The existing literature shows consistent focus on the importance of the group *task* in forming the hot group state of mind. Despite the interpersonal challenges that may arise in such groups, in which members are not necessarily friends, the commitment to the task takes priority over such conflicts. Such an instrumental focus often leads task-cohesive groups to superior levels of performance and renders them less prone to groupthink (Bernthal and Insko 1993; Zaccaro 1991; Zaccaro and Lowe 1988).

The intrinsic challenge of a task is related to the capacities and skills of the members. If there is a match between these two elements, where the task is neither too easy to cause boredom, nor too difficult to discourage participation, then it is 'optimally challenging' (Cskiszentmihalyi 1990). Such tasks have been shown not only to captivate attention and interest to the exclusion of everything else, but also to be a source of fulfillment for the people engaged in them.

If a task is both meaningful and optimally challenging, it promotes task-centred cohesiveness and also contributes to the state of mind that characterizes hot groups. All the same, we propose that at the heart of the potentially transformational practice of *Thinking from Within*, is *much more than just passion for a task*. While the task is important, there are other factors contributing to the manifest peak experience of teams of managers *Thinking from Within*. The literature helps us shed more light on this issue.

Aesthetic interaction

The idea of aesthetic interaction draws on the work of Taylor (2002), who conceptualizes organizational members' aesthetic experiences as being based on the involvement of both the performer and audience:

> Verbal performance is the closest in form of any of the arts to the art of management. Most of a manager's work is verbal and interactive, which makes it more like storytelling than dance, theatre, painting, writing or other arts ... the aesthetic transaction includes both performer and audience, and because for organizational action, the roles of performer and audience may switch back and forth rapidly as managers interact with each other and their staffs. (ibid. p. 824).

This constant interplay makes the distinctions between performer and audience disappear in a group setting. If we consider group performance a form of art, then we can imagine an aesthetic experience also occurring in a community of people interacting, like in the examples we have already alluded to. In that respect peak performance *emerges* (see Chapter 7) from people interacting, and thus can be neither predicted nor directly controlled.

'Aesthetic muteness' challenges peak experience in groups (Taylor 2002). As discussed in Chapter 1, people in organizations are typically trained to think rather than feel. Extracting feelings about personal issues such as identity and relationships with others can be a delicate and difficult issue. Directly addressing aesthetic concerns such as beauty and per-

	Flow (Csikszentmihalyi 1990)	Timelessness (Mainemelis 2001)	Aesthetic Experience (Sandelands and Buckner 1989; Beardsley 1982)	Peak Experiences in Groups
Level of analysis	Individual	Individual	Individual	Group
Qualities of manifest experience	• Merging of action and awareness • Intense concentration • Sense of heightened control • Forgetting of one's self • Forgetting of time	• Feeling of immersion • Recognition of time distortion • Sense of mastery • Sense of transcendence	• Felt freedom • Detached effect • Active discovery • Wholeness	Flow + Timelessness + Aesthetic experience
Source of experience	Task/Activity	Work	Art	Group performance
Qualities of above source	• Clear goals • Optimally challenging • Immediate feedback • Autotelic	• Clear goals • Optimally challenging • Immediate feedback • Rites of passage	• Boundary • Dynamic tensions • Growth and development • Unresolved possibilities	• Authentic • Spontaneous

Exhibit 11.1 Types of peak experiences
Source: Marotto et al. (2004).

ception may be perceived as soft and disconnected from organizational concerns of efficiency and the bottom line. Discussions of aesthetics certainly make the picture of organizational life somewhat more complex, and strategy practice less tidy and controlled.

Exhibit 11.1 summarizes the theoretical findings of the phenomena discussed above.

To further illustrate some of the peak-like experiences described in this chapter consider the story of TalkCo.

Case: Peak experiences in TalkCo[2]

During the 1990s TalkCo grew from a small local player in the German telecom service industry into a major regional one. As part of the industry's ongoing consolidation in early 2002, TalkCo needed a more international strategy that brought people from different countries together into the growing TalkCo organization, brand and culture. The CEO asked the director of strategy to prepare and implement a new strategy process that would encourage strategists from the acquired organizations to bring forth an innovative, shared strategy. In his words, 'Plot the course and steer the ship' should be the spirit and metaphor of this exercise. The process was initiated in mid-2002.

The head of corporate strategy delegated the task of leading the strategy work to a senior member of his team, who immediately sketched a three-phase, traditional planning process, involving more than 70 planning people from the various businesses. Yet, the project leader questioned this approach. Was there a better way? Should other people be involved too? What should be done in the planning process, and for what purpose? At this stage Johan agreed to design and facilitate a retreat during which the corporate strategy group was invited to develop and share new ideas about how to proceed, given the new organizational and competitive landscape. In the invitation to his colleagues, the project leader set the objective of the retreat to 'develop a coherent view of the upcoming strategy process'. The shared expectation was that anything could happen. The retreat took place in June 2002.

What happened?

What started out as a way to discuss how to design and proceed with the upcoming strategy practice became a deep and introspective conversation about basic values within the strategy group. As the group collaboratively built a representation of the new TalkCo organization, as a way to position the strategy work, people revealed and discussed differences in their views. For instance, one participant argued for a smooth flow-like description, whereas another suggested the organization was more like a political network of personal connections. Eventually, they agreed on an elaborate model showing the organization as both. From here, they began to populate the model with 'key people' such as leaders of functions and units they felt were part of their own 'landscape' as a strategy group. Together they discussed and selected various attributes for each of these key people: for example, whether they were in dark or light colours, or were large or small. Eventually, they also built and placed themselves as individuals representing different skills and values within their unit on the table.

During this work they came to spend much time on representing their immediate boss as protecting an enclosed zone – their group of people. Suddenly their position within the organization looked precarious. As the conversation continued, they felt increasingly under threat from other senior people and they modified the symbol of their boss to have two faces: a live one and a skull – 'the living Karl and the dead Karl'. One person asked if the group could trust him to continue to protect them to champion the strategy work within the organization. Their opinions differed.

Next, they began to focus on what they could contribute as a group to the strategy process. A decisive moment was when one participant challenged what he considered his colleagues' lack of passion for the upcoming strategy work. 'What is our passion here? 'What is our dynamism?' he burst out, while grabbing a bottle of soda and violently shaking then opening it. As the content sprayed over the stunned participants and the construction he exclaimed, 'That is passion! That is dynamism! That's what we need in this strategy process!' Then he calmed down and placed the bottle in the construction. Others joined the theme and readily shared views about their jobs, responsibilities and individual aspirations. The conversation continued with unchanged intensity and, suddenly, it was time to call it a day.

To be continued in Chapter 12 ...

Quick reflection

Like other illustrations in this book this case can be interpreted in many ways. For our purposes in this chapter we highlight the similarities of what unfolded in the TalkCo group with the notions of flow, timelessness and aesthetic experience. We are not sure these people were in flow, except for a brief moment when they were sprayed by soda. Perhaps only the person doing the spraying was. We do think the introspection about their group created the conditions for a qualitative feeling of loss of time. 'Time just went by' as one participant witnessed afterwards. Recall that the timelessness idea ties together personal factors such as intrinsic motivation, task factors such as clear goals and optimal challenges and work environment factors such as autonomy and meaningful work, to account for the manifest experience of timelessness.

The extent to which they shared an aesthetic experience is more difficult to assess. Much of what makes up an aesthetic experience seems to have been in place: the required willingness to invest attention in a visual stimulus; the experience was not taken literally; people immersed into the challenges described and developed a sense of exhilaration from the involvement; afterwards they seem to have felt self-acceptance (not described in the case). The off-site, beautiful and unusual milieu might have generated a sense of harmony that preempted everyday concerns. To the extent these conditions were in place, we also think they shared this experience.

Why are peak experiences important for strategy practice? The instrumental motivation is that peak experiences bring *peak performance*. The answer more in line with the idea of potential benefit, is that it is in peak-like experiences we freely and willingly practise our imagination, construct together with virtuosity and thoroughly enjoy object-mediated communication. If circumstances are stable and we really neither need nor expect a different outcome, who cares? But, when circumstances call for new outcomes and we intentionally want this, creating the context for potential peak experiences may both reinforce and amplify the intricate processes of *Thinking from Within*. Peak experiences are rare but that may say more about the local conditions in organizations and during strategy practices than anything about the people involved. We are all able humans and just need the right conditions to get into the flow, perceive timelessness and truly think what we do is beautiful.

Conclusion

The experiences of flow, timelessness and aesthetic experience are qualitatively similar to stories told by people who engage in practices of *Thinking from Within*. The purpose of this chapter was to reflect on the theoretical explanations of such phenomena, seen as emergent benefits of *Thinking from Within*.

When work is done in a group the experience of flow and timelessness is contingent on an aesthetic experience of others' performance. When we think of the process of *Thinking from Within* as art, we may be closer to understanding why certain groups have peak experiences and others do not. Just as beauty and art can enthral the human spirit, so can work 'evoke and sustain a play of mind at the fringe of awareness' (Sandelands and Buckner 1989: 122). The aesthetic theory forces us to look beyond the technical and functional aspects of organized life and to focus on the sensual, perceptive, communicative and emotional, which since Chapter 1 has been a clear thread throughout this book. If we remove the aesthetic from human interaction, this can only lead to *anaesthesia*, or numbness. Perhaps this lack of feeling is what the BrassCo and TechCo cases illustrate.

Although peak experiences fundamentally occur at an individual level, in our experience and as manifested in the case illustrations throughout this book, we suggest they may also occur at the group level. While we cannot prescribe peak experiences during strategy practice, as already indicated, we can speculate under what conditions they will not emerge. If people are not open to truly listening, watching, feeling and sensing what others are doing, then such peak experiences cannot emerge.

Peak experiences in groups may suddenly arise in even the most mundane and routine of circumstances, not just during strategy practice. When a group of people can seize that moment and be open to their own transformational performance, they may very well have an experience that is deeply meaningful and memorable. *Thinking from Within* creates the conditions for the emergent benefit of peak experiences.

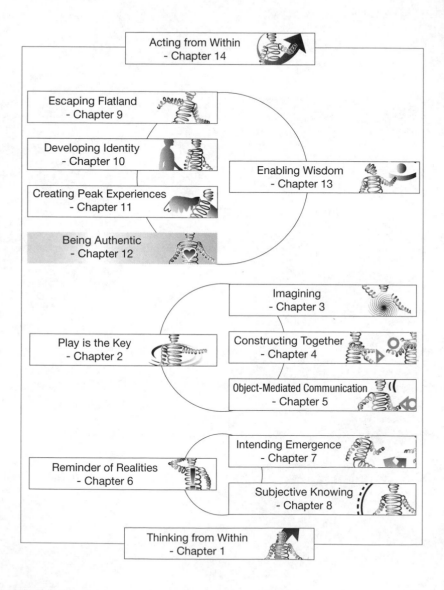

12
Being Authentic

Madeleine Roos and Johan Roos

Introduction

The American 19th century author Ralph Waldo Emerson is known to have said that what lies behind us and what lies before us are tiny matters compared to what lies *within* us. *Thinking from Within* implies that what is said and shown correspond to what is imagined and spontaneously done, which is a way to define authenticity. In metaphorical terms we are authentic when we 'follow our heart'. As discussed in Chapter 1, we agree with David Whyte (1994) on the necessity to also take our inner self seriously at work and on the importance of making 'the heart aroused'.

Thinking from Within is often a profound experience that manifests authenticity or inauthenticity which is an emergent benefit in itself. To put it more strongly, *Thinking from Within* enables authenticity and, our claim is, the more authentic the better. If people try to apply the ideas in this book in inauthentic ways, in our decade of experience with early prototypes and more developed versions of various techniques aimed at *Thinking from Within*, they are likely to be disappointed and disappoint others involved. So, in this chapter we focus on issues of authenticity: we explain what it is, what it means, what it implies and illustrate with examples situations when people were authentic and when they were inauthentic. To this end we go back to some of the previous cases, as well as contribute two new case stories.

To be or not to be authentic

The famous TV-doctor in USA, 'Dr Phil' (McGraw 2001), describes that if the eagerness to please others, for example the boss and important colleagues, is too incongruent with our honest thoughts, or if we seek the additional bliss of entering the 'comfort zone' at the price of rather too many compromises than our true self would really like, we have given up our authentic selves. He goes so far as to state that if we deny ourselves the opportunity to live authentic lives, we create stress that might even shorten our lifespan. In his book *Real Age*, Michael Roizen (1999) calculates how many years a life is shortened by stress deriving from living in a 'cage of fiction' and not in congruence with the authentic self. But it is not just a question of alignment, but also of giving all of what we have in a situation when it is needed; like swearing the oath in court: ' … the whole truth and nothing but the truth … ' To contribute, in boardrooms or courtrooms, we need to tap into our full potential.

However, in order to change anything in our existence we first have to acknowledge what it is we need and want to change. An example of how *Thinking from Within* effectively may help in bringing to the surface such recognition and subsequent acknowledgement is PackCo in Chapter 7. While constructing together and engaging in object-mediated communication the four managers became aware of patterns of actions in their organization that traditional flipchart-based discussions had difficulties in showing. In their representation of the company in its landscape, the participants had portrayed some connections as straightforward and based on common sense, whereas other connections were seen as more or less weird. In the process, participants made statements like: 'This is absurd! We have to change this.' The emotional intensity of the conversation about contradictions and absurdities sparked by the model the four had built led the CEO to ask the group: 'Are we just like the dance band on the Titanic, trying to keep spirits high after the ship has hit the iceberg?' Encouraged by such an eye-opening experience, ideas came up in the following discussion that no one had dared to explore in previous strategy conversations.

The TalkCo story in Chapter 11 illustrates how insights and subsequent acknowledgment of important issues were achieved on day one. As we will see below the accomplishments were seriously threatened by lack of authenticity on day two. Still, the positive spirit of day one, especially represented by a project leader who 'followed his heart', led the way forward to a imaginative outcome for the changing circumstances.

Case: Turn-around with TalkCo[1]

Recall that on the first day a new kind of strategy process had been explored which included only a few of the 70 people identified as 'planning' staff from the company's many business units and instead involved a range of people from business operations and functions not usually invited to take part in corporate strategy practices, including brand, culture, customer service and HR. A variety of symbolic and colourful materials represented the more diverse people they now collectively thought should be involved.

As they described the story of their model, they emphasized the need to involve people rather than to impose a strategy conceived without them. Henceforth, the discussion centred on how to proceed to make this happen and was particularly sensitive, as it implied that the project leader had to cancel the existing plan, including dates already set for a number of meetings for the 70 strategy planners. He also had to reassess the already approved €700,000 budget.

Day two

During the morning of the second day events took a dramatic turn. One of the strategy group members, who had excused himself the previous day, suddenly reappeared. As a courtesy to the new arrival, the project leader proudly asked one of his colleagues to share their new 'story'. The person selected reacted very awkwardly, as if reluctant to share the meaning of the construction. He visibly struggled to depersonalize the story and even physically distanced himself from the model by not pointing to its various elements, as they had all done the previous day. After a short while, the newcomer interrupted the appointed speaker in a deprecatory manner. He was very critical about the content of what had been said, especially the idea of involving more and other people. Strategy, the newcomer was arguing, 'had to be done by a team of experts, not by involving a bunch of operational managers.' At one stage he also said: 'We need a new mission? Well, just give me 15 min in another room, and I will write it just like I wrote the last one.'

Moreover, he also used some of the group's vocabulary in a derisive way – for example the notion of 'being a missionary of strategy' when going out to operational units, became the 'missionary position'. These interventions and interruptions caused neither laughs nor complicit grins among the people in the original group. On the contrary, their body language indicated great discomfort. The ambience had shifted dramatically and the participants clearly felt awkward.

The project leader was still convinced about the benefits of staying with what had been decided the previous day, but he also realized that a traditional approach may have some advantages. Acknowledging that a double approach was the best way to acknowledge all facets of the strategy process he stood up after the 'presentation' and, pointing to various features of the model they had built, told the rest of the group that he had changed his mind about what the right way forward was. As project leader he would use his authority to cancel the already planned strategy process, adding that this was a risk he was willing to take. The bulk of the work ahead, he explained, would be to 'identify and invite key people from a variety of units and functions, beyond strategy, to be part of a more bottom-up process of strategy making.'

Looking at the newcomer he also said that there was value in the kind of top-down approach they had previously used and invited him to contribute in whatever way he could. Then, he thanked everybody and ended the retreat a few hours before schedule. People were visibly shaken. On his way back to the office after the retreat the project leader summarized his views: 'I am shocked about the split in our strategy group. I knew we all weren't on the same page, but this ... ' He added: 'I am glad it came to the surface so that I can deal with it.' In interviews immediately after the event and a few weeks later, other participants said it was one of the more memorable strategy discussions they had ever had.

Both these stories illustrate how *Thinking from Within* can vigorously assist participants in visualizing and acknowledging hidden patterns in their organization. However, the following example will show that *Thinking from Within* did not always reach all the way through to such desired effects.

Case: Lacking courage in GadgetCo[2]

'I cannot understand it,' the CEO told Johan during a meeting, 'I have been explaining and motivating the strategy over and over again. Yet, it is like they do not hear me. Why don't they do something to move us ahead?' His second in command, the COO, nodded and added: 'Just think of how many days we have been touring various sites to present and take questions about our strategy. Was it all wasted?'

A few years earlier the CEO of GadgetCo had recruited a new COO to take over the daily operations and eventually the firm. The remaining part of the leadership team consisted of ten senior executives with distinct functional or business unit responsibilities. Six months earlier the CEO had asked the COO to help him develop and advocate a new company strategy, in which the company would work in a different way, while remaining true to its vision and mission. In a typical top-down manner the COO, supported by the CEO, had 'communicated' this strategy to the rest of the leadership team, and in turn to the rest of the organization.

At its core, this strategy outlined the goals and actions that both leaders felt were necessary to make the company more adaptive to increasing competition and new technological innovations. It was also intended to inject more life into an organization, traumatized by a major cost-cutting campaign following two years of declining results and significant layoffs. As the new strategy trickled through the organizations, the results did not improve and the leadership duo became increasingly frustrated.

At this stage Johan agreed with the CEO to stage a retreat for him, the COO and a few staff members of his choice, during which they would take a fresh look at the company and its strategy. If it were to lead to new insights, the CEO would be prepared to follow it up with a similar retreat for the additional leadership team of ten. The retreat took place during November 2004 in a comfortable hunting lodge a few hours' drive from the headquarters.

What happened?

The CEO took the lead in constructing a representation of the company in its business landscape, but was soon challenged by the two staff members. The CEO had especially asked them before the retreat not to withhold their views. After a few hours of gradually depicting how they saw the realities of the organization, the group centred on three issues. Firstly there was the 'difficult and dangerous crossing' the organization was currently making, represented by a lava stream. The problem, they said, was that too many people still remained on 'the other side' of the bridge together with some 'dead elephants', which represented parts of the organization that were not yet restructured. However, they praised the parts that had already made the crossing. These people, they said, were both enthused and forward looking, and some were even 'running so fast the rest of the organization cannot keep up'.

Secondly, they spent much time representing and discussing the huge supply chain, which they felt was still lagging behind in its evolution. In their model, although the 'wrong values' were gradually being dismantled, a ghost was lurking behind the wall ready to appear when things went sour (see Exhibit 12.1 in the plate section).

Thirdly, there was the problem of the relationship between the leadership duo and the management team (MT) of ten. The representation put the two leaders physically above and somewhat detached from the MT group. The COO insisted, 'the MT members are gathered around a table underneath our strategic priorities.' During this part of the process the COO took the lead in the discussion. He elaborated extensively on internal barriers and infighting, represented by black bricks, between MT executives. He said that these people had a tendency to 'pass the buck' along, meaning they did not act responsibly. He also talked about a 'cold wind', represented by a polar bear, blowing among MT members, which symbolized politicking and infighting. Finally, he placed a whip in the hand of the figure representing himself in the construction and jokingly said that it could be one of two things: a conductor's baton or a whip.

After this introspection the focus changed to GadgetCo's business environment. Despite four people co-constructing, only a handful of elements appeared on the table, including a subcontractor in India, portrayed as both friend and foe, since they were fearful this company would steal their intellectual property. Another player was a major software company, with whom they had developed very good personal relationships. A third player was their largest supplier of raw materials for the manufacturing process. They had a particular problem agreeing on how to portray this supplier to show that it was both a dear friend and a cause for possible concern, because of environmental issues regarding raw materials. Only then did these executives add a representation of the customers, followed by very simplistic symbols of a few competitors and alliance partners.

The COO was now challenged to give further meaning to and make sense of the largest customer, a retail chain. What did it really look like according to him? The CEO had used a simple plastic brick with the same colour as the customer's logotype. Encouraged by the CEO, the COO reluctantly went away to make a richer representation. After a few minutes he returned with a plate with just the customer's name written on it in bricks. 'This is a sufficiently good representation of them,' he said in a way that prevented any further comments from anyone in the room. The difference between this simplistic model and a much more elaborate one built by the CEO was striking. On the whole, the group spent much more time discussing the firm than the world outside it.

At the end of the retreat all four participants politely said they thought it was a 'useful' process. What they found new and insightful were the many connections that they had with external players and a few ideas for additions were offered. As a consequence the CEO gave the COO the task of reviewing the scope and nature of these connections. The two staff members did not offer any views during this debrief and instead took careful notes about what their two bosses said.

While the COO seemed to act according to his true self, we suspect that the other three participants were not authentic, especially from the perspective of not giving their all in a situation where it was needed. During the analogous workshop in PackCo (Chapter 7) the atmosphere was creative all the way. In the example of TalkCo it was creative and positive on day one and only turned awkward on day two, something that could be saved through a spontaneous and imaginative intervention by the project leader. But in the example of GadgetCo, we have to realize that there was never any experience of peaks (see Chapter 11) and limited imagination and spontaneity that could help in the necessary progress to develop new outcomes for changing circumstances. In addition, a similar experience is also described in the continuation of the BrassCo story (Chapter 6). Despite their attempts to *Think from Within* the existing roles and positions prevailed and constrained. They stayed in their 'fictional cages' of prescribed thinking (see Exhibit 1.1 in Chapter 1) and did not come close to practising their imagination or making way for the spontaneity of their wisdom. Instead they continuously glanced at the COO who, seemingly authentically, continued his autocratic ways.

What can we do to enhance the passing of the threshold that sometimes separates participants from their individual imagination and spontaneity as well as simultaneously strengthen the dynamics of the group? Recall that *Thinking from Within* is an example of a creative arts process and shares many traits with creative arts therapies (see Chapter 2 for the theoretical foundations, Chapter 4 for more on the process and Chapter 5 for theories on physical media) so consequently we return to this vital source for further inspiration. Just like creative arts therapists have found it beneficial to include other media in their ongoing activity, without losing its original character but rather *enhancing its depth and benefits* (for example Blatner 1996; Moreno 1999), we see analogous opportunities to enrich the media dimension of *Thinking from Within* with conceptual media in general and non-scripted dramatic techniques especially.

Drama therapy and psychodrama

For thousands of years drama has been used in healing rituals. Drama therapy is the heir to the ancient shamanic traditions of healing through ritual drama (Casson 1984, 1997–8). In the 20th century many creative workers rediscovered its therapeutic values and developed the related methods of drama therapy and psychodrama. For many people the word drama is connected with theatre, but there is a difference. Drama is a personal experience (the word comes from the Greek *drao*: 'I do' or 'struggle') and theatre is communicating the experience to others (the word comes from the Greek *theatron*: 'a place for seeing/showing').

Drama therapy and psychodrama both employ drama as therapeutic methods but in slightly different ways; for example spontaneity and imagination are even more emphasized in psychodrama (see for example

Blatner 1996). They are not, as in theatre, specialized skills that people can or cannot do. Anyone can role-play.

Drama has the potential to 'arouse the heart'. As early as 440 BC, in Sophocles' play *Antigone*, the chorus sang a hymn to Dionysus invoking his 'swift healing', *'katharsios'* (Sophocles 1994). The Greek word *katharsis* comes from *kathairein* (to purge) and from *katharos* (pure). Aristotle in his Poetics recognized catharsis as an effect of tragedy (Fyfe 1967). At that time catharsis was focused on pity and fear (Dayton 2005). The catharsis that originally was thought of as an emotional purging or cleansing, experienced by an ancient Greek audience at the end of a tragedy, has in modern psychotherapy come to imply a release of ideas, thoughts and repressed material from the unconscious, accompanied by an emotional response and relief (Breuer and Freud 1895; Malchiodi 1998; Dayton 2005). The value of drama is manifested in the theatres, operas, musicals, movies and other shows we enjoy as often we can (see Exhibit 12.2 in the plate section for an example).

Origins of psychodrama

While drama therapy in general has its roots in ancient Greek culture, psychodrama is rooted in multiple traditions of psychoanalysis and role-play as well as Greek drama and further developed within the tradition of humanistic psychology. It was founded in the 1920s by Jacob Levy Moreno (1889–1974), an MD, not a psychoanalyst, but in his work as a doctor he took a great interest in contemporary Freudian theories.

Educated at the University of Vienna Medical School, where Sigmund Freud lectured, Moreno believed that he started where Freud left off. While Freud interpreted his patients' dreams, Moreno said to Freud when they met in Vienna in 1912: 'You analyze their dreams, I try to give them courage to dream again' (Moreno 1946: 5–6). Both men agreed on the importance for a healthier future of achieving catharsis, with its successive emotional relief, but in comparing his work with Freud on how to approach the patients, he found himself at the opposite end of the scale. Like some of Freud's less orthodox followers at that time, Moreno also believed in the positive forces of the inner resources of the human mind and that a symbolic communication from within, via a creative process that was healing in itself, was beneficial to achieving a healthier future. He saw spontaneity and creativity as propelling forces in human progress and advocated his ideas on how people could experience catharsis from *acting out* their issues in a creative group process of role-play, instead of just talking about them from the traditional, Freudian perspective.

In 1921, still in Vienna, the concept of psychodrama was born and only a few years later came the first publication on 'spontaneity theatre' (Moreno 1923). Later Moreno published *Psychodrama* in three volumes, the first alone and the two following with his wife Zerka, who also has had a great influence on the development of psychodrama (Moreno 1934, 1946; Moreno and Moreno 1959, 1969). A pioneer in group psychotherapy, in the 1930s he also came up with a technique to measure internal group relations called sociometry, as well as a different approach to group drama called sociodrama, in which one does not address personal issues but roles that participants have in common. The three methods are closely related. We do not exclude sociodrama and sociometry as future sources of inspiration for *Thinking from Within*, but in this chapter we will focus on psychodrama, because it emphasizes the importance of the personal deep experiences in each participant, which can happen when people think from within.

Using psychodrama

The basic idea in psychodrama is that it is only when individuals have been given the chance to express themselves in a *subjective, spontaneous, imaginative* and *authentic* manner that the time is ripe to merge the group's individual views of an issue into a new pattern that can only emerge at the group level. In this manner, the finding of the strong interrelation between what happens within the individual and within group will be intentionally considered. Dayton (2005: 51) writes: 'A catharsis that is successful within an individual should have the effect of increasing the spontaneity of the entire group, which should then reduce both the individual and group-dynamic disturbances.' Although far from structured as psychodrama this appears similar to what happened in the story of the five business unit leaders in the ConglomerateCo anecdote in Chapter 11 and some of the other examples of peak experience discussed in that chapter.

In psychodrama no audience or traditional performance is expected.[2] Beginning with the warm-up, all participants are engaged in the play as *protagonist, director, auxiliary roles* or *spectators* who can be engaged in the play at any given time. The protagonist is at the centre of a psychodrama with a concrete situation. There is the stage set by the director in collaboration with the protagonist, based on the initial 'psychodramatic interview' with the protagonist. Open questions are asked in order to clarify and illuminate what might be going on in the upcoming scene or within the mind of the protagonist. What comes out will guide the director's intuition on how to guide the protagonist to unfold the problem by building up a spontaneous, intuitive and imaginative drama around the protagonist. Auxiliary figures and characters are subsequently added and different dramatic techniques are employed, like for example *role reversal* (taking another person's role), which is often carried out with frequent role changes back and forth to increase the understanding of the character of the portrayed persons, things, animals, phenomena and so on; anyone or anything can be given a voice in psychodrama. To play *the double* is a way of clarifying and strengthening somebody in his/her role by acting as a duplicate of the role one is the double for; and this person considers the statements made by the double as part of him/herself. It is thus of extreme importance not only that the director proceeds with care, but that the whole situation is one of trust and safety.

In *the soliloquy* (monologue), the protagonist can drop out of the scene for a moment and soliloquize about what is going on in his/her inner world. With *the mirror* technique, the protagonist can see him/herself as if in a mirror, which also can be played with a stand-in for the protagonist allowing him/her to see from the outside how the scene progresses (see Moreno 1946; Moreno and Moreno 1959, 1969; Blatner 1996; Dayton 2005).

To heighten the expression of emotion and awareness the director may use a rich palette of other techniques such as *asides, videotape playback, behind-your-back, audience feed-back, chorus, non-verbal projection, future projection* (for example Blatner 1996; Blatner and Blatner 1997).

First person

A very important basic trait of psychodrama is that all roles are always played in *first person* form, 'I am … ,' which enables the participants to fully take on and live the roles they play. As mentioned, the roles can be of any kind, for example oneself from another perspective, another person (existing or non-existing), an event, a thing, an idea, a thought, a feeling, a state of mind. Thus, the reality as it is in the presented situation is not the limit, but the reality that exists within the person(s) playing, which Moreno called *surplus reality* (Moreno 1965; Moreno et al. 2000) is of vast importance for the creative and spontaneous experience. It gives the players the possibility of exploring 'what if?' questions (Blatner 1996; Dayton 2005). It also gives the participants the opportunity to think from within in the most truthful manner as *the inner authentic reality often exceeds the outer imposed reality*, and thus has to be expressed metaphorically in a way the ambiguity of play (Chapter 2) can convey.

The technique of identifying with a role, as oneself or as an external identity in role reversal, is a powerful way to develop the capacity for understanding others, other parts of oneself and other things that matter to the situation at hand. Moreno implied that because role reversal is the operational method for building the capacity for imagination and empathy, he felt that the activity of extending oneself empathically was an ethical obligation (Blatner 2000).

Chronicles from Within

Role-play with role reversal and double, in the present as well as in surplus reality, can also be carried out in writing, a psychodramatic technique called *psychodramatic journaling* (Dayton 2005). It can be an activity in itself or combined with educational exercises and counselling. Based on this concept we have developed a tool we call *Chronicle from Within*, which is the participants' written reports of their experiences, in terms of both process and content, from practising *Thinking from Within*. Our preliminary experiments suggest that this additional application fulfils busy managers' need to obtain ('flatland') 'take home values'. In addition, we have seen that it fills the gap between the imaginative thinking and spontaneous doing during an intensive experiential retreat or workshop, and the more routine-like analytical practice the participants meet in their daily management practice. In other words, it connects the practice from *Thinking from Within* with the more 'prescribed' practices in organizations.

Dangers in psychodrama

There are dangers to be avoided when working dramatically with deep and personal issues. One of the contemporary authorities on psychodrama and related methods, Blatner (1996) puts words to our concern that psychodrama, which can, when used carefully by trained therapists, work wonders with many people, also presents pitfalls that have to be considered and avoided.

One risk is *pathological spontaneity*, which often comes as an prescribed reaction from the director, or possibly a co-player, and which might at first sight seem like true spontaneity, but in reality is mere countertransference (that is, the reaction relates not to the ongoing session but to a different experience within the director or co-player) expressed in an impulsive way. Impulsivity is the opposite of creative spontaneity. Impulsive behaviour can lead to chaos, wherein a pain-filled inner world surfaces in action. It is thus a novel response but not right for the situation. Another risk is *stereotyped spontaneity*, which is an adequate response without novelty and creativity. Unlike the two above, true spontaneity is an adequate, authentic and novel response (Dayton 2005).

Respecting the above concerns, Moreno early encouraged a cross-disciplinary view on the benefits of psychodrama (Blatner 1996). Blatner continues to describe the benefits of psychodramatic techniques in meeting the challenges of developing a broader imagination with regard to the implications of industry's actions in contemporary society as well as the building of psychological-interpersonal sophistication in management. Based on our experiments, we have found that role-play should be an integral part of practising *Thinking from Within*. We have followed the advice from experienced psychodramatists to employ selected dramatic techniques, which we find appropriate for our focus on non-clinical issues.

In our experience many managers find it difficult to overcome the initial threshold of daring to let go of the distance and 'objective' neutrality they have been taught for so long to keep up. Thus, we were amazed by the smiles of relief and emotional presence and engagement once they felt as one with what they individually or as a group had constructed. During the subsequent sharing, we learnt how people said they could never again distance themselves too far from their construction-based roles, but rather felt the urge to take the necessary responsibility and commitment to follow through in understanding, as well as in future actions, on the insights gained in the process.

Quick reflection

We have taken part in and closely observed the development of *Thinking from Within* from its infancy in the mid-1990s. Over the years, we have tried many versions, used many kinds of physical media with predominantly very positive results. Yet, when we integrated dramatic techniques the quality of the process reached significantly higher levels. Moreover, we began to see more often the emergent benefits described and illustrated in previous chapters. Let us illustrate with a recent example.

Case: Go deep with UtilityCo

A large European utility company asked us to help develop the 'strategic thinking' of a group of senior leaders, especially in the area of post-acquisition integration. The company was very successful and had recently gone through a series of large and small acquisitions, some of which they considered successful and others more 'ongoing'. We split the leaders into two parallel groups, and guided them through the same process.

During the warm-up phase we first practised creative movements, using their bodies in new ways for such discussions. Then we practised making and sharing stories, which emerged from co-construction and object-mediated communication. More than this, in line with psychodrama, we spent much time practising role-playing and speaking in the first person, that is, taking on the role of an individually and/or co-constructed object. After initial resistance and discomfort most of them eventually learnt the process and we embarked on the action phase.

During this phase we asked them to describe their organization, and to do so in the first person. Here are the two stories, visually depicted in Exhibits 12.3 and 12.4 in the plate section.

Group 1

My heart is in [the home country]. I have a chain inside, which connects my different parts, but the chain is too short so it does not connect all of them. I have a periscope to look for opportunities, but currently the glass is foggy, so I am not sure what I am seeing. I really like that my various parts are making good progress in their own way. Formally and officially, I am fully 'integrated', but in reality I am full of holes and gaps. This really concerns me. I need to grow the chain some way to close these gaps before they cause damage to the rest of me. Looking outside I must satisfy customers more than I do now. In fact, I need to remove the barrier between the customers and me, but I am not sure how.

Group 2

I have an outer and inner world. I am firmly anchored to my monopolistic and 'fat cat' past [pointing at a big red block], which I would like to see reduced in size. Internally, I consist of three regional parts. At my centre I have my rational, technical knowledge [green soft apple]. From that core I have built many bridges to my various internal parts, but they look different. Specifically, I have a solid bridge to Region A, a thin line to Region 2, and a complex structure connecting Region C, which among the mess consists of a small shining bridge to country X. This unevenness doesn't feel right.

In my outer world I see a prosperous future in Europe, but the financial markets constrain me. I really try to treat my customers well, but there is a barrier between us [fence]. Just outside me, and next to the past I want to shy away from, is complicated political machinery [different wheels], which is spinning around in strange ways. One of the wheels, the most imposing one, is the political system in our home country.

A range of energy issues, like alternative fuels, which I think I understand, circumvents me. Yet, what I cannot really comprehend are the many 'soft' issues [pink mushy brain], like attitudes among young people. I am afraid these issues, which I cannot fully grasp, are incompatible with my own technical knowledge and attitudes. Look, I'll show you [illustrates this by moving the pink soft brain and fails to connect it with the green apple inside].

Overall, I am concerned about my ability to better connect my inner and outer worlds. I really want to rid myself from my past [illustrates this by removing the chains to it], and open up towards my customers [illustrates this by removing the barrier].

After Group 1's presentation not much happened. Early on during Group 2's presentation, however, people in the first group said 'wow', 'incredibly good', and 'that's fantastic', causing proud smiles in Group 2. At the end of their presentation all participants were either laughing or smiling cheerfully. Following the end, people broke into spontaneous applause. People closed in and began to repeat the moves made by the presenter, like moving the pink brain and trying to connect it to the hard, green apple, or fiddling with the 'spinning wheels' of the political system. And, they did not want to stop doing this. They also prompted their colleagues in Group 2 for more input, calling on them to explain parts of the story over and over again, even the most miniscule parts of their construction.

From here they discussed what their stories revealed about their officially successful post-acquisition strategy, zooming in on the 'gaps' and 'bridges' presented in both models and how this related to 'integration' issues.

In our view, the conversation engaged all of them to authentically put on the table several unresolved issues. As indicated by psychodrama theory and captured in the *Thinking from Within* concept, role-play can bring forth the reality that exists within, that is, what Moreno called surplus reality (see above). In this case example we observed the importance of the surplus reality within the participants, as captured in the constructions and vivid stories in the form of 'I am ... ' which turned the object-mediated communication into an imaginative, spontaneous and very authentic experience.

Moreno described how role-play created the context for empathy. We also observed how their role-play improved these leaders' capacity for understanding one another, the organization and the 'integration' issues at hand. Their concluding remarks suggest a higher level of understanding than before:

Our push towards a unified integration is too much for the organization. We need more local adaptation of our initiatives.

We lack a common business language on the operational level.

We need to engage middle managers in strategic, not just operational issues.

Integration should be a natural choice, not as imposed is we do it now.

We need to create the context in which integration is naturally seen as an opportunity, not a risk of losing one's job; we need integration 'from within'.

On a more subtle level we also observed how these managers treated one another with more respect after the exercise. Gone was any trace of early harsh comments and instead they remained in the room helping one another to gather papers and personal items that had become scattered around.

During our debriefing, all of them testified about the impact of this new experience. Comments indicated authenticity ('I was more honest'), precision ('I was forced to be more precise'), initial discomfort then feeling good ('I was terrified at first but when I let go it felt great'; 'I have been taught to never be subjective, but I liked it'). Most of them said they were taken aback by the profound impact of allowing themselves to be subjective and take on a different role from within, for example, 'I just couldn't distance myself from what I talked about.' It was altogether an unusual and engaging experience in this context.

We have repeated the drama-inspired approach to *Thinking from Within* in many different companies and situations and seen the same pattern of enhanced authenticity over and over again, for example OilCo in Chapter 1. Psychodramatic methods can escalate the experiential process to a more authentic level of imaginative, spontaneous and, thus, emotional encounters. Not only does this approach facilitate a more productive exploration of problems in psychotherapy, education, personal development, counselling, and religion (Blatner 1996; Gershoni 2003), as we have described and illustrated in this chapter it can be applied in the serious context of organizations and strategy practice.

Why is authenticity important in strategy practice? When we care about people's personal views and stances there is nothing like it. *Thinking from Within* both calls for and enables authenticity. If you need further motivation we suggest you review again some of the case illustrations in this book.

Conclusion

Despite the past decades of increased acceptance of subjective and personal values, it is clear that rationality and pure intellectual reason from the Enlightenment (see Chapter 1) still set many standards. We do by no means deny the necessity of such values at times, but we advocate the obligation to complement the strong impulses from the outside with the inner imaginative and genuine spontaneity that comes from being authentic.

In this chapter we have described and illustrated how object mediated communication, which constitutes the base for *Thinking from Within*, can be significantly enhanced with the use of dramatic techniques. We have, however, also noted that the subjectivity it implies can at first be a challenge to take on for managers trained in praising rational and objective thinking. Like musicians and actors, sometimes the more trained we are the more we seem to be dependent on interpreting compositions made by others, perhaps even seeking to 'resurrect' the composer, or the 'boss'. 'Prescribed thinking' leaves only marginal room for our own views, at the expenditure of our ability to improvise spontaneously. Our formal training and institutionalized behaviour in organizations do not naturally promote *Thinking from Within* with its play-based facets of imagination, ethics and intentional emergence (see Chapter 2).

Blatner (1996) said that action approaches are good not just for people with problems but also for those who tend to over-intellectualize their experiences. We would like to add, 'like managers in general, and managers practising strategy in particular.' Once the timidity and hesitation is overcome with the help of a competent facilitator and in a safe and secure environment, which respects the vulnerability that comes with opening up our protective shell to the vast resources of imagination and spontaneity, we benefit from the true authentic self hidden deep inside each and every one of us. This is *Thinking from Within* in practice.

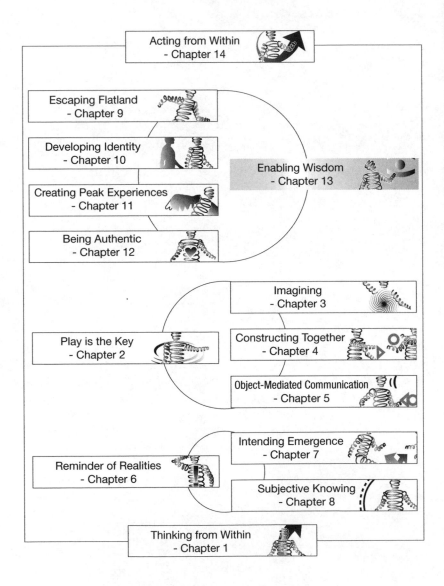

13
Enabling Wisdom
Johan Roos

Introduction

From its early development many years ago, it was clear that practising *Thinking from Within* changed the way participants saw the world they created during the session. Participants expressed their engagement and enthusiasm in terms of understanding of and commitment to the issues explored, but also sometimes seemed to become more aware of others and the potential impact on such others. In Chapter 12 we reported how dramatic techniques took such benefits to new heights of quality.

More than compelling, three-dimensional constructions and associated communication, peak experiences, commitment and authenticity, the overarching emergent benefit of *Thinking from Within* is to make way for the spontaneity of our wisdom. When we are wise we are always a little warmed-up, like in the metaphor the 'iron is always hot', so that when we face the unexpected, we take the 'right' actions and make the 'right' decisions. At this stage we are ready to develop new outcomes when changing circumstances call for it.

To reach the state of continuous warm-up we need to over and over again go through the process of *Thinking from Within* until no new and unexpected information can rock our stability and throw us into impulsive behaviour. When we are wise we use our inner potential of imagination and spontaneity to size up novel situations, make good decisions and take competent actions. We do not engage in mindless execution for the sake of just taking action. With increased wisdom we reduce the risk of doing the same thing over, and over, and over again, while, for some reason, expecting a different outcome. The purpose of this chapter is to shed light on what wisdom is and how *Thinking from Within* nurtures this habit.

First I describe the concept of wisdom as it has evolved over the past two and a half millennia, with a particular emphasis on Aristotle's definition. Second, I describe how *Thinking from Within* cultivates wisdom because it is a multimodal rather than solely intellectual experience; because the constructed artifacts can play a crucial role in helping articulate and express people's value judgements; and because dramatic techniques for the object-mediated communication put the storyteller at the centre of action. Finally, I discuss how wisdom developed and expressed by management teams can be manifested in simple guiding principles within the frame of a 'chronicle from within'.

The concept of wisdom

Psychologist Robert Sternberg (2003: 3) opens his book on wisdom by saying, 'To understand wisdom fully and correctly probably requires more wisdom than any of us have', and I agree. A concept with considerable intellectual history and many evolutionary trails, wisdom enjoys a wealth of scholarly interpretations of what it means and implies in practice. Popular culture often presents it as wise elderly men with long white beards and hair like Albus Dumbledore in *Harry Potter* and the wizard Gandalf in *The Lord of the Rings* (see Exhibit 13.1). Even the mature images of Albert Einstein, Charles Darwin and Abraham Lincoln and could play these roles. In addition to the generic representation of God, Christian history prominently features the three 'wise men' precisely in

Exhibit 13.1 A wise man?

this way. Another acknowledged wise man, Mahatma Ghandi may not have had the same hairy features but was perhaps the wisest of all men. In the same line of thinking I have met several women who I consider wise and who don't look like any of these old men.

Exceptional self-knowledge, understanding of others, a broad outlook, interpersonal skills, practical experience, sagacity, judgement and reasoning ability are just a few of the terms used to capture what wisdom is.[1] Some argue that wisdom is an advanced stage of intellectual development; that is a personal and rewarding experience from pure intellectual reflection. Some even go as far as to say that it is a rare gift to some selected philosophers who are concerned with questions more than answers – which leaves nothing for the rest of us.

Others claim that wisdom is a virtue guiding our actions so that we can be more conscious about how to improve our lives. Exemplifying this view, Jacob Levy Moreno argued the necessity of going back on the life-stage again and again until we have trained our imaginative and intuitive spontaneity to reach the level of wisdom (see Dayton 2005). Yet others claim wisdom to be the basic mechanics of information processing, even contingent on genetic differences. Despite the different views, scholars all seem to agree that wise people have exceptional insight into life matters based on good judgement, and that this is rare.

Good judgement implies a fundamental ethical dimension in wisdom, which is embodied in character and manifested through habits. Wise people seem to have the ability to combine and balance technical, practical and self-reflective, values-based knowledge. Scholars also seem to agree that wisdom potentially, but not necessarily, matures and grows with age. Hence, wise men may have 'grey beards' but not all elderly men are wise, and some wise women may frown on this cliché.

Intellectual heritage

Some of the early Greek dialogues contain the first known records of the concept of wisdom (and Socrates et al. are indeed often portrayed as elderly grey men with white beards). These records reflect how different aspects of life require different types of wisdom in general. Aristotle's (1962) categories developed in his *Nicomachean Ethics* may be particularly useful to grasp the meaning of wisdom, especially vis-à-vis related concepts. In this treatise he claimed that natural scientific knowledge (Gr. *episteme*) seeks to understand the necessary laws and principles for things in the natural world. This is knowledge about principles or laws that do not change, but hold by necessity to eternity. His claim is an intellectual cornerstone for modern traditions of inquiry also in some of the social sciences, for instance the views of the world (ontology) discussed in Chapter 7 and the view of knowledge and knowing (epistemology) discussed in Chapter 8.

A second category from Aristotle is the ambiguous intelligence, which he described as cunning (Gr. *metis*), which seeks not truth but personal advantage at the expense of the well-being of others (see Detienne and Vernant 1978). Distinct from the knowledge of natural scientists, the philosopher Aristotle said this is the knowledge that military generals use when they wage war, politicians use when they seek to win arguments, and doctors use to fight ill health. The story of Odysseus returning from Troy to Ithaca represents an idealized version of this form of knowledge. His entire journey magnificently displays example after example of how he cunningly sized up and spontaneously coped with unexpected dangers and arrived just in time to save his lonely wife from increasingly desperate suitors. Sure, most of his crew died but Odysseus-the-cunning-hero survived. While necessary for survival, Aristotle argues that cunning alone is not appropriate to govern the state (Gr. *polis*), because it may encourage both deception and corruption in pursuit of self-advantage. Aristotle's words still seem remarkably wise today, in light of continuous scandals in corporate and governmental life.

Wisdom for everyday readiness

Many researchers have argued that wisdom is needed when human knowing is characterized by uncertainty (for example, Kitchener 1983; Taranto 1989). The argument is straightforward: routines and well-structured problems do not call for great wisdom. It is when we reach the limits of our personal knowledge and knowing that we rely on our wisdom to guide our actions and decisions away from routinized, deductive analytical thinking (or impulsive behaviour) towards imagination and spontaneity. Thus, as Socrates is known to have argued, wise people are aware of their own ignorance.

Aristotle judged the *social* world too complex and unpredictable to be known with any natural scientific certainty. Thus, in uncertain times we cannot bet only on *episteme*. Known to be generally sceptical about using the goals of an action to justify its means, he no longer believed that *metis* alone promoted the 'good life' (Gr. *eudaimonia*) that ensured stability in society. Thus, from an Aristotelian perspective neither natural scientific knowledge nor cunning intelligence was sufficient to understand and improve organized life. The 'best' course of action simply cannot be reduced to an algorithm, nor can we rely on individuals seeking competitive advantage only for themselves. The solution in ancient Greece was to cultivate the governing elite's habits of thinking and doing so that they were able to make good decisions and do the *right* things in everyday life, especially when they faced uncertainty and vagueness. Aristotle called this ability, embodied in character and manifested in habit, *phronesis*.

In between natural science and cunning intelligence, where explanation and prediction do not work and where our cunning intelligence is not sufficient, Aristotle defined *phronesis* as the virtuous habit of making decisions and taking actions that serve the common good: 'a true and reasoned state of capacity to act with regard to the things that are good or bad for man'.[2] We can review how various choices might influence others, but when we think from a *wise* standpoint we add on the dimension of what is good for the community and then reflect on how we best reach that good.

To do this we ought to have a broad and deep understanding of what is good for humankind and we need the ability to make judgements accordingly. Aristotle used the metaphor of a 'good eye' to illustrate wise people's ability to identify certain situations as worthy of action (in light of what is 'good') and then move ahead, decide and act positively. The basis for such actions is *thus thoughtful deliberation in light of the common good and moral sensitivity in everyday life.* In this light wisdom can be seen as an intrinsically ethical habit. All our actions and decisions have a moral dimension and the ones we (have to) make spontaneously manifest our values and put our wisdom to the test.

In turn, this also suggests an affective dimension since our emotions influence how we interpret situations: 'right readings of situations are often only possible when we have certain feelings, whether those emotions are compassion, anger, love, or revulsion' (Fowlers 2003: 418). The emotional dimensions for wisdom are also prominent in, for example, psychodrama, where the exercising of spontaneity comes from the players opening up in order for their true inner selves to access the rich human source of emotions. When we 'follow our heart' we draw strongly on our authentic emotions to make wise decisions, which in turn feed back to our emotional depths for evaluation of decisions. Thus, our emotional reactions also manifest, or indicate, the moral dimensions of the situation at hand. For example, we usually feel good when we have made the 'right' decision. For most of us the opposite works too. Similarly, when we suppress our emotions, that is, reducing our authentic selves, we risk also suppressing what we perceive.

Everyday strategic preparedness

In our book *Everyday Strategic Preparedness,*[3] Matt Statler and I discuss how and why wisdom, especially *phronesis*, is particularly important in organizational circumstances of ambiguity and uncertainty. When our view of the world (organization and environment) shifts from static to dynamic (see Chapter 7), and when our ways of knowing shift from the objective and pre-given to the subjective and constructed (see Chapter 8), we face more situations in which our natural science breaks down and our cunning intelligence is not necessarily appropriate. When we stretch our thinking towards the 'unimaginable' and our doing towards the 'impossible' the risk we accept is based on the (emotionally laden) value judgements of our wisdom. It is precisely when we are in doubt that we *spontaneously* need to do the 'good' and 'right' rather than the 'bad' and 'wrong' thing, and hope for others do so too. This is the reason why the Aristotelian notion of *phronesis* holds a key to how everyday strategic preparedness helps us to deal positively with the unexpected.

This is also the reason why practising *Thinking from Within* is a way to keep growing our spontaneity to still higher levels of wisdom. As seen also in Chapter 12, this matter is influenced by ancient Greek theories and drama (a cornerstone in psychodrama which greatly inspires the practice of *Thinking from Within*) where Aristotle played an important role for the concept of catharsis. Also, recall that as a practice, *Thinking from Within* includes the necessary dimensions of experiential and multi-modal aspects (see Chapters 3–5), which I discuss below.

It is precisely when the predictive capacity of natural scientific knowledge breaks down that wisdom, as it is defined by social sciences, helps us not just adapt to, but also shape the situation at hand. Similarly, although wisdom draws on our cunning intelligence to realize our goals, it urges us not to reap advantages solely for our own benefits. Wisdom guides us in selecting the features of situations that we choose to act upon. Said differently, *we are wise when we act with split-second swiftness to cope with a surprising situation in a way that also benefits others*. To this end, Aristotle has thus contributed two different concepts, *phronesis* and *catharsis*, which separately have been taken further by many scholars over the centuries. In the shape of imagination and spontaneity *phronesis* and *catharsis* meet again in the practice of *Thinking from Within*, to potentially give rise to habits others may call wise.

Practising

Such a view on what wisdom is can be contrasted with the scholarly view of wisdom on a pedestal onto which only a selected few 'philosopher kings' (or Plato's 'guardians' of the city state, Gr. *polis*) have access. Aristotle suggested that to be wise is to 'know oneself', including our own limitations, and to continually develop our identities, including knowing more about our 'blind-spots', towards moral perfection or virtue (Gr. *arete*) in life. I see wisdom just as much among all the anonymous heroes, men and women, who by managing their daily lives in a wise way, in silence make up the pedestal onto which the esteemed stars have mounted to receive the admiration of the masses.

Like Moreno and others, I also believe that wisdom needs training – practice – to reach its peak and that *Thinking from Within* is a good way to do so. From this perspective, in each and every case story (perhaps with the exception of Chapter 6) what people experienced developed their *potential* wisdom. What may first have appeared to some of them as only a superficial and playful activity (read: non-threatening leisure) that would neither affect their world view (Chapter 7), their ways of knowing (Chapter 8), their ways to capture and present information (Chapter 9) and their perceived identity (Chapter 10), nor touch upon their vulnerability as authentic leaders (Chapter 12) came out as something that did just about *all* of those things. Managers were taken aback by these new experiences and also integrated them in their speech and behaviour outside the session, perhaps with the exception of GadgetCo in Chapter 12. We can only imagine what might have happened if the managers described in Chapter 6 also had practised *Thinking from Within*.

Indicating wisdom in artifacts

Not only Aristotle reflected on what wisdom is but so too did, for example, Socrates, who in Plato's *Republic* argued that music and sports (broadly defined) are appropriate methods to develop potential wisdom. In today's context, consider how music can transform our inner experiences, for example within the context of 'guided imagery and music' (GIM), which involves listening to music in a relaxed state to achieve a deep experience of self-understanding (Bonny and Savary 1973). Also consider the inherent spontaneity that is often illustrated in jazz music, which has come to symbolize the spontaneity and improvization that can lead to peak experiences and which calls for authenticity. In the words of Welsh (1999: 22): 'jazz emerges from the awareness of who the other musicians are, what they are doing at the moment, and their particular configuration of strengths and weaknesses.' Some scholars have been so enticed with the apparent fluidity of exchange within the group, fuelled by individual effort, creativity and technique, they proposed jazz as a model for organizations (for example Weick 1998; Hatch 1998; Crossan 1998).

Similarly sports, especially team sports, seem to naturally develop not only our cunning intelligence or an identity (see Chapter 10) but also the 'good' spontaneous actions that help us avoid the unnecessary penalty that may harm the entire team and hobble intra-team relationships.

When we practise sports we often use artifacts like balls, clubs and rackets to create movement, and when we practise music we use instruments to create sound. Artifacts are thus important for our capacity to express ourselves and this notion is an important part of how we practise *Thinking from Within*. Halversen (2004) suggested the development and use of *artifacts* can be used to 'track' expressions of wisdom and drew the analogy with artisans, who develop material and abstract artifacts as a result of their work.

The objects, *intentionally* constructed together during the strategy workshops and retreats described and illustrated in the company examples in this book, qualify as such artifacts, but so do the stacks of PowerPoint slides used in BrassCo and TechCo (Chapter 6.) So, what is the difference? The point here is that, under the right circumstances, wisdom can be manifested in the co-constructed objects resulting from *Thinking from Within*. The reason is that the object-mediated communication embodied the local and value-laden habits of the people involved, *indicating* wisdom. In the *Republic*, Plato suggested that philosophical dialogue as 'serious play' (Gr. *spoudaious paidzein*) promotes the wisdom required of leaders (Roos et al. 2004). When objects constructed together mediate the dialogue, and *when the dialogue is inspired by dramatic, playful techniques that involve the very core of the person's authentic self*, it nurtures wisdom more effectively than pure intellectual reasoning.

The case examples in this book illustrate how co-constructed artifacts can capture the little things that can mean a lot – trade-offs, priorities and the situational ethics of the situation at hand. Consider the sensitive and normative narrative about the 'two-faced customers' among the leaders of PrintCo in Chapter 4; or the surprising concern and call for more passion represented by the soda bottle (and the remains of its sparkling content) in TalkCo's construction in Chapter 11. As we discussed in Chapters 4 and 5, deep conversations around co-constructed artifacts can capture people's normative value judgements, which open a door to their true and authentic inner self, which manifests itself in wisdom. Non-scripted drama enhances it to new heights (Chapter 12).

A few of the examples in this book exemplify how the constructions come to life when their creators move inside them by saying 'I am ... ' Consider, for example, the detailed interpretations of the 'journey' construction OilCo leaders did in Chapter 1, or the portrayal of the state of affairs in UtilityCo in Chapter 12. This additional depth can be particularly relevant when people are known to say one thing and then do another. It is more difficult to construct together one thing, which indicates potential wisdom, and not act accordingly.

As discussed in Chapters 4 and 5 the artifacts that come from constructing together can be extraordinarily inclusive (presuming an appropriate variety of hard and soft materials to construct from), and this richness enables and promotes careful and normative deliberation. It is difficult to stay outside an object-mediated communication when we, not others, have constructed the objects. When we construct, reconstruct and deconstruct we sometimes reach cognitive and emotional depths that motionless, intellectual abstraction does not. Because it is based on playful, imaginative co-construction and object-mediated communication, *Thinking from Within* provides the opportunity for people, like a group of strategists, to reflect on their values and how these are reflected in action. This is why *indicators of wisdom can be found in the details of the carefully constructed artifact;* in the way people identify and solve problems, set goals and the basis for making a 'good' decision.

In sum, *Thinking from Within*, practised in a safe and secure environment, cultivates people's habits to act for their own as well as for the common good in two ways: (1) by its very experiential, multi-sensual and aesthetic character that captures people's ideas, hopes and fears in symbolic artifacts; and (2) by capturing the true and authentic inner self in subjective object-mediated communication that trains our inherent capacity for spontaneity.

Wisdom in simple guiding principles

Based on intensive fieldwork in several organizations, David Oliver and I have used the concept of 'simple guiding principles' to capture how managers in highly dynamic environments make decisions (see Oliver and Roos 2003, 2005; also Lissack and Roos 1999). We found that managers operating in particularly dynamic business environments use rules of thumb, *heuristic reasoning* to making decisions and cope with critical incidents rather than follow rules. Such heuristics, we found, draw on *emotionally laden organizational narratives.* The management teams we studied took actions, made decisions and behaved in ways that appeared to be guided by these kinds of simple and normative principles, highly meaningful to team members. The following excerpt from Oliver and Roos (2003: 1074) exemplifies the emotional and narrative nature of simple guiding principles:

The principles were developed through discussions within the team, and they would go on to guide team members' actions in many ways.

Each of the team's principles functioned in much the same way as the headline of a narrative – a short phrase that called to mind a more elaborate, shared story intended to influence behaviour, action, and decision-making within the team. These stories appeared to evoke emotional – as well as rational – responses in team members. We observed three main guiding principles that were invoked on numerous occasions by team members and the team leader in responding to critical incidents: 'stay in orbit', 'parallel process', and 'be a real partner'.

Thus, simple guiding principles are *not* rules. Whereas rules unconditionally restrict our imagination and spontaneity *simple guiding principles, loaded with emotions and narrative meaning, provide the flexibility required to cope effectively and responsible with unexpected situations.* Experts appear seamless both from the perspective of observers and the actors themselves because they act with spontaneity rather than impulsivity. Add the ethical dimension and we approach our previous discussion about wisdom rather than expert knowledge. Simple guiding principles are not wisdom as such, but can conserve potential wisdom. To indicate wisdom, guiding principles should call upon people's *phronesis*, not just their cunning intelligence.

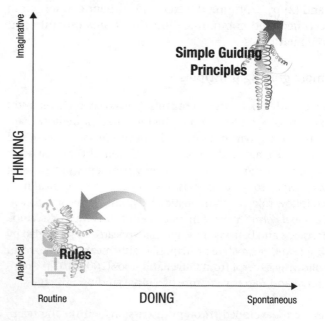

Exhibit 13.2 Prescribed rules and simple guiding principles (from within)

Simple guiding principles are far from ready-made, corporate propaganda statements about great vision, the virtue of winning, wonderful teamwork and delighted costumers available on the Internet for a fistful of dollars. Unlike such generic half-truths simple guiding principles come *from within* and are not necessarily applied broadly. In terms of the framework developed in Chapter 1 analytical routines form the intellectual home for the 'prescribed thinking' of rules. In contrast, simple guiding principles reside in the landscape of our spontaneous imagination – *Thinking from Within* (see Exhibit 13.2).

Although such principles can be developed by conventional meetings this will take considerable time. David Oliver and I followed the group in the example above for 18 months, and the three guiding principles evolved during this time period. The practice of *Thinking from Within* intensifies the experience to an extent that a group of managers can more effectively and responsibly develop, express and conserve simple guiding principles. Recall that the very idea of *Thinking from Within* is to create the context in which people are comfortable to reach inside for ideas and views. That is the fertile ground for identifying and expressing in meaningful, three-dimensional and dramatic ways simple guiding principles.

Case: Developing guiding principles in ChemCo[4]

Recall the ChemCo case in Chapter 3. As an integral and final part of the workshop we facilitated an object-mediated communication about appropriate responses to emergent change. The purpose was to create a context to develop simple guiding principles. To this end we invited people to imagine what might happen to the situation represented by their constructions. Thus, the managers continued to think from within and, sufficiently warmed up (see Chapter 4), they engaged with passion and intensity.

In the Fine Chemicals group they suddenly realized what happened in their division might have dramatic effects for other divisions of ChemCo. As their worldview had changed from static to dynamic (see Chapter 7), they engaged in a discussion about relationships on various levels of scale. They concluded that any important decisions about their own division must also include such considerations. The simple principle *Understand impacts on the whole group* became a way to describe the desired behaviour needed by all of them in their respective roles throughout the organization. Reflecting with their hands about their organizational identity as a complex 'interpersonal and informational network', they also expressed the simple principle *Don't depend on single individuals*.

Finally, realizing the intricate web of relationships with key players in the industry, prominently featured in their construction, they developed the principle *Maintain trusting relationships*.

All three principles express their shared potential wisdom about what is the 'right' course of action, which would not just give them and their own division advantage, but also be beneficial for others. In each case the guiding principle was integrated into their construction, either directly as an object or indirectly as the result of a change or reconstruction of their model. In their case, the model became a conserve for potential wisdom.

Quick reflection

We have facilitated similar attempts to develop simple guiding principles with the managers in some of the other examples of this book. For instance, the TelCo managers (Chapter 5) expressed their potential wisdom as 'control the whole narrative' and 'control the whole story.' The TalkCo strategists (Chapters 11 and 12) were unable to manifest potential wisdom on the group level, which perhaps is not surprising because of the political split in the group. Because simple guiding principles, as defined in this chapter, are so specific to the organizational and managerial context, they cannot be generic.

Conserving potential wisdom

Thinking from Within remains for most people in organizations an unusual experience. Although valuable in itself most people need a guided transition back into 'ordinary' life. Consider the ChemCo Fine Chemicals story in Chapter 3. These leaders carefully deconstructed their model into manageable pieces, put them in boxes and reconstructed it for display elsewhere. As impractical as this may seem, their intention was worthy: to both retain an aide-mémoire and convey to others the potential wisdom gained. This is easier said then done. How can a finished form of something convey the imagination and spontaneity of its creator? Well, we can all listen to Bedrich Smetana's 'The Moldau,' or Pink Floyd's 'The Dark Side of the Moon' and enjoy an aesthetic experience from the imagination and spontaneity captured forever in their music. Like a tin can of conserved food, this book is the 'conserve' of the thoughts, musings, engaging conversations and hands-on experiences that Peter, Madeleine, Mark, Roger and I have had together and with the many other people who have indirectly contributed to it: Bart, Paul, Matt, David, Claus, Carla, Jennie, Cliff, Kari, Göran, Susan, Wendelin, Jim, Marjorie, James, Richard, Marco, Hugo, Joachim, Christian, Torben, Kendra and of course

Kjeld. It is not the 'real thing' and nor is it as enjoyable as the CD version of Floyd's 'Money', but it can still be valuable.

Return to the ChemCo leaders for a moment. Anyone who came into the room and saw the original model would, unaided, not see any of these things. Instead we would see a finished product, a conserve of their experience that would need a fair bit of explanation to make sense to people who were not involved. How then can the artifact – the context-specific conserve – be transformed into a conserve that serves the two purposes listed above?

Inspired by Moreno's (1947/1983) notion of 'cultural conserve' the 'chronicle from within' technique, which Madeleine Roos and I are developing, is the dramatic, *written* and, thus, 'flat' continuation of the experience of *Thinking from Within*. Although not the 'real thing', this chronicle seeks to conserve what was spinning around in participants heads, what they constructed together and how and what they conversed about – *including their value judgements* – while holding, changing, perhaps even smashing their creations and playing different roles *from within*. The *Chronicle from Within* combines semi-structured and open-ended dramatic writing with pictures and maps. Anything deemed important from the experience can be conserved this way. This technique makes it possible to conserve expressions of potential wisdom in the relevant artifacts constructed, and in the total experience. Simple guiding principles make up an important part of chronicles from within. To further illustrate this approach, consider the story of BankCo.

Case: Conserving wisdom in BankCo

During the morning the Austrian bankers had constructed together a model of their bank, a subsidiary of a larger international bank, which included a wide range of hard and soft material (see Exhibit 13.3 in the plate section). Their objective was to take a strategic look at the bank's relationship with customers, and what in the bank's ways of working could be changed to improve customer relationships.

As they constructed and conversed with one another, a certain tension in the organization surfaced, prominently featured in the construction. In line with what we described in Chapter 12, we applied drama techniques to enhance their authenticity, which the dramatic narrative manifested:

> I am stretched between three corners: corporate vision, our long-term goals and our short-term goals. Big brother [corporate] is looking down

on me, in fact, stressing me. Just below him lies the amorphous IT system that he imposes on me and which takes up so much of my attention. I feel chained by it [pushed a metal chain into the soft material used]. Too close to my heart there is the political knife I use to cut off people I do not like. Sometimes a part of me uses this knife to backstab another part, which I cannot seem to control ... [and so on.]

The story went on for quite some time and took into account virtually all parts of the construction. Their comments and body language suggested they felt relieved to have talked about issues that were not usually part of such management meetings; they experienced a sort of catharsis.

An important part of their narrative focused on three groups of customers, which cut across the existing and official segments and that they featured in different ways. Instead of accepting the existing definition of segments, they had spent much time constructing new, and to them, meaningful representations of particular groups of customers. Much time was spent on retired people who some of them thought were troublesome. Said one manager: 'They just complain about our service, threatening to take their account elsewhere ... fine with me.' The feelings were mixed and others offered the opposite view. Eventually they constructed a figure that they thought represented their shared, mixed feelings about such customers. This was a strange-looking character pushing a chair full with green stuff (money) and with a 'head' with huge eyes looking (critically) at their organization (at the top of Exhibit 13.4a in the plate section). On top of the head they placed 'horns' that reminded them of certain aggressiveness they all seemed to agree these people featured. Unlike other customers groups the connection between these customers and the bank was extremely thin – only a narrow paper strip (see Exhibit 13.4b in the plate section). Prominently featured next to this symbolic representation was a black cross, indicating that these people were close to death.

When they took turns to act out how these customers might regard the bank they had to physically stand at their side of the table bending down and sharing a story in the first person. Over the course of these, ever more dramatic stories, their shared view of these particular customers changed. Suddenly one of them interrupted her story and exclaimed 'I am not dead yet!' which led to a deep conversation about demography, health care, life expectancy, wealth management and the role of the bank in their community.

One of them complemented the back cross with a candy bar (see Exhibit 13.4b) from his bag and made the point that these people had perhaps another 25 years to live and that both parties could benefit from a more mutually respectful relationship.

After completing the action phase of *Thinking from Within* we concluded the session with a debrief, which included several exercises aimed to conserve the experience in a kind of 'chronicles from within' where as much as possible of their individual and shared experience was captured. The chronicles included illustrations and text in the form of several dramatic narratives chosen by each person based on personal preferences about what was important. Exhibit 13.5 in the plate section illustrates how participants formulate abbreviated versions displayed on the wall, passionately narrated by its author. It also included the overall narrative shared by the group members.

The group spent considerable time extracting indicators of wisdom, or lack thereof, as represented in the various artifacts. For instance, we discussed at length the intrinsic value judgements of the black cross and the wisdom called for to transform the relationship with these older customers, who they previously had looked upon more derogatively. In turn, this allowed the group to develop emotionally laden 'headlines' for what to do next, that is, a form of simple guiding principles, which became an integral part of their chronicle.

Conclusion

Wisdom is our habit of thinking and doing that determines and makes us follow courses of intentional action to serve also others, especially when we face ambiguous and uncertain circumstances. *Thinking from Within* encourages us to express and even act out our deliberations and reasoned choices. The company examples in this book illustrate how relatively short episodes of *Thinking from Within*, in ways previously not achieved, enabled leaders to be deliberately hands-on about the 'right' way of meeting known and unknown opportunities and challenges and, to some extent, also how to act in life in general. When we do this over and over again we cultivate the spontaneity of our wisdom, so that we are ready to respond as is required. *Thinking from Within* enables wisdom.

Why is such wisdom important for strategy practice? Perhaps this is less of an issue in circumstances where strategy practices is seen as a routine of 'strategic' analysis about a pre-given objective and stable environment. In those situations we need people who execute as instructed without tapping too deeply into their brains and hearts. But, in all other circumstances, when we doubt (read: meet new circumstances calling for new outcomes) wisdom is what makes us 'do the right thing'.

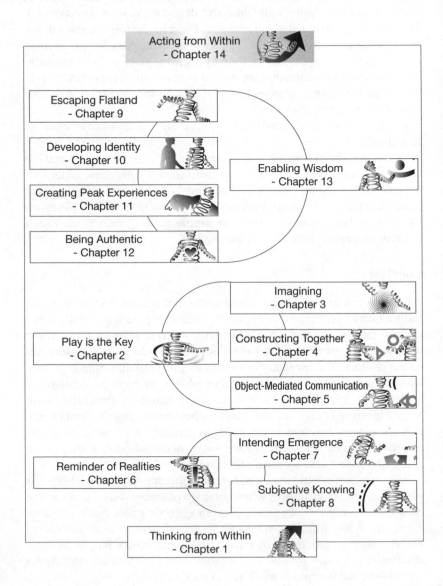

14
Acting From Within

Johan Roos

Introduction

In this book we have described and illustrated a way of practising strategy (thinking and doing) appropriate for developing new outcomes to meet new circumstances: *Thinking from Within*. By definition, this type of strategy practice is not for all managers all the time. It is suitable for those managers who aspire to realize the potential benefits discussed in Chapters 9–13: escaping the conventional flatland of papers, computer screens and whiteboards; the opportunity to naturally develop and adapt organizational identity; experience peak performance; encouraging more authenticity; and develop a habit to act wisely. *If circumstances are stable and we do not need or seek new outcome, 'prescribed' strategy is often adequate and we can calmly retain the routine of repeating the same analyses we did the last time.* The problem is that such calm circumstances are becoming more endangered by the minute. Perhaps this is why so many scholars have pointed out the need for new ways of thinking and doing strategy.

In *Strategy Bites Back* Henry Mintzberg et al. (2005) use irony, sarcasm, ridicule, analogy and humour to make us see the apparent insanity of contemporary strategy practice. In their experience 'the most interesting companies we know, often the most successful, are not boring. They have novel, creative, inspiring, sometimes even playful strategies' (ibid. p. 2). Although it is often an unexpected benefit, the purpose of *Thinking from Within* is not to 'have fun' for its own sake. *Thinking from Within* is a carefully crafted attempt to bring the emergent benefits of *play* – imagination, ethics and intentional emergence (described in Chapter 2) – to the serious work of organizations in general, and to strategy in particular. Sure, sometimes it is fun but that is an effect, not the starting point.

Mintzberg et al. suggest that 'Strategy can be awfully boring ... it often gets us worse [strategies] – standard, generic, uninspiring ... an uninspiring strategy is really no strategy at all' (ibid. p. 2). Better strategies, they continue, have 'to come out of a creative process conducted by thoughtful people' (ibid. p.5). *Thinking from Within* is way beyond a general 'creative' process – it is a creative arts process. As described in Chapters 3–5 when we think from within we use our bodies to imagine, construct together and engage each other in object-mediated communication spiced with drama. This makes a huge difference, which the examples included in this book illustrate.

Cummings and Wilson's (2003) *Images of Strategy* is a scholarly survey of 'maps' of strategy. In their volume researchers offer a broad range of perspectives: strategy as ethos, as organizing human resources, as anticipation and intention, as orchestrating knowledge, as combining data and sense-making, as creative thinking, as exploration and connection, as systems thinking, as process, power and change, as marketing and market value, as decision-making, and as numbers. After their extensive survey they urge us to develop our own maps of strategy and make combinations that make sense to us. *Thinking from Within* uses the map metaphor too, but escapes the flatland of all the above maps. Three-dimensional maps, which should be constructed by the people involved and used in dramatic ways, are put into space itself, not just left flat on a surface. This makes a huge difference, which the examples included in this book illustrate.

In sum, *Thinking from Within* offers a solid theoretical foundation and many illustrations for how to positively transform strategy practice. Our starting point is not the lack of fun, but the widely acknowledged *emergent* benefits of play for how we think and learn, act and interact also have the potential to, in David Whyte's terms, arouse people's hearts. Again, *I am not claiming that this practice is indiscriminately needed all the time and everywhere.* I am the first to acknowledge that sometimes leaders legitimately have to suppress people's imagination and restrict their spontaneity, which also applies to the practice of strategy. At others times, however, the very same leaders have to do the opposite, which is much more difficult. *This book offers a way to think and act that is suitable when we really want people to use more of their imagination and encourage more of the spontaneity of their wisdom.*

Review

Chapter 1 framed the problem of traditional strategy practice for changing circumstances as lacklustre, superficial and therefore also irresponsible. I described the Enlightenment heritage of rational and disembodied thinking as particularly problematic as it promotes the kind of routine-like and wasteful management practices illustrated in some of the cases in this book. I framed the problem as too much deductive, analytical thinking and routine-like doing. When we think *from within* our thinking is imaginative, not only 'analytical', and our actions come spontaneously, not just from routines. The practice of *Thinking from Within* fuels many parts of our minds by engaging our senses in ways pure intellectual reason does not. The OilCo case illustrated *Thinking from Within*.

Chapter 2 described the conceptual foundation of *Thinking from Within* as the inherently human and ambiguous activity called play. Not because play necessarily is 'fun' but because this activity comes with benefits for how we think and learn, act and interact and also has the potential to engage people's feelings. Therefore, we paid particular attention to what we can learn about play from psychology in its many forms.

Thinking from Within involves three interrelated and playful ways of thinking and doing, which Chapters 3–5 described and illustrated with case stories (ChemCo, PrintCo and TelCo). First, we practise our conceptual, behavioural and material imagination, which by definition implies we have to move rather than sit still. Second, we use our bodies in general and our hands in particular to construct together meaningful, metaphorical representations of things, events and processes that we regard as important. Third, we use these physical objects to mediate deep communication, which influences profoundly how we think and act.

As a reminder that *Thinking from Within* is an exception rather than the rule in organizations, Chapter 6 presents two longer cases of how leadership teams struggled with their rather conventional strategy practice (BrassCo and TechCo). In turn these two cases help illustrate the huge difference certain assumptions have for what we do, which is what we discussed in the subsequent two chapters.

On a philosophical level *Thinking from Within* calls for us to view the world as intrinsically dynamic with stability as an exception, which means that we should expect to be surprised and even intend such emergence. Chapter 7 described and illustrated these ontological assumptions, also by means of an additional case – PackCo. *Thinking from Within* also requires us to see knowledge and knowing as private and delicate subjective processes, which unfold within each one of us. Chapter 8 uses the previous cases to describe and illustrate this critical, epistemological assumption.

The emergent benefits from *Thinking from Within* were presented in Chapters 9–13. In each chapter we added case illustrations; HandyCo, InfCo, DiscCo, ConglomerateCo, TalkCo, GadgetCo, UtilityCo and BankCo.

Specifically, we argued that when we think from within we escape the 'flatland' of two-dimensional papers and screen and are free to describe, create and challenge in three dimensions images of our organizational and business landscapes. Because what we see and express depends on who we are, issues of identity underlie most practices in organizations. Regardless of in what background we do this, when we think from within we always touch upon issues of organizational identity and, as such, we get an opportunity to develop and adapt who we are and want to become. When we think from within we create the conditions for 'peak' experiences, which others have described in terms of flow, timelessness, and aesthetics. Our practices become enjoyable and beautiful, and sometimes perhaps time seems to disappear. Compared with conventional practices of pure, intellectual reasoning, *Thinking from Within* ups the ante for the emergence of such peak experience and peak performance. When we enrich our object-mediated communication with dramatic techniques *Thinking from Within* can become a deep, personal experience of our authentic self. With such authenticity we cannot but follow our hearts and often arouse those of others. Without such authenticity the imagination and spontaneity of our wisdom remains hidden within and we risk slipping back into the world of prescribed thinking.

When we think from within, in a safe and secure environment, we practise our habit for acting for our own best interest as well as for the common good in two ways, which was the message of Chapter 13. First, its experiential, multi-sensual and aesthetic character captures people's thinking and emotions into symbolic artifacts. Second, it captures the true and authentic self in a deep and subjective object-mediated communication, which trains our inherent capacity for spontaneity. Just like the ancient Greek ideal of leadership, wise people are ready to strike a balance between adapting to changes caused by others and seizing fleeting opportunities to shape the situation in ways that also benefit the common good. When we use 'chronicles from within' people can capture in effective and responsible ways the potential wisdom gained while *Thinking from Within*. Previous cases in the book illustrate such potential wisdom and the lack thereof.

The purpose of this book was to show a different path forward to positively influence strategy practices in organization when this is required. Strategy is just an application and does not constrain where *Thinking from Within* can and should be applied – wisely. The only limit is your own imagination.

Fertile grounds?

Chapter 1 alluded to Sumantra Goshal's recent and biting critique of management theory and managerial practice. The result of *amoral* theories combined, as depicted by Goshal, does not seem to provide a fertile ground for *Thinking from Within*:

> Combine agency theory with transaction costs economics, add standard versions of game theory and negotiation analysis, and the picture of the manager that emerges is one that is now very familiar in practice: the ruthlessly hard-driving, strictly top-down, command-and-control focused, shareholder-value-obsessed, win-at-any-cost business leader. (2005: 85)

Ouch. So, if we teach managers to be *cunning* for one's own good only and encourage their ability of emotionless reasoning we should not be surprised that their *thinking* in strategy practice is biased towards deductive analysis and their *doing* biased towards processes for cunningly reaping advantage rather than how to wisely act to contribute to society at large (see Margolis and Walsh 2001).

Again, what we have described and illustrated in this book is *not* for everybody, all the time. For some, particularly those in stable environments, conventional ways of working may be sufficient for strategy practice – regardless of the mind-set of those involved. Managers who consciously or unconsciously have a habit of restricting people's imagination and constraining their spontaneity are likely to consider *Thinking from Within* threatening nonsense that distracts from the 'real' issue: instruction and execution. In stable circumstances they may be right, but analogous to the well-known 'Law of Requisite Variety' in systems theory (Ashby 1956), this stable attitude may be less appropriate when circumstances are unstable. The following anecdote, inspired by recent events in a company I have observed for many years, illustrates this point:[1]

> A multinational manufacturing company was nearing the end of its planning cycle. On the encouragement of a board member, the CEO had arranged for an innovative series of aesthetically rich, play-based experiences for the worldwide management team to take place in conjunction with the upcoming period of planning meetings. After learning about this approach (from Johan) his idea was to provide the team with an opportunity to enhance their understanding of the organization's identity by engaging in interpretative dialogue. He was assured

that corollary benefits such as team building and commitment to the next phase of strategy development would also emerge through the course of the experience.

One month before the event was to have taken place, preliminary performance reports began to come in from the firm's various divisions and regions. The picture did not look good. Not only had sales suffered from increased competition in some markets and decreased demand in others, operational efficiency had actually declined across the board and a series of unexpected costs had plagued a rationalization measure, severely diminishing the anticipated savings.

On closer inspection of the reports, it became clear to the CEO that the plan which had been formulated had not been implemented. He became concerned that the management team had engaged in the strategy process without understanding the vision that he had set for the organization. As he considered this possibility, he remembered the axiom of strategy which states that '95% of strategy is execution' and cursed himself for not putting in place the performance objectives and control that would have required the members of his team to submit their resignations along with their bleak reports.

Determined not to let people off the hook so easily this time around, he composed an e-mail announcing that instead of participating in the aesthetically rich, play-based experiences together, his team would be required to spend that time preparing detailed analyses of the factors that had contributed to their poor performance. The CEO resolved to kick off the upcoming strategy process with a forceful presentation of his vision for the firm and a detailed outline of the objectives for which each and every team member would be held accountable. As he sent off the e-mail he felt satisfaction that the team members as well as the board would respect his take-no-prisoners commitment to success.

As this book has discussed and exemplified the problem is perhaps not just one of 'execute or risk execution', but rather of how we think of strategy practice, what we do when we practise it and what we use when we engage in this important work to create value for all our stakeholders and society at large. Taking a hint from Goshal I guess our kind should start teaching theories that are intrinsically ethical and hope they are deemed 'relevant'.

Thinking from Within is a concept and practice aimed to enable thoughtful people in organizations to complement the necessary 'prescribed' thinking with the imaginative spontaneity of their wisdom (see Exhibit 14.1 in the plate section). What could be more ethical?

Chapter 1 framed the problem of strategy practice in terms of inapt thinking and doing for dynamic circumstances, grounded in assumptions from another era. In any case the root cause is much more profound than what we see on the surface (for example the apparent difference between Exhibits 1.2 and 1.3 or what is illustrated in Exhibit 14.1 in the plate section) and this is probably why so few people – scholars, consultants and managers – have come up with so few ideas about HOW to *practise* strategy differently. 'Fun' and new maps may help, but the 'pathological' behaviour Goshal (2005) sees in management practices, partly caused by our kind, may not be enough. As Goshal pointed out, managerial behaviours are difficult to change because social science theories tend to be self-fulfilling (Gergen 1973).

Deep change

In the language of the ancient Greeks (see Chapter 13), over the last decades management professors have managed to indoctrinate a whole generation of managers to use *episteme* and *metis* to deal with the world as they see it, including in strategy practice. Business school education has yet to include the necessary elements to nurture wisdom. Although valuable in themselves, I am not talking about the token 'outdoor' exercise in the mountains, nor watching Apollo 13 in the classroom – nurturing wisdom calls for much more. *Without that wisdom it is not surprising that, when we are in doubt, we do not necessarily do the 'right' thing.* This holds true for the CEOs featured in handcuffs on CNN, who apparently were a bit too cunning even for their own good, and equally for professors teaching managers to be cunning and then turning them into role models for the next generation of MBAs. Learning from the ancient Greeks, to foster the wisdom-as *phronesis* we need the kind of experiential, multi-sensuous and aesthetically rich activities discussed in this book. In a world of e-learning this seems perhaps a bit over the top. Yet, *to nurture people's wisdom we need intensive face-to-face and hand-to-hand interaction. Thinking from Within* is built on this ancient idea.

The same principle applies to strategy practice. If strategy practice (in which we repeat the same thing over and over again while expecting a different outcome) bears such a close resemblence to insanity, which I suggested in Chapter 1 and which Mintzberg and others seem to think too, perhaps the problem is one of imbalance between *episteme, metis* and *phronesis* (see Chapter 13 for the full discussion) in the actual *practice* of strategy. From this angle, strategy practices are *simply not wise enough* and I can make the same point as I did for education: to nurture *wisdom-as-*

phronesis in strategy practice we need the kind of experiential, multi-sensuous and aesthetically rich activities discussed in this book. This is easier said than done and the barriers can be significant. At first, many people are somewhat sceptical of the apparently bizarre concept that serious strategy practice *should* be playful and that it *should* involve more than austere and intellectual reasoning. Others, for their own personal reasons, do not want to venture into the unknown. When people get to grips with the concepts and try the practice, few hearts remain untouched, few hands rest motionless and they become 'delightfully petrified' rather than sceptical. Ideas spring to their minds and they create and perceive serious business issues in new ways. After they return to their daily, unstable life with a 'chronicle from within' in their hand and a smile on their face, in my experience when they meet the next unexpected issue they are more likely to act wisely by doing the 'right thing'.

Unless we can practise our imagination and act spontaneously (NB, not impulsively!) we cannot expect anything but the prescribed thinking that rarely encourages more than repeating the same thing over and over again and, perhaps, even continues to expect a different outcome the next time. *By virtue of its philosophical assumptions, cross-disciplinary foundations and emergent benefits Thinking from Within is a practice that has the potential to break this pattern.*

Responsibility included

Whereas Goshal, Mintzberg and many other brilliant observers are somewhat gloomy over what can be done I am more optimistic. Over the past decades humanistic values in general have regained their place in the centre of society and *even natural sciences* recognize the importance of the actor for the outcome of an experiment or observation, for example the famous Einstein saying that imagination is more important than knowledge. In the humanities the boundary between social science and arts blurs and even business schools have taken seriously the potential of learning from the practice and theory of arts, not just ethics. Taking Goshal's critique seriously we *who seek to influence managers must be self-critical in what we profess*. His critique was that the *amoral* theories professed profoundly shape managers' *worldview* and ways of working. So, how does the practice of *Thinking from Within* hold up?

The ways of thinking and doing that make up *Thinking from Within* rest on the assumption that the world is a complex, living system (Chapter 7) and that knowledge is a sensitive process within each unique human being (Chapter 8). Moreover, the practice draws on the human activity called play that, by definition, is imaginative, ethical (we need to follow the rules of play) and intentionally emergent (Chapter 2); it encourages multi-dimensional imagination, which means we should be handymen, storytellers and architects (Chapter 3); and it calls for us to construct things with our hands and do this together (Chapter 4); and engage in deep communication mediated by such crafted objects (Chapter 5) and also enhance these conversations and communications with drama (Chapter 12). We have framed the benefits in terms of three-dimensionality, identity development, peak experiences and authenticity and on an overall level, in terms of the wisdom, which concerns others (*phronesis*).

Goshal talked about 'ruthlessly hard-driving, strictly top-down, command-and-control focused, shareholder-value-obsessed, win-at-any-cost business leader' (2005: 85). In light of the above and the many illustrations of behaviour conserved in stories of preceding chapters, *Thinking from Within* seems profoundly incompatible with this kind of manager. Instead, when *Thinking from Within* imaginative, reflective and responsible managers engage each other in respectful and profound dialogue about potentially wise actions, which are also good for others. Therefore, *Thinking from Within* is by definition a responsible practice.

Thinking from Within represents and promotes the kind of intellectual pluralism Goshal calls for. In this book we have drawn on anthropology, neuroscience, philosophy, psychology, sociology, and theories of complex adaptive systems, knowledge, imagination and play. We have not taken on board the hubris that comes from assuming we can predict human behaviour in general and in strategy practice in particular. Personal preferences guide the choice of these theoretical perspectives. For instance, I happen to really like the idea that work should be more play-like and I expect emergence on a daily basis (and love to change things). *Thinking from Within* should be without boundaries.

Conclusion

In the spirit of 'phronetic' social science (Flyvbjerg 2001; Roos 2005), I conclude that *Thinking from Within* is good for precisely those circumstances I discussed in Chapter 1 and illustrated in Exhibit 1.1. That is, not for everybody all the time. Facing changing circumstances calling for new outcomes, *Thinking from Within* helped the OilCo leaders (Chapter 1) to make sense of and do something about their abstract Customer Service Champion concept; it turned the minds of ChemCo leaders (Chapter 3) to see new threats and new ways of working; it enabled the PrintCo leaders (Chapter 4) to address taboos; it encouraged the TelCo managers (Chapter 5) to develop a coherent view of their organization; it made the PackCo (Chapter 7) CEO try out a new strategy; it crystallized the strategy for the HandyCo strategist (Chapter 9); it made the InfCo and DiscCo leaders (Chapter 10) see their organizations in a new light; it made the leaders about to be divested in ConglomerateCo (Chapter 11) experience peak performance; it stimulated people in UtilityCo to be more authentic; revealed a sense of emptiness in GadgetCo (Chapter 12); and it prepared the managers in BankCo (Chapter 13) to act more wisely. Whether or not such benefits also means the 'better' strategies that Mintzberg et al. (2005) call for are for the people involved to tell over time. If it does, it is because of a simple idea built into *Thinking from Within*: If you want to change the content of your strategy, innovate the practices.

To make strategy practice more 'from within' means using more of our imagination and making way for the spontaneity of our wisdom. In my experience such profound transformation in thinking and doing does not happen by itself. We need to do it over, and over, and over again, and because of its emergent nature, when *Thinking from Within* we *should* expect a different outcome.

Notes

Chapter 1

1 In our paper 'The Normativity of Strategy Practice' Matt Statler and I (2005b) identified that Giddens (1984) views practice as a recursive relationship between structure and agency; Bourdieu (1990) sees it as a dialectical relationship between a structured environment and the structured dispositions engendered in people; MacIntyre (1981) sees it as a collaborative human activity realized in search of excellence; and de Certeau (1984) sees it as ways of operating within organizational structures.

2 The boundary between routines and non-routines is not clear but whereas routine activty is guided by procedures established in advance based on past experience, non-routine activity is adapted while unfolding (see for instance, Cheng and Miller 1985).

3 Some have argued that spontaneity is always mediated by structure, just as structure must be mediated by spontaneity. Thus, spontaneity and routine are perhaps not two separable or even separate things, but rather different moments of the same process, so that one cannot exist without the other.

4 To protect the real identity of the companies, I have altered names and contextual information of all cases in this book.

5 Elster's (1983) well known schema about how different sciences uses different forms of explanation makes it manifestly clear why the ways of thinking in the natural sciences are on the whole inappropriate in the humanities, which included strategy practice. Causal explanation (if … then) works well to explain the movements of comets, and functional explanation (in terms of benefits, evolution and progress) can shed light on our immune system, but have limited, if any place in the humanities. Why? Unlike inorganic and organic 'matter', our human mind has intentions that cannot be decoupled from normativity. Every decision and action, by implication, comes with an explicit or implicit value judgement about what is right, wrong, good, bad, beautiful or ugly. The only appropriate form of explanation (finding causal patterns and seeking prediction) in management studies is 'intentional explanation', which recognizes that intentions are mental states that cannot be separated from everything else that potentially influences it in unpredictable ways.

6 Stated at the *2005 Leaders in London Conference*, London, October 19 2005.

Chapter 2

1 This chapter extends three Working Papers from Imagination Lab Foundation, Switzerland: Statler, M., Roos, J., and B. Victor, 'Ain't Misbehavin: Taking Play Seriously in Organizations' (2002: 17); and Roos, M., and M. Statler, 'Play and the Creative Arts: A Review of Concepts and Techniques in the Psychotherapeutic Tradition' (2004: 58); and Linder, M., Roos, J., and B. Victor, 'Play in Orga-

nizations' (2001: 2). We are particularly re-using the review of the play literature presented in Statler et al. (2002: 17) above.

2   Briggs and Myers found Jung's types and functions so revealing that they
developed the well-known Myers-Briggs Type Indicator based on his ideas.

3   This technical case is notably also the first one in which a child's symptoms
were attributed to emotional causes, rather than to the child's education and
training (Reisman 1966; Landreth 2002).

4   A childhood reading of how H. G. Wells and his sons played Floor Games in the
early 1900s inspired the creator of 'World Technique', Margaret Lowenfeld.
Father and son Wells chose miniature play materials stored on bookshelves to
create dramatic play scenes on the floor (Wells and Turner 2004).

5   In *Sandtray Network Journal*, De Domenico (1998) also gives other examples of
how therapists, teachers, consultants, and researchers with very diverse theoretical orientations convey their particular ways of seeing the 'sandtray' process
to their clients and research subjects.

6   First, an egalitarian relationship is established; second, the lifestyle is
explored; third, insights are gained about the lifestyle; fourth, a reorientation/
re-education takes place.

7   For example, in the USA the National Association for Music Therapy was
founded in 1950; the American Dance Therapy Association was founded in
1966; the American Art Therapy Association was founded in 1969.

Chapter 3

1   A word of caution: the schema we propose is meant to be an intuitively useful
one, and not one deduced from exhaustive analysis. The thumbnail history of
the imagination concept and its meanings we offer in this chapter shows, at the
base, that an exclusively deductive enterprise has been attempted by analytical
philosophers for over 2000 years – and our goal here is not to contribute
directly to the stream of philosophical discourse. As such, we claim simply a
fundamental heurism for our schema: its value lies in offering an interrelated,
tripartite set of ways to analyse what imagination creates in social contexts. The
schema is, moreover, not meant to be mutually exclusive or collectively
exhaustive in the design of its various categories.

2   This case description is adapted from Bürgi and Roos (2004). Used with
permission.

3   The individual was referring to the prescriptions on strategy found in Porter,
(1980).

Chapter 4

1   This chapter extends ideas published in Bürgi et al. (2005).

2   This case is adapted from Roos and Said (2005). Used with permission.

3   This section is inspired by and significantly extends Roos and Statler (2004).

Chapter 5

1 This case is adapted from Bürgi et al. (2005). Used with permission.

Chapter 6

1 Although there were two facilitators in this case, to simplify the case description it is written as if I was acting alone. Much of the workshop structure was developed by a colleague in a business school, who was not involved in the research.

Chapter 7

1 The origin of the word 'complexity' comes from the Latin word *complexus*, which means 'braided together', and therefore is not the same as its everyday usage as a synonym for 'complicated'. Complexity refers not just to the number of parts in a system, but to their interconnectedness.
2 The literature review in this chapter draws on the literature review in Oliver and Roos (2000) and Oliver (2002).
3 Source: http://www-chaos.umd.edu/misc/poincare.html. For additional information about this remarkable man see http://www-groups.dcs.st-and.ac.uk/~history/Mathematicians/Poincare.html.
4 This part of the story is adapted from Roos et al. (2004). Used with permission.
5 This case is adapted from Roos et al. (2004). Used with permission.

Chapter 8

1 The underlying theory of autopoiesis was developed in the field of neurobiology to describe the composition and structure of living systems (Maturana and Varela 1980). Others have subsequently used the theory to propose new theories of knowledge of social systems (Luhmann 1986; Teubner 1991; von Krogh and Roos 1995a).
2 Some research in this field has discussed the role of the individual. For example, Nisbett and Ross (1980) suggested individuals develop rudimentary 'knowledge structures' by making guesses, resolving ambiguities, and inferring causal relationships. Prahalad and Bettis (1986) claimed that problem-solving behaviour ingrained in such knowledge structures creates 'dominant logics' of how to view the business. Still, these authors do not discuss how knowledge structures develop, and instead rely on the assumptions discussed in this chapter.

Chapter 9

1 This chapter extends ideas published in Bürgi and Roos (2003).
2 This case is adapted from Bürgi and Roos (2003). Used with permission.

Chapter 10

1 This section is based on the following Working Papers by Oliver, D. and J. Roos published by Imagination Lab Foundation, Switzerland: 'Studying Organizational Identity: A Review' (2003: 31); 'Creativite et Identite Organisationelle' (2004: 49); and 'Constructing Organizational Identity' (2004: 52); as well as 'Organizational Identity, Imagination, and Strategy' (2002: 17) by Oliver, D. Burgi, P. and J. Roos; as well as Oliver and Roos (2000).
2 This case is adapted from Statler and Roos (2004).
3 This case is adapted from Oliver and Roos (2004).

Chapter 11

1 This section uses the literature review developed in the following Working Papers published by Imagination Lab Foundation, Switzerland, all by Marotto, M., Victor, B., and J. Roos: 'Leadership as Collective Virtuosity' (2001: 08); 'Collective Virtuosity: Reclaiming Aesthetic Experience in Teams (2002: 12); 'Collective Virtuosity: An Aesthetic Experience in Groups' (2003: 27); and 'The Fragile Beauty of Work Well Done' (2003: 39, and 2004: 53).
2 This case is adapted from Roos and Said (2005). Used with permission.

Chapter 12

1 This case is adapted from Roos and Said (2005). Used with permission.
2 This case is adapted from Roos and Said (2005). Used with permission.
3 Moreno (1947/1983) was very critical of conventional theatre, which he referred to as dedicated to the worship of the dead and dead events. By 'filling the minds' of actors with a manuscript theatre practices de facto render creative people uncreative, he claimed. His notion of 'theatre of spontaneity' contrasted these practices by making the whole audience the cast, co-actors interacting with all. Suddenly, spontaneity and imagination flourished.

Chapter 13

1 For an excellent summary of elements of wisdom discussed in the literature see Birren and Fisher (2003).
2 Taken from Ross's translation of *Nicomachean Ethics*, 1984, New York: Oxford University Press, III.3, 1112b11.

3 Statler, M. and J. Roos, *Everyday Strategic Preparedness: The Role of Practical Wisdom in Organizations* (2005 manuscript under review with several publishers). Contact johan@imagilab.org for information about publisher. See also Statler and Roos (2005) and Statler et al. (2006).

4 This case description is adapted from Bürgi and Roos (2004). Used with permission.

Chapter 14

1 This story is adapted from Statler et al. (2003).

References

Abelson, R. (1963). 'Computer simulation of hot cognitions', in Tomkins, S. and Mesnick, S. (eds) *Computer Simulation of Personality*, New York: Wiley.

Abrams, M.H. (1953). *The Mirror and the Lamp: Romantic Theory and the Critical Tradition*. New York: W.W. Norton.

Ackoff, R. (1981). *Creating the Corporate Future*. New York: Wiley.

Albert, S. and Whetten, D. (1985). 'Organizational Identity', in Cummings, L. and Staw, B. (eds) *Research in Organizational Behavior* (vol. 7). Greenwich, CT: JAI Press, pp. 263–95.

Albert, S., Ashforth, B.E., Gioia, D.A., Godfrey, P.C., Reger, R.K. and Whetten, D.A. (1998). 'What does the concept of identity add to organization science?' in Dave Whetten and Paul Godfrey (eds) *Identity in Organizations: Building Theory Through Conversations*. New York: Sage.

Andrew, A. (1989). *Self-organizing Systems*. New York: Gordon and Breach Science Publishers.

Ansbacher, H.L. and Ansbacher, R.R. (1956). *The Individual Psychology of Alfred Adler*. New York: Basic Books.

Aristotle. (1962). *Nicomachean Ethics*. Indianapolis: Bobbs-Merrill.

Arthur, B. (1996). 'Positive feedbacks in the economy', *Scientific American*, February, pp. 92–9.

Ashby, W.H. (1956). *An Introduction to Cybernetics*. London: Methuen.

Ashforth, B. and Mael, F. (1989). 'Social identity theory and the organization', *Academy of Management Review*, **14**: 20–39.

Axline, V. (1947). 'Nondirective play therapy for poor readers', *Journal of Consulting Psychology*, **11**: 61–9.

Bakhtin, M.M. (1984). *Rabelais and his World*. Bloomington: Indiana University Press.

Barney, J. (1991). 'Firm resources and sustained competitive advantage', *Journal of Management*, **17**: 99–120.

Barry, D. (1994). 'Making the invisible visible: using analogically-based methods to surface unconscious processes in organizations', *Organizational Development Journal*, **12**(4): 37–47.

Beardsley, M.C. (1969). 'The instrumentalist theory of aesthetic value', in Hospers, J. (ed.) *Introductory Readings in Aesthetics*, pp. 308–19. New York: The Free Press.

Beardsley, M.C. (1982). 'Aesthetic experience', in Wreen, M.J. and Callen, D.M. (eds) *The Aesthetic Point of View: Selected Essays of Monroe C. Beardsley*. New York: Cornell University Press.

Becker, A. (1991). 'A short essay on languaging', in Steier, F. (ed.) *Research and Reflexivity*, pp. 226–34. London: Sage.

Bell, C. (1840). *The Hand, Its Mechanisms and Vital Endowments, As Evincing Design: The Bridgewater Treatises on the Power, Wisdom, and Goodness of God as Manifested in the Creation*. Treatise IV, New York: Harper and Brothers.

Bernthal, P.R. and Insko, C.A. (1993). 'Cohesiveness without groupthink', *Group & Organization Management*, **18**(1): 66–88.

Betensky, M. 'Phenomenalogical art therapy', in Rubin, J.A. (2001). (ed.) *Approaches* to Art Therapy, Theory and Technique, pp. 121–33. (2nd edn). Philadelphia: Brunner-Routledge.

Birren, J., and Fisher, L.M. 'The elements of wisdom: overview and integration', in Sterneberg, R. (ed.) (2003). Wisdom: Its Nature, Origin, and Development, pp. 317–32. Cambridge: Cambridge University Press.

Blatner, A. and Blatner, A. (1997). The Art of Play. Helping Adults Reclaim Imagination and Spontaneity. New York: Brunner/Mazel.

Blatner, A. (1996). Acting In: Practical Applications of Psychodramatic Methods (3rd edn). Springer.

Blatner, A. (2000). Foundations of Psychodrama: History, Theory, and Practice (4th edn). Springer.

Boje, D. (1991). 'The storytelling organization: a study of story performance in an office-supply firm', Administrative Science Quarterly, 36: 106–26.

Bonny, H.L. and Savary, L.M. (1973). Music and Your Mind. New York: Harper & Row.

Bourdieu, P. (1990). The Logic of Practice. Stanford, CA: Stanford University Press.

Boynton, A. and Fischer, B. (2006). Virtuoso Teams: Lessons from Team that Changed their Worlds, London: Financial Times/Prentice Hall.

Brann, E. (1991). The World of the Imagination: Sum and Substance. USA: Rowland and Littlefield.

Breuer, J. and Freud, S. (1895, 1982). Studies on Hysteria. Basic Books.

Brown, J.R. (1991). The Laboratory of the Mind: Thought Experiments in the Natural Sciences. London: Routledge.

Brown, A. (2001). 'Organization studies and identity: towards a research agenda', Human Relations, 54. 113–21.

Bruner, J (1960). The Process of Education. Cambridge, MA: Harvard University Press.

Bruner, J. (1986). Actual Minds, Possible Worlds. Cambridge, MA: Harvard University Press.

Bundy, M.W. (1927). The Theory of Imagination in Classical and Medieval Thought. Illinois: University of Illinois Studies in Language and Literature XII.

Bürgi, P. and Roos, J. (2003). 'Images of strategy', European Management Journal, 21(1): 69–78.

Bürgi, P. and Roos, J. (2004). 'Crafting strategy at ChemCo', in Johnson, G. and Scholes, K. (eds) Exploring Corporate Strategy, (7th edn, online version). London: Financial Times/Prentice Hall.

Bürgi, P., Jacobs, C. and Roos, J. (2005). 'From metaphor to practice in the crafting of strategy', Journal of Management Inquiry, 14(1): 78–94.

Cane Detre, K., Frank, T., Refsnes Kniazzeh, C., Robinson, M.C., Rubin, J.A. and Ulman, E. (1983). 'Roots of art therapy: Margaret Naumburg (1890–1983) and Florence Cane (1882–1952) – a family portrait', American Journal of Art Therapy, pp. 113–16.

Case, C. and Dalley, T. (1992). The Handbook of Art Therapy. London: Routledge.

Casson, J. (1984). 'The therapeutic dramatic community ceremonies of Sri Lanka', The Journal of the British Association for Dramatherapists, 7(2): 11–18.

Casson, J. (1997–8). 'Shamanism, dramatherapy and psychodrama', Cahoots magazine, 62: 52–6; 63: 55–6; 64: 56–60; 65: 49–56.

Caves, R.E. (1980). 'Industrial organization, corporate strategy and structure: a survey', Journal of Economic Literature, 18(1): 64–92.

Chakravarthy, B. and Lorange, P. (1991). *Managing the Strategy Process*. Englewood Cliffs, NJ: Prentice Hall.

Cheng, J.L.C. and Miller, E.L. (1985). 'Coordination and output attainment in work units performing nonroutine tasks: a cross-national study', *Organization Studies*, 6: 23–39.

Cocking, J.M. (1991). *Imagination: A Study in the History of Ideas*. London and New York: Routledge.

Collins, J. and Porras, J.I. (1994). *Built to Last: Successful Habits of Visionary Companies*. New York: HarperCollins.

Crossan, M.M. (1998). 'Improvisation in action'. *Organization Science*, 9(5): 593–600.

Csikszentmihalyi, M. (1990). *Flow: The Psychology of Optimal Experience*. New York: HarperCollins.

Csikszentmihalyi, M. and Robinson, R.E. (1990). *The Art of Seeing: An Interpretation of the Aesthetic Encounter*. Malibu, CA: The Getty Center for Education in the Arts.

Cummings, S. and Wilson, D. (2003). *Images of Strategy*. London: Blackwell.

Cyert, R.M. and March, J.G. (1993). *A Behavioral Theory of the Firm*. Englewood Cliffs, NJ: Prentice Hall.

Damasio, A.R. (1994). *Descartes' Error: Emotion, Reason, and the Human Brain*. New York: Grosset/Putnam.

Dayton, T. (2005). *The Living Stage: A Step-by-Step Guide to Psychodrama, Sociometry and Experential Group Therapy*. FL: Health Communications.

Deacon, T.W. (1997). *The Symbolic Species: The Co-evolution of Language and the Brain*. New York: W.W. Norton.

de Certeau, M. (1984). *The Practice of Everyday Life*. Berkeley: University of California Press.

De Domenico, G.S. (1998). 'What's in a name?', *Sandtray Network Journal*, 2(3).

Derrida, J. (1978). 'Structure, sign and play in the discourse of the human sciences', *Writing and Difference*, (trans.) A. Bass, Chicago: University of Chicago Press, pp. 278–93.

Detienne, M. and Vernant, J.P. (1978). *Cunning Intelligence in Greek Culture and Society*. Sussex: Harvester.

Dewey, J. (1958). *Experience and Nature*. Mineola, NY: Dover.

Diderot, D. (ed.) (1751–1780) *Encyclopédie ou Dictionnaire Raisonné des Sciences des Arts et des Métiers*. Paris: l'Académie Royale des Sciences.

Doyle, J.R. and Sims, D. (2002). 'Enabling strategic metaphor in conversation: a technique of cognitive sculpting for explicating knowledge', in Huff, A.S. and Jenkins, M. (eds), *Mapping Strategic Knowledge*. London: Sage.

Drazin, R. and Sandelands, L. (1992). 'Autogenesis: a perspective on the process of organizing', *Organization Science*, 3(2): 230–49.

Eco, U. (1976). *A Theory of Semiotics*. Bloomington: Indiana University Press.

Eden, C. and Huxham, C. (1996). 'Action research for the study of organizations', in Clegg, S.E.A. (ed.), *Handbook of Organization Studies*, pp. 526–80. Thousand Oaks: Sage.

Eikeland, O. (2001). 'Action research as the hidden curriculum of the western tradition', in Reason, P. and Bradbury, H. (eds) *Handbook of Action Research: Participative Inquiry and Practice*. London: Sage.

Elster, J. (1983). *Explaining Technical Change*. Cambridge, UK: Cambridge University Press.

Elsbach, K. and Kramer, R. (1996). 'Members' responses to organizational identity threats: encountering and countering the *Business Week* rankings', *Administrative Science Quarterly*, **41**: 442–76.

Fiol, C.M. (1991) 'Managing culture as a competitive resource: an identity-based view of sustainable competitive advantage', *Journal of Management*, **17**(1): 191–211.

Flyvbjerg, B. (2001). *Making Social Science Matter: Why Social Inquiry Fails and How it Can Succeed Again*. Oxford: Cambridge University Press.

Fombrun, C. (1996). *Reputation: Realizing Value from the Corporate Image*. Boston: Harvard Business School Press.

Fowlers, B.J. (2003). 'Reason and human finitude', *American Behavioral Scientists*, **17**(4): 415–26.

Freedheim, D. (ed.) (1992). *History of Psychotherapy: A Century of Change*. Washington DC: American Psychological Association.

Freud, S. (1955). 'Analysis of a phobia in a five-year old boy', in Strachey, J. (ed.). *The Standard Edition of the Complete Psychological Works of Sigmund Freud*, **10**: 1–152. London: Hogarth (original work published 1909).

Freud, A. (1946). *The Psychoanalytic Treatment of Children*. London: Imago.

Fyfe, W.H. (1967). *Aristotle's Art of Poetry*. Oxford: Clarendon Press.

Geertz, C. (1973). *The Interpretation of Cultures*, New York: Basic Books.

Gergen, K.J. (1973). 'Social psychology as history', *Journal of Personality and Social Psychology*, **26**(2): 309–20.

Gershoni, J. (ed.) (2003). *Psychodrama in the 21st Century: Clinical and Educational Applications*. Springer.

Gibbs, R. (1993). 'Process and products in making sense of tropes', in Andrew Ortony (ed.) *Metaphor and Thought*, pp. 252–71. Cambridge: Cambridge University Press.

Gibson, K. and Ingold, T. (1993). *Tools, Language, and Cognition in Human Evolution*, New York: Cambridge University Press.

Giddens, A. (1984). *The Constitution of Society*. Cambridge: Polity Press.

Gioia, D. (2003). 'Give it up! Reflections on an interpreted world (A commentary on Meckler and Baillie)', *Journal of Management Inquiry*, **12**(3): 285–92.

Gioia, D. and Thomas, J. (1996). 'Identity, image and issue interpretation: sensemaking during strategic change in academia', *Administrative Science Quarterly*, **41**: 370–403.

Glaser, B.G. and Strauss, A.L. (1967). *The Discovery of Grounded Theory: Strategies for Qualitative Research*. Chicago: Aldine.

Goffman, E. (1974). *Frame Analysis: An Essay on the Organisation of Experience*, New York: Harper & Row.

Goldstein, K. (1939, 1963). *The Organism*. Boston: Beacon Press.

Goldstein, J. (1999). 'Emergence as a construct: history and issues', *Emergence*, **1**(1): 49–72.

Goldstein, J. (2000). 'Emergence: a construct amid a thicket of conceptual snares', *Emergence*, **2**(1): 5–22.

Goshal, S. (2005). 'Bad management theories are destroying good management practice', *Academy of Management Learning & Education*, **4**(1): 75–91.

Halverson, R. (2004). 'Accessing, documenting, and communicating practical wisdom: the phronesis of school leadership practice', *American Journal of Education*, **111**: 90–121.

Harel, I. and Papert, S. (eds) (1991). *Constructionism*. Norwood, NJ: Ablex Publishing Corporation.

Haslam, S., Postmes, T. and Ellemers, N. (2003). 'More than a metaphor: organizational identity makes organizational life possible', *British Journal of Management*, **14**: 357–69.

Hatch, M.J. (1998). 'Jazz as a metaphor for organizing in the 21st century', *Organization Science*, 9(5): 556–8.

Hatch, M. and Schultz, M. (1997). 'Relations between organizational culture, identity and image', *European Journal of Marketing*, **31**: 356–65.

Hatch, M. and Schultz, M. (2000). 'Scaling the tower of Babel: relational differences between identity, image and culture in organizations', in Schultz, M., Hatch, M. and Holten Larse, M. (eds). *The Expressive Organization*, pp. 11–35. Oxford: Oxford University Press.

Hatch, M. and Schultz, M. (2002). 'The dynamics of organizational identity', *Human Relations*, **55**: 989–1018.

Hayek, F.A. (1945). 'The use of knowledge in the society', *The American Economic Review*, **xxxv**(4): 519–30.

Heidegger, M. (1968). *Identity and Difference*, (trans.) Stambaugh, J. New York: Harper & Row.

Heidegger, M. and Farrell, D. (ed.) (1993). *Basic Writings*. Oxford: Routledge.

Hinkle, B. (1923). *The Recreating of the Individual*. New York: Dodd, Mead and Company.

Holland, J. (1995). *Hidden Order: How Adaptation Builds Complexity*. Reading, MA: Addison-Wesley.

Holland, J. (1998). *Emergence: From Chaos to Order*. Reading, MA: Addison-Wesley.

Holton, G. (1996). 'Imagination in science', in his: *Einstein, History and Other Passions: The Rebellion Against Science at the End of the Twentieth Century*, pp. 78–102. Reading, MA: Addison-Wesley.

Hopcke, R.H. (1989, 1999). *A Guided Tour of the Collected Works of C.G. Jung*. Boston: Shambhala Publications.

Huff, A. (1990). *Mapping Strategic Thought*. Chichester: Wiley.

Huff, A. and Jenkins, M. (2002). *Mapping Strategic Thought*. London: Sage.

Huizenga, J. (1950). *Homo Ludens: A Study of the Play Element in Culture*. Boston: Beacon Press.

Jantsch, E. (1980). *The Self-organizing Universe: Scientific and Human Implications of the Emerging Paradigm of Evolution*. Oxford: Pergamon Press.

Jarvis, P. (1995). *Adult and Continuing Education: Theory and Practice* (2nd edn). London: Routledge Kegan.

Johnson, G., Melin, L. and Whittington, R. (2003). Guest editors' introduction. 'Micro strategy and strategizing: towards an activity based view', *Journal of Management Studies*, **40**(1): 3–22.

Jung, C.G. (1965). *Memories, Dreams and Reflections*. New York: Vintage.

Kalff, D. (1980). *Sandplay: A Psychotherapeutic Approach to the Psyche*. Santa Monica: Sigo Press.

Kant, I. (1781, 1950). *Critique of Pure Reason*, (trans.) N. Kemp-Smith, New York: St. Martin's Press.

Kant, L. (1790, 1987). *Critique of Judgment*, (trans.) W.S. Pluhar, Indianapolis: Hackett.

Kauffman, S. (1995). *At Home in the Universe*. New York: Oxford University Press.

Kearney, R. (1988). *The Wake of Imagination: Toward a Postmodern Culture*. Minneapolis: University of Minnesota Press.

Kierkegaard, S., Hong, H.V. and Hong, E.H. (ed.) (1996). *The Essential Kierkegaard (Kierkegaard's Writings)*. Princeton University Press.

Kirsh, D. (1995). 'Complementary strategies: why we use our hands when we think', *Proceedings of the Seventeenth Annual Conference of the Cognitive Science Society*, 212–17.

Kitchener, K. (1983). 'Cognition, metacognition, and epistemic cognition'. *Human Development*, 26: 222–32.

Klein, M. (1955). 'The psychoanalytic play technique', *American Journal of Orthopsychiatry*, 25: 223–37.

Kolb, D. and Fry, R. (1975). 'Toward an applied theory of experiential learning', in Cooper, C. (ed.) *Theories of Group Process*. London: John Wiley.

Krauss, R.M. (1998). 'Why do we gesture when we speak?', *Current Directions in Psychological Science*, 7: 54–59.

Lakoff, G. and Johnson, M. (1980). *Metaphors We Live By*. Chicago: University of Chicago Press.

Landreth, G. (2002). *Play Therapy: The Art of the Relationship* (2nd edn). New York: Brunner-Routledge.

Landreth, G. (2001). *Innovations in Play Therapy: Issues, Process, and Special Populations*. New York: Brunner-Routledge.

Latour, B. (1987). *Science in Action*. Cambridge: Harvard University Press.

Levinas, E. (1969). *Totality and Infinity*, (trans.) A. Lingis, Pittsburgh: Duquesne University Press.

Leavitt, H.J. and Lipman-Blumen, J. (1995). 'Hot groups', *Harvard Business Review*, July/August.

Levitt, T. (1960) 'Marketing myopia', *Harvard Business Review*, July–August.

Lewin, K. (1949). *Resolving Social Conflicts: Selected papers on group dynamics*. Lewin, G. (ed.) New York: Harper & Row.

Lieberman, E.J. (1985). *Acts of Will (The Life & Work of Otto Rank)*. New York: Free Press.

Linder, M., Roos, J. and Victor, B. (2001). 'Playing with Strategy', Working Paper 2001:1, Lausanne: Imagination Lab Foundation.

Lissack, M. and Roos, J. (1999). *The Next Common Sense: Mastering Corporate Complexity through Coherence*. London: Nicolas Brealey.

Lorenz, E. (1963). 'Deterministic nonperiodic flow', *Journal of the Atmospheric Sciences*, 20: 130–41.

Lowenfeld, M. (1979). *The World Technique*. Melbourne: Allen & Unwin.

Lowis, M.J. (1998). 'Music and peak experiences: an empirical study', *The Mankind Quarterly*, XXXIX(2): 203–24.

Luhmann, N. (1986). 'The autopoiesis of social systems', in Geyer, F. and van der Zouwen, J. (eds), *Sociocybernetic Paradoxes*, pp. 172–92. Beverly Hills, CA: Sage.

Luhmann, N. (1990). *Essays on Self-Reference*. New York: Columbia University Press.

Lyotard, J.F. (1984). *The Postmodern Condition: A Report on Knowledge*. Minneapolis: University of Minnesota Press.

MacIntyre, A. (1981). *After Virtue: A Study in Moral Theory.* Notre Dame: University of Notre Dame Press.

McGraw, P.C. (2001). *Self Matters, Creating Your Life from the Inside Out.* New York: Free Press.

McInman, A. and Grove, J.R. (1991). 'Peak moments in sport: a literature review', *Quest*, **43**: 333–51.

McNiff, S. (1998). *Trust the Process.* Boston: Shambhala.

Mainemelis, C. (2001). 'When the muse takes it all: a model for the experience of timelessness in organizations', *Academy of Management Review*, **26**: 548–65.

Malchiodi, C.A. (1998). *The Art Therapy Sourcebook.* Lincolnwood, IL: Lowell House.

March, J.G. and Simon, H.A. (1958). *Organizations.* New York: Wiley:

Margolis, J. and Walsh, J. (2001). 'Misery loves companies: rethinking social initiatives by business', *Administrative Science Quarterly*, June, **48**(2): 268–306.

Maslow, A.H. (1968). *Toward a Psychology of Being* (2nd edn). New York: Van Nostrand.

Maturana, H. and Varela, F. (1987). *The Tree of Knowledge* (in Danish). Copenhagen: Ask.

Maturana, H. and Varela, F. (1980). *Autopoiesis and Cognition: the Realization of the Living.* London: Reidl.

May, R. (1985). *My Quest for Beauty.* Dallas, TX: Saybrook Publishing Company.

Mead, G.H. (1934, 2001). *Mind, Self and Society*, Chicago: University of Chicago Press.

Miller, A.I. (1984). *Imagery in Scientific Thought: Creating 20th Century Physics.* Boston, MA: Birkhauser.

Minsky, M.A. (1975). 'A framework for representing knowledge', in Winston, P.H. (ed.), *The Psychology of Computer Vision*, pp. 211–77. New York: McGraw-Hill.

Mintzberg, H. (1987). 'Crafting Strategy', *Harvard Business Review*, **65**(4): 66–75.

Mintzberg, Henry (1994). *The Rise and Fall of Strategic Planning: Reconceiving Roles for Planning, Plans, Planners.* New York/London: Free Press.

Mintzberg, H. and Waters, J. (1985). 'Of strategies, deliberate and emergent'. *Strategic Management Journal*, **6**: 257–72.

Mintzberg, H., Ahlstrand, B. and Lampel, J. (2005). *Strategy Bites Back: It is a Lot More, and Less, Than You Ever Imagined.* London: Pearson.

Mitchell, R.R. and Friedman, H.S. (1994). *Sandplay: Past, Present and Future.* London: Routledge.

Mook, B. (2003). 'Phenomenological play therapy', in Schaefer, Ch.E. *Foundations of Play Therapy.* New York: Wiley.

Moreno, J.L. (1923). Das Stegreiftheater [Spontaneity theatre]. Berlin_Potsdam: Kiepenheuer Verlag. (Part translated in *Sociometry*, 4, 205–26. Published in English by Beacon House in 1947; second enlarged edition, 1973. Selections also reprinted in *Psychodrama*, vol. 1, 1970 and 1972 editions.)

Moreno, J.L. (1934). *Who Shall Survive? A New Approach to the Problem of Human Interrelations.* Washington, DC: Nervous and Mental Disease Publishing Co. Psych. Abs., 8, 5153.

Moreno, J.L. (1946). *Psychodrama*, vol. 1. Ambler, PA: Beacon House.

Moreno, J.L. (1947, 1983). *The Theatre of Spontaneity.* Ambler, PA: Beacon House.

Moreno, J.L. (1965). 'Therapeutic vehicles and the concept of surplus reality'. *Group Psychotherapy*, **18**: 211–16.

Moreno, J.L. (1999). *Acting Your Inner Music: Music Therapy and Psychodrama.* Mmb Music.

Moreno, J.L. and Moreno, Z.T. (1959) *Psychodrama*, vol. 2. Ambler, PA: Beacon House.

Moreno, J.L. and Moreno, Z.T. (1969) *Psychodrama*, vol. 3. Ambler, PA: Beacon House.

Moreno, Z.T., Blomkvist, L.D. and Rutzel, T. (2000). *Psychodrama, Surplus Reality and the Art of Healing*. London: Routledge.

Morgan, G. (1997). *Images of Organization* (2nd edn). Beverley Hills, CA: Sage.

Naumburg, M. (1947). 'Studies of the "free" art expression of behaviour problem children and adolescents as a means of diagnosis and therapy'. *Nervous and Mental Disease*, 71.

Naumburg, M. (1950). *Schizophrenic Art: Its Meaning in Psychotherapy*. New York: Grune and Stratton.

Naumburg, M. (1953). *Psychoneurotic Art: Its Function in Psychotherapy*. New York: Grune and Stratton.

Nelson, R.R. and Winter, S.G. (1982). *An Evolutionary Theory on Economic Change*. Cambridge, MA: The Belknap Press of Harvard University Press.

Nisbett, R. and Ross, L. (1980). *Human Inference: Strategies and Shortcomings of Social Judgement*. Englewood Cliffs, NJ: Prentice Hall.

Oliver, D. (2002). *Building Collective Capacity in Self-Managed Teams: A Complex adaptive systems perspective*, Unpublished doctoral thesis, Ecole des Hautes Etudes Commerciales, University of Lausanne, Switzerland.

Oliver, D. and Roos, J. (2000). *Striking a Balance: Complexity and Knowledge Landscapes*, Berkshire UK: McGraw-Hill.

Oliver, D. and Roos, J. (2003). 'Dealing with the unexpected', *Human Relations*, 56(9): 1055–80.

Oliver, D. and Roos, J. (2004). 'Constructing Organizational Identity', Working Paper 53, Lausanne: Imagination Lab Foundation.

Oliver, D. and Roos, J. (2005). 'Decision making in high velocity environments: the importance of guiding principles', *Organization Studies*, 26(6): 889–913.

Oswick, C., Keenoy, T. and Grant, D. (2002). 'Metaphor and analogical reasoning in organization theory: beyond orthodoxy', *Academy of Management Review*, 27: 294–301.

Owen, A.R.G. (1971). *Hysteria, Hypnosis and Healing: The Work of J.-M. Charcot*. New York: Garrett Publications.

Parker, D. and Stacey, R. (1994). *Chaos, Management and Economics*, Hobart Paper 125, London: The Institute for Economic Affairs.

Patton, M.Q. (2002). *Qualitative Research and Evaluation Methods* (3rd edn). Thousand Oaks, CA: Sage.

Penfield, W. and Rasmussen, T. (1957). *The Cerebral Cortex of Man; A Clinical Study of Localization of Function*. New York: Macmillan.

Piaget, J. (1958). *Etudes d'épistémologie génétique*, V, Paris: Presses Universitaires de France.

Piaget, J. (1971). *Biology and Knowledge*. Chicago: University of Chicago Press.

Porter, M. (1980). *Competitive Strategy. Techniques for Analyzing Industries and Competitors*. New York: Free Press.

Prahalad, C.K. and Bettis, R.A. (1986). 'The dominant logic: a new linkage between diversity and performance', *Strategic Management Journal*, 7(6): 485–502.

Privette, G. (1982). 'Peak performance in sports: a factorial topology', *International Journal of Sport Psychology*, 12: 51–60.

Privette, G. and Bundrick, C.M. (1997). 'Psychological processes of peak, average, and failing performance in sport', *International Journal of Sport Psychology*, **28**: 323–34.

Rank, O. (1989). *Art and Artist: Creative Urge and Personality Development*. New York, NY: WW Norton & Company.

Reisman, J. (1966). *The Development of Clinical Psychology*. New York: Appleton-Century-Crofts.

Reynolds, C. (1987). 'Flocks, herds, and schools: a distributed behaviour model', *Computer Graphics*, **21**(4): 25–34.

Rogers, C. (1951). *Client-centered Therapy*. Boston: Houghton Mifflin.

Rogers, C. (1961). *On Becoming a Person: A Therapist's View of Psychotherapy*. New York: Houghton Mifflin.

Rogers, N. (1993). *The Creative Connection: Expressive Arts as Healing*. Palo Alto, CA: Science and Behavior Books.

Roizen, M.F. (1999). *Real Age, Are You as Young as You Can Be?* HarperAudio, Abridged Edition.

Roos, J. (1996). 'Distinction making and pattern recognition in management', *European Management Journal*, **14**(6): 590–5.

Roos, J. (2005). 'I matter: remaining the first author in strategy research', in Floyd, S., Roos., J, Kellerman, F. and Jacobs, C. (eds). *Innovating Strategy Processes*, pp. 252–62. Oxford: Blackwell.

Roos, J. and Said, R. (2005). 'Generating managerial commitment and responsibility', *European Management Review*, **2**: 48–58.

Roos, J. and Victor, B. (1999). 'Towards a model of strategy making as serious play', *European Management Journal*, **17**: 348–55.

Roos, J. Victor, B. and Statler, M. (2004). 'Playing seriously with strategy', *Long Range Planning*, **37**: 549–68.

Roos, J. and von Krogh, G. with Simcic Brønn, P. (1996). *Managing Strategy Processes in Emergent Industries: The Case of Media Firms*. Basingstoke: Macmillan – now Palgrave Macmillan).

Roos, M. and Statler, M. (2004). 'Play and the Creative Arts: A Review of Concepts and Techniques in the Psychotherapeutic Tradition', Working Paper 58, Switzerland: Imagination Lab Foundation.

Rorty, R. (1991). *Objectivity, Relativism, and Truth*. Cambridge, UK: Cambridge University Press.

Sandelands, L.E. and Buckner, G.C. (1989). 'Of art and work: aesthetic experience and the psychology of work feelings'. *Research in Organizational Behavior*, **11**: 105–31.

Schaefer, Ch. E. (ed.) (2003). *Foundations of Play Therapy*. Hoboken, NJ: John Wiley.

Schaverien, J. (1987). 'The scapegoat and the talisman: transference in art therapy', in Dalley, T., Case, C., Schaverien, J., Weir, F., Halliday, D., Nowell-Hall, P. and Waller, D. *Images of Art Therapy*, 74–108. London: Routledge.

Schiller, F. (1983). *On the Aesthetic Education of Man*, (eds) E. Wilkinson and L.A. Willoughby, Oxford: Clarendon Press.

Schön, D.A. (1983). *Reflective Practitioner: How Professionals Think in Action*. London: MT Smith.

Schön, D. (1963) *Displacement of Concepts*. New York: Humanities Press.

Schön, D. (1993). 'Generative metaphor: a perspective on problem-setting in social policy', in *Metaphor and Thought*, Andrew Ortony, (ed.) pp. 137–63. Cambridge: Cambridge University Press.

Schopenhauer, A. (1969). *The World as Will and Representation*, E.F.J. Payne (trans.) Mineola, NY: Dover.

Simon, H. (1989). *Models of Thought*, vol. 2. New Haven, CN: Yale University Press.

Simon, H.A. (1996). *The Sciences of the Artificial*. Cambridge, MA: MIT Press.

Skinner, B.F. (1974). *About Behaviorism*. New York: Random House.

Smith, P.K. (1982). 'Does play matter? Functional and evolutionary aspects of animal and human play', *The Behavioral and Brain Sciences*, 5: 139–84.

Sophocles, translated by Kitto. (1994). *Antigone, Oedipus the King, Electra*. Oxford: Oxford University Press.

Sproull, L. and Kiesler, S. (1991). *Connections: New Ways of Working in the Networked Organization*. Cambridge, MA: MIT Press.

Starbuck, W.H. (1992) 'Strategizing in the real world', *International Journal of Technology Management*, Special Publication on Technological Foundations of Strategic Management, 8(1/2): 77–85.

Statler, M. and Roos, J. (2005). 'The Normativity of Strategy Practice', Working Paper 68, Lausanne: Imagination Lab Foundation.

Statler, M. Roos, J. and Victor, B. (2002). 'Ain't Misbehavin', Working Paper 5. Lausanne: Imagination Lab Foundation.

Statler, M., Roos, J. and Victor, B. (2003). 'Dear Prudence: An Essay on Wisdom in Strategy Making', Working Paper 25, Lausanne: Imagination Lab Foundation.

Statler, M., Roos, J. and Victor, B. (2006). 'Illustrating the need for practical wisdom', *International Journal of Management Concepts and Philosophy*, (forthcoming).

Sternberg, R.J. (2003) *Wisdom, Intelligence, and Creativity Synthesized*. New York: Cambridge University Press.

Sutton-Smith, B. (1997). *The Ambiguity of Play*. Cambridge, MA: Harvard University Press.

Sveningsson, S. and Alvesson, M. (2003). 'Managing Managerial Identities: Organizational Fragmentation, Discourse and Identity Struggle'. Institute of Economic Research Working Paper Series. Sweden: Lund University.

Tajfel, H. and Turner, J. (1985). 'The Social Identity Theory of Intergroup Behaviour', in Worchel, S. and W. Austen (eds) *Psychology of Intergroup Relations*, pp. 7–24 (2nd edn). Chicago: Nelson-Hall.

Taranto, M.A. (1989). 'Facets of wisdom: a theoretical synthesis', *International Journal of Aging and Human Development*, 29: 1–21.

Tattersall, I. (1998). *Becoming Human; Evolution and Human Uniqueness*. New York: Harcourt Brace.

Taylor, J. (1999). 'The other side of rationality', *Management Communication Quarterly*, 13: 317–26.

Taylor, Frederick W. (1911). *The Principles of Scientific Management*. New York: Harper.

Taylor, S.S. (2002). 'Overcoming aesthetic muteness: researching organizational members' aesthetic experience', *Human Relations*, 55(7): 821–40.

Teubner, G. (1991). 'Autopoiesis and steering: how politics profit from the normative surplus of capital', in R.J. in't Veld, Schaap, L. Termeer, C.J.A.M. and van Twist, M.J.A.W. (eds), *Autopoiesis and Configuration Theory: New Approaches to Social Steering*, pp. 127–43. Dordrecht: Kluwer.

Thomas, H. and Hafsi, T. (2005). 'The field of strategy: in search of a walking stick', *European Management Journal*, 23(5), October.

Thomas, N. (1997). 'Imagery and the coherence of imagination: a critique of white', *The Journal of Philosophical Research*, 22: 95–127.

Thomas, N. (1999). 'Are theories of imagery theories of imagination? An active perception approach to conscious mental content', *Cognitive Science*, 23(2): 207–45.

Thomas, N. (2001). 'Mental imagery', in Stanford Online Encyclopedia of Philosophy, [http://plato.stanford.edu/entries/mental-imagery/]

Thornton, F., Privette, G. and Bundrick, C.M. (1999). 'Peak performance of business leaders: an experience parallel to self/actualization theory', *Journal of Business and Psychology*, 14(2): 253–64.

Tufte, Edward (1990). *Envisioning Information*. Graphics Press.

Turner, V.W. (1982). *From Ritual to Theatre: The Human Seriousness of Play*. New York: Performing Arts Journal Publisher.

Tsoukas, H. (1993). 'Analogical reasoning and knowledge generation in organizational theory', *Organization Studies*, 14: 323–46.

Tweney, R.D., Doherty, M. and Mynatt, C. (eds) (1981). *On Scientific Thinking*. New York: Columbia University Press.

Varela, F.J., Thompson, E. and Rosch, E. (1992). *The Embodied Mind*. Cambridge, MA: MIT Press.

von Bertalanffy, L. (1968). *General System Theory*, New York: Braziller.

von Foerster, H. (ed.) (1984). *Observing Systems*. Salinas: Intersystems Publications.

von Krogh, G. and Roos, J. (1995a). *Organizational Epistemology*, Oxford: Macmillan.

von Krogh, G. and Roos, J. (1995b). 'Conversation management', *European Management Journal*, 13(4): 390–4.

von Krogh, G. and Roos, J. (1997). 'A phraseologic view of organizational learning', in Huff, A.S. and March, J. (eds), *Advances in Strategic Management*, pp. 53–74. JAI Press.

von Krogh, G. and Vicari, S. (1991). 'An autopoiesis approach to experimental strategic learning', in Lorange, P., Chakravarthy, C., Roos, J. and Van de Ven, A. *Implementing Strategic Processes: Change, Learning and Co-operation*, 394–410. Oxford: Blackwell.

Vygotsky, Lev. (1934/1986). (translation), *Thought and Language*, Cambridge: MIT Press.

Walsh, J.P. and Ungson, G.R. (1991). 'Organizational memory', *Academy of Management Review*, 16: 57–91.

Warnock, M. (1976). *Imagination*. Berkeley and Los Angeles: University of California Press.

Wartofsky, M.W. (1979). *Models: Representation and Scientific Understanding*. Boston: Reidel.

Weber, M. (1958). *The Protestant Ethic and the Spirit of Capitalism*. New York: Scribner's Press.

Weick, K.E. (1995). *Sensemaking in Organizations*. Thousand Oaks, CA: Sage.

Weick, K.E. (1998). 'Improvisation as a mindset for organizational analysis', *Organization Science*, 9(5): 543–56.

Weick, K.E. and Roberts, K.H. (1993). 'Collective mind in organizations: heedful interrelating on flight decks'. *Administrative Science Quarterly*, 38(3): 357–81.

Wells, H.G. and Turner, B.A. (eds) (2004). *Floor Games: A Father's Account of Play and Its Legacy of Healing*. Cloverdale, CA: Temenos Press.

Welsh, S.D. (1999). *Sweet Dreams in America: Making Ethics and Spirituality Work*. New York: Routledge.

Wernerfeldt, B. (1984). 'A resource-based view of the firm', *Strategic Management Journal*, (5): 171–80.

White, A. (1990). *The Language of Imagination*. London: Basil Blackwell.

Whittington, R. (2003). 'The work of strategizing and organizing: for a practice perspective'. *Strategic Organization*, 1(1): 117–25.

Whyte, D. (1994). *The Heart Aroused*. New York: Doubleday.

Whyte, W.F. (ed.) (1991). *Participatory Action Research*. Newbury Park: Sage.

Wilson, F. (1998). *The Hand: How Its Use Shapes the Brain, Language, and Human Culture*. New York: Pantheon Books.

Wilson, D. and Jarzabkowski, P. (2004). 'Thinking and acting strategically: new challenges for interrogating strategy', *European Management Journal*, 1: 14–20.

Winnicott, D.W. (1971). *Playing and Reality*. London: Tavistock.

Wood, D. (1993). *The Power of Maps*. London: Routledge.

Wundt, W. (1874). *Grundzüge der physiologischen Psychologie*. Leipzig: W. Engelmann. In English 1904: *Principles of Physiological Psychology*. New York: Macmillan.

Yocits, M.C., Jacobi, J. and Goldstein, G. (1962). *Self-organizing Systems*. Washington: Spartan Books, cited in: Andrew, A. (1989). *Self-organizing Systems*. New York: Gordon and Breach.

Zaccaro, S.J. (1991) 'Nonequivalent associations between forms of cohesiveness and group-related outcomes: evidence for multidimensionality', *Journal of Social Psychology*, 131(3): 387–400.

Zaccaro, S.J. and Lowe, C.A. (1988). 'Cohesiveness and performance on an additive task: Evidence for multidimensionality', *Journal of Social Psychology*, (128): 547–58.

Notes on Contributors

Madeleine Roos is the co-founder and Director of spAcademy, a Swiss-based professional service company offering corporate clients innovative workshops, retreats and comparative engagements based on the *Thinking from Within* concept. Madeleine has a general interest in human interrelations and a specific interest in creative arts processes, especially drama. She earned her MD degree in 1987 and a Ph.D. in Medicine in 1991, both from the University Hospital in Lund, Sweden, where she worked at the Dep. of ORL. In the early 1990s she worked with acute psychiatry in Norway. In the late 1990s she founded an innovative kindergarten (Les Jeux Educatifs) in Switzerland, combining hands-on play with children's educational software. After actively contributing to the *Thinking from Within* idea, in 2005 Dr Roos founded the company she now leads. Madeleine can be reached at madeleine@spacademy.com.

Peter Bürgi is the Director of PTB Consulting, a Chicago-based firm which aligns international management teams to strategic business needs using customized learning interventions. He was a Research Fellow from 2001 to 2005 with Imagination Lab Foundation, where he researched how the imagination boosts innovation, strategy-making and teamwork. Previously, with ISR Corporation and IOR Global Services he directed employee attitude research projects in international corporations, coached executives on global assignments, and helped management teams improve their cross-cultural effectiveness. Dr Bürgi holds a Ph.D. in anthropology from the University of Chicago, and has published original research in several leading academic journals. His current research focuses on culture and identity in organizations. Born in the USA and a holder of American and Swiss citizenship, he is a native English speaker fluent in French, German, Swiss-German dialect, and Spanish. Peter can be reached at peter@ptbglobal.com.

Mark Marotto is the co-founder of Voix d'Espérance, a not-for-profit association that addresses humanitarian needs through classical music. Mark is a professional musician and does freelance conducting with orchestras and choirs throughout Switzerland and abroad. Prior to this Mark was a researcher at Imagination Lab Foundation from 2000 to 2004 where he led a three-year action research project on peak experiences in orchestras. In the late 1990s he was also a research associate at IMD in Lausanne. Mark is the co-author of several research papers, articles and book chapters, especially in the field of aesthetics, leadership and 'collective virtuosity'. He obtained a Bachelor of Arts in music from Duke University and his Master's degree in orchestral conducting at the National Music University of Bucharest, Romania. Mark can be reached at marotto@voixdesperance.org.

Roger Said is an independent consultant and writer who works with non-governmental organizations on aspects of communication, strategy and sustainability. In 2001 and 2002 he was a researcher at Imagination Lab Foundation, focusing on issues of time, on simple guiding principles, and on the use of objects in conversations. Prior to this, Roger worked in journalism, public relations, and advertising. He holds a licentiate in philosophy from the University of Basel and a Master's degree in artificial intelligence from the University of Edinburgh. Roger can be reached at rogersaid@yahoo.com.

Thinking from Within® Programme for Facilitators

The concepts and techniques described and illustrated in this book have evolved during a decade of basic and applied research, executive education and consulting work in the United States, Europe, Middle East and Australia.

Emergent Thinking Pty Ltd, which is based in Melbourne, has the exclusive rights to offer facilitators, educators and managers the formal training and official certification needed to effectively and responsibly apply *Thinking from Within*® in organizations.

Emergent Thinking is affiliated with the de Bono Institute, a not-for-profit organization dedicated to the research, development and facilitation in the areas of creativity, innovation and new thinking.

Consult www.emergentthinking.com for additional information about Emergent Thinking programmes.

Index

The letter *n* following a page number refers to an item in the notes; for example *n*1/2 refers to note number 2 relating to Chapter 1